Accessible, clear, an[...]
Praise for Ran[...]
Searching for the [...]

"A serious look at the canonization process, the abundance of translated resources... and the consistency of Bible translations...A fine book for lay and professional readers alike."

—*Publishers Weekly* magazine

"Randall Price is to be commended for this fine comprehensive treatment of the technicalities of textual criticism in language that pastors, students, and informed laypeople can understand. He also refutes the notion of so-called alternative Christianities (based on such noncanonical works as *The Gospel of Thomas and The Gospel of Judas*)."

—**Kenneth L. Barker, ThM, PhD**
General editor, *The NIV Study Bible*

"Dr. Randall Price, in his characteristic style of careful research and clarity of expression, has produced a book that should be in the hands of every pastor and parishioner who cares about the integrity of the Bible and its reception as God's truth....

"The general public is being offered a liberal diet about the origin and nature of Scripture, Christ, and early Christianity that is undermining the faith of many—and confusing those who might be attracted to Christ. Dr. Price's book is the medicine for these attacks. I heartily recommend it."

—**Dr. H. Wayne House**
Distinguished Research Professor of Biblical and Theological Studies
Faith Evangelical Seminary, Tacoma, WA

"Dr. Price's *Searching for the Original Bible* has graphically and accurately traced the long but exceedingly important work that lies behind obtaining the authentic words that our Lord revealed to his prophets and apostles in the Scriptures. Very few scholarly endeavors, if any, could be as significant for our obtaining an authoritative message in the Scriptures now in our possession.

"While the task of textual criticism involves a good deal of academic work, Randall Price has carefully and patiently explained it so that men and women in all walks of life can grasp what has happened and why it is significant for our faith. This story is a must for all who are grateful to God for the gift of his powerful word."

—**Walter C. Kaiser Jr.**
President Emeritus and
Colman M. Mockler Distinguished Professor of Old Testament,
Gordon-Conwell Theological Seminary, Hamilton, Massachusetts

Searching for
THE
Original
Bible

To Roger & Valerie,

Randall Price

With gratitude for your friendship,

Psalm 119:38

HARVEST HOUSE PUBLISHERS

EUGENE, OREGON

ERRATA

The section entitled "What About 'Errors' in the Manuscripts?" on pages 115 to 116 contains original statistical information produced by Daniel B. Wallace and is taken from his chapter "Can We Trust the New Testament?: The Quality and Quantity of Textual Variants" as contained in J. Ed Komoszewski, D. James Sawyer, and Daniel B. Wallace, *Reinventing Jesus: What the Da Vinci Code and Other Novel Speculations Don't Tell You* (Grand Rapids, MI: Kregel Publications, 2006), pp. 59-61.

SEARCHING FOR THE ORIGINAL BIBLE
Copyright © 2007 by World of the Bible Ministries
Published by Harvest House Publishers
Eugene, Oregon 97402
www.harvesthousepublishers.com

Library of Congress Cataloging-in-Publication Data
Price, Randall.
Searching for the original Bible / Randall Price
  p. cm.
Includes bibliographical references.
  ISBN-13: 978-0-7369-1054-5 (pbk.)
  ISBN-10: 0-7369-1054-9 (pbk.)
1. Bible—Inspiration. 2. Bible—Evidences, authority, etc. I. Title.
  BS480.P754 2007
  220.1—dc22
                                                         2007014163

Printed in the United States of America

07 08 09 10 11 12 13 14 15 / VP-KB / 12 11 10 9 8 7 6 5 4 3 2 1

In memory of my mother
Maurine Grace Atkins Price
A woman of the Word
who taught me to be
a man of the Word

Dedicated to
Marsha Ginzel Stuckly
A faithful friend
who knows the greatest gift
is the giving of God's Word

Acknowledgments

As with each of my books, I owe the successful completion of this one to many who have graciously given of their time, resources, and permission. My gratitude is extended to the many evangelical scholars who have helped me understand and respond to the recent critical challenges to the biblical text. Particular thanks are given to Dr. Daniel B. Wallace (Dallas Seminary, Executive Director of the Center for the Study of New Testament Manuscripts) for his kind attention to my questions concerning historical and textual questions; and to Dr. Walter C. Kaiser Jr. (Gordon-Conwell Seminary) for taking time to discuss with me some of the difficult issues related to the text of the Old Testament. I am also grateful to Richard Averbeck (Trinity Evangelical Divinity School) for sharing with me some of his ongoing research concerning the early development of the Hebrew text. Special thanks is given to Ken Stanford, Operations Manager of World of the Bible Ministries, for research assistance, and for his and Mrs. Lori Davis's help with the charts and tables.

I especially wish to thank my friend and former professor Dr. Charles C. Ryrie, one of the foremost authorities on the Bible and especially the extant biblical manuscripts and versions, for writing the foreword. I also am grateful for the kind endorsements of Dr. Kenneth Barker and Dr. H. Wayne House, and those of Dr. Wallace and Dr. Kaiser. All of these have been my teachers through their own valuable writings.

Finding sufficient seclusion to complete a manuscript is always a necessity for me, and I wish to thank Rev. Tommy and Sue Jenkins for the use of their home during some of the writing process. Leon and Linda Hewlett also graciously offered their hospitality and provided use of their "casita," which enabled me to meet my deadline. Thank you both so much for your kindness and encouragement! I am grateful to the following friends for their photographic assistance or use of photos from their archives: Paul Streber (Qumran), Rick Schuler (Jerusalem), and Alexander Schick (Bibelausstellung Sylt, Germany). Appreciation is also given to the following institutions for permission to photograph or use photographs from their collections: Bible Society (Jerusalem), Cairo Museum, Coptic Museum (Cairo), British Museum/British Library (London), Freer Gallery of Art & Arthur M. Sackler Gallery (Washington, DC), Shrine of the Book (Jerusalem). I am also grateful to Bob Hawkins Jr. for his working with me when circumstances required the extension of our original publication schedule, to Paul Gossard for his editorial oversight of this project, and to the production staff of Harvest House Publishers for their skill at their craft.

Finally, the dedication of time and attention necessary for each book I write only increases my love for my wife Beverlee and my now grown children and their spouses (Eric and Elisabeth Ream, Pavel and Eleisha Tabares, Erin Price, Jon Price, and Emilee Price), who have shared with me in different ways in the authorial process. Their own devotion to the Bible as the Word of God and diligence in following its precepts have been a constant joy in my life and a witness to the reality of its divine origin. May whatever use the Lord makes of its publication give a sense of reward to each who have in some way helped bring it to life.

Contents

Part One:
Searching for Evidence of the Original Bible

Part Two:
Searching for the Reliability of the Original Bible

Part Three:
Searching for the Truth About the Original Bible

Part Four:
Searching for the Restoration of the Original Bible

List of Photographs

*For photograph credits and source information, see "Acknowledgments for Photographs"
at the end of this book.*

List of Charts

Foreword
by Dr. Charles Ryrie

New School. Higher criticism. Textual criticism. The Jesus Seminar. The Judas Gospel. Gnosticism. Postmodernism. The Apocrypha. Inerrancy. What do they mean? Should we be concerned about them? How do they affect our attitude toward and our understanding of the Bible?

In this important book, Dr. Price deals with these matters for a variety of readers. Those who affirm inerrancy, those who are less certain of it or even what it means, those who outright deny it, those who do not know or ignore the wealth of evidence for the preservation and transmission of the biblical text, and those who are indifferent or uniformed about these issues—all of them need to read this excellent work.

Thorough research, informative sidebars, charts, photographs, and clear writing all combine to make this book a significant, up-to-date defense of the inerrancy and reliability of our Bible. How anyone could read this book without having more confidence in the accuracy and dependability of the biblical text we have today would be a mystery to me.

—Charles Caldwell Ryrie
July 2007

Why Believe
the Bible?

When I graduated from seminary, my wife, Beverlee, gave me a graduation gift: a new Bible with my name personalized on the outside. This Bible, however, was not like any other I had previously bought, either in my growing-up years as a Christian or even as a seminary student. My wife had contracted with a bindery to put together in a leather cover a copy of the critical editions of the Hebrew Old Testament and the Greek New Testament.

I immediately treasured this "Scripture for the scholar," and over the last 30 years have tried to use it exclusively in my own personal study and preparation for teaching. Consequently, when people through the years have asked me what version of the Bible I use, it has been with a little amusement on my part, and surely consternation on theirs, that I have answered, "I use the *Original* Bible!"

What I mean, of course, is that I try to work from the original-language texts of the Bible rather than from translations of them. Even so, my playful comment has usually been misunderstood. Many in the Christian world do not know that the Bible has ever existed in any form other than that which they use. Worse, there are some who think their particular English translation *is* the Original Bible!

Worse still are those on the other end of this spectrum, who have abandoned the Bible as a reliable source of knowledge about God—preferring the existential approach or becoming agnostic. Many of these people began to doubt the biblical text after encountering the seemingly endless versions that fill bookstore shelves. Or perhaps they have compared the many different Protestant versions with the significantly different versions of other persuasions (Jewish, Catholic, Eastern Orthodox) and concluded it is simply impossible to know what the Original Bible said.

This book is written in the confident conviction that, in the critical editions of our present Hebrew and Greek texts, we have substantially all of the words given by God, and that the work of textual critics today is bringing us ever closer to the Original Bible. Despite the thousands of translations made—necessary for distributing the Bible to the common person—the text has remained essentially unchanged. And certainly nothing that affects doctrine or practice has been lost or altered through thousands of years of the history of textual transmission. This is a conviction that can be maintained even in the current marketplace of ideas, where skepticism reigns and the integrity of the Bible is daily maligned in the media.

The Need to Take Up the Challenge

I was initially asked to write a book like this when Dan Brown's fictional novel *The Da Vinci Code* was released. I hesitated at that time to offer a response because so many capable scholars were adequately meeting the challenge. Also, I realized that the problem was greater than the issues raised by *The Da Vinci Code,* because it has been a dismal lack of knowledge (or knowing too many *wrong* things) about the Bible that permitted Brown's novel to persuade so many (especially those who claim to be believers).

Now that *The Da Vinci Code* and its Hollywood screen version are on the wane, a flood of other books has followed, with the purpose of enlightening society concerning the "Alternative Christianity" introduced in Brown's novel. Alongside these books have come others, written by many *formerly* in the faith, whose "inside information" as scholars has convinced them that 1) the text of the Bible has been hopelessly corrupted by the church, 2) Jesus was misquoted, and 3) the real truth of Christianity (or "Christianities") has been lost for at least 1500 years. Because some of these books have risen to the New York Times bestseller list (which at least means they are being bought, if not read) I felt it was finally time for me to get into the arena.

However, this book has not been written in haste. After spending a year in research I was compelled to take an additional year to read the latest books on this subject. You will see by consulting the footnotes (for the books of critical scholars) and my list of Recommended Reading (for the books of conservative scholars) that the recent production of such works has been prolific. There have also been unexpected family interruptions of significant proportions (death, cancer, surgeries), not to mention a computer meltdown in the final stages of writing! Such incidences coming all at once at the very time of writing is a reminder that the subject of this book is one that is firmly a part of spiritual warfare.

More than three decades ago Harold Lindsell published his book *The Battle for the Bible*. He predicted that the rest of the twentieth century would see an unprecedented attack on the inerrancy of the Bible.* That predicted attack surely came, but it was confined for the most part to the arcane world of scholars, who could argue for the "essential trustworthiness" of the Bible while affirming only that it "*contained* the word of God." The fallout for the public came largely through pastors who, influenced by seminaries that abandoned their former commitment to inerrancy, drifted away from preaching certain portions of Scripture as authoritative (for example, Genesis 1–11).

However, even the attempt to "water down" the scientific and historical interpretation of the Bible has, ironically, revealed the strength of its supernatural source, as New Testament grammarian Professor A.T. Robertson once quipped: "The greatest proof that the Bible is inspired is that it has stood so much bad preaching!" Nevertheless, the attack on the Bible's integrity has continued into the twenty-first century. But it has now become more publicly focused, with dissenting scholars (for example, the Jesus Seminar) announcing their wholesale rejection of the Bible as even "historically reliable" while advocating that Gnostic Gospels (such as Thomas) replace canonical Gospels (such as John)!

Fortunately, in response to these recent popular attacks on the Bible, a number of excellent books by competent Christian scholars have been written to counter such claims and present the facts about the origin

---

*For more about inerrancy, see pages 34–35.)

and transmission of the biblical text (see Recommended Reading). I am indebted to these many scholars, since much of the technical discussion in this book lies outside of my own field of expertise—though I have been trained in textual criticism and practice it in my own exegesis of the biblical text. This book joins with their works in answering questions about what happened to the Bible after it left the hands of its original authors, and what degree of confidence we can place in our modern text, now more than two millennia removed from its ancient source.

We Can Believe the Bible

What should the response of spiritual leaders be to the present confusion concerning the origin of the Bible and the integrity of its text? They should inform people of the actual state of the text, and how conservative textual critics are laboring to align it to the original, a task that is not only possible, but has admirably succeeded in its goal. If people of faith are presented with such facts and are willing to think through them, they will be equipped to understand and respond to the critical attacks on the Bible that are assaulting the church in increasing quantity and persuasiveness.

This book seeks to help you, the reader, better understand how the text of sacred Scripture has been transmitted from the ancient world to ours and to answer the claims of modern critics against its integrity. As a text that has been handed down to our generation by martyrs' hands, it is worthy of such a pursuit. It is my hope that our search for the Original Bible will result in your having a greater confidence in the biblical text and a renewed trust in its Divine Author.

PART ONE

Searching for
EVIDENCE OF
THE
Original
Bible

Chapter 1

Why Does It Matter?

Those in ministry must close the gap between the church and the academy. We have to educate believers. Instead of trying to isolate laypeople from critical scholarship, we need to insulate them. They need to be ready for the barrage, because it is coming. The intentional dumbing down of the church for the sake of filling more pews will ultimately lead to defection from Christ.

—DANIEL B. WALLACE

Scholars are often accused of being out of touch with the average person and of writing only about matters that have significance to themselves and their ivory-tower colleagues. In reading the title of this book you might think that its subject belongs with academicians rather than the average person who walks the streets. However, as a local church pastor and a professor at the university level, I have found that both the church member and the student, exposed to controversial documentaries and the cynical classroom teacher, have very practical concerns about the origin of the Bible.

I spend a good deal of my writing time in a neighborhood coffee shop. Conversations with other regulars have revealed that they share a basic confusion about the Bible. One common misunderstanding is that different Bibles exist because no one really knows what the Bible says. One gets the impression that they believe translators make up the words of the Bible as they go! Too, like church members and university students, my coffee-shop companions have also heard reports in the media of newly discovered "missing" Gospels and of other books "lost" or deliberately "left out" of the Bible.

Moreover, they have been told that the text of the Bible is filled with errors and has been altered as the result of a political (church) conspiracy. Figures such as Moses and Jesus, for instance, are mythical creations of religious movements whose principal aim has been to manipulate the masses. Popular books and movies such as *The Da Vinci Code*—and the myriad of spin-offs that have sought to capitalize on its success—have increased (if not caused) this confusion, and have produced a skepticism that has undermined the traditional sacred status of the Scripture in secular society.

Scholarly Skepticism

One of my coffee-shop companions recently asked me where the Greek legend of Dionysus was in the New Testament. He said that in his philosophy of religion class he had been told that the myth of Jesus' virgin birth had been based on that of Dionysus, so he had assumed the Greek legend was there also! The school of higher (historical) criticism that likely informed this student's professor has now been joined by the "new school" of early church interpretation, whose theories concerning the origins of Christianities (yes, they refer to them as plural) are being taught today as fact, not only in secular colleges and universities, but also in theological seminaries.[1] However, less radical but equally antisupernaturalist descendants of the school of higher (historical) criticism had already been plowing this ground and planting the seeds of skepticism for over a century. Higher criticism of the Bible rejects a literal reading of the text and, in general, denies its historical basis. As a result, most higher critics have adopted an agnostic position toward religion in general—and an antagonistic position toward evangelical Christianity in particular.

To be sure, there are varying extremes among these schools, ranging from the old-school liberalism that values social issues over spiritual doctrines to the Jesus Seminar (a product of the school of form criticism[2]) that barely allows the Jesus of the Gospels to have existed. Having allowed the tenets of form criticism to deconstruct their own faith, they have weaned themselves from what they call theological superstition and have made it their mission to challenge traditional belief in the Bible (as divinely inspired and historically credible).

The New School

Some scholars of the new school have marshaled the science of textual criticism to attack the reliability of the Bible. The goal of these new-school textual critics is no longer to recover the original text of the Bible, as had been the aim of scholars for hundreds of years. Rather, owing to their emphasis on textual corruption, they believe it is impossible to even speak of "an original text." They argue that the text remained in an unstable form for many centuries, constantly being changed in accord with the church's theology—until it was forced into a static form by a state-controlled orthodoxy. Therefore, instead of searching for the Original Bible, they search for textual errors they believe justify their convictions and then write books about how few words in the New Testament actually reflect a historical Jesus.

The Aftermath of Skepticism

One of the most pointed critiques of new-school skepticism came from the late Professor David Flusser of the Hebrew University. Although Flusser was not a Christian, he held Jesus and the New Testament in high esteem and produced scholarly works defending the integrity of the historical account. During an evening in his home he told me a story of how he once presented a lecture to a group of Christian pastors at a prominent university in Germany. He says that when he asked the pastors how many of the words of Jesus in the New Testament they considered authentic, they replied, "Only one." When he asked, "Which one?" they replied, "We forgot." Flusser loved to tell this story—although I'm sure it was midrashic (created to teach a lesson)—to illustrate the apathetic aftermath that is the result of the destruction of the "Jesus of faith" by the scholarly skeptics.

Today, scholars like those ridiculed by Professor Flusser have banded together as "The Jesus Seminar."[3] They attempt to demythologize the Bible by deciding which words represent the actual words of Jesus and by then seeking to paint a largely legendary and nonhistorical portrait of the so-called founder of Christianity. After all, they maintain, the Jesus of history has been lost to us; we know only a Jesus invented by the church. Consequently, his image has to be pieced together not from the four canonical Gospels (which are unreliable sources), but from other ancient writings, such as the Gospel of Thomas and the Gospel of Peter.

The resulting image—though documentarized by Peter Jennings on ABC-TV's *The Search for Jesus*—is unrecognizable to the everyday Christian: a peasant Jewish Cynic born in Nazareth (not Bethlehem), who as a political dissident (veiling his call for revolt against Rome in his parables) became a nuisance to the Roman government and was executed by crucifixion. However, before he could be buried, he was eaten off of the cross by dogs. Yet, somehow, on the basis of this pathetic story, his handful of followers overcame persecution and martyrdom and grew into a global religion, some three billion strong! A similar approach has been taken with respect to the Old Testament, transforming it from a historical record of the people of Israel in their land into a late propagandistic account used to justify an imperialistic occupation of other people's land.

In both cases, the road to this state of pessimism and despair about the Bible began with an undermining of the trustworthiness of its text. In other words, if you can't believe the *words* of the Bible, you can't believe the *Bible!* Now, the entire Bible should not be accused of being untrustworthy because of a few discrepancies (and they are *few*—see chapters 5 and 6). However, Western culture tends to rush to judgment too easily on such matters, possibly because materialistic people are looking for reasons not to believe and the media is looking for provocative things to keep such people entertained (and make money from them). How else could programs like "The Gospel of Judas" or "The Lost Tomb of Jesus" capture an audience?[4]

The Bible in the Western World

The degree to which the general public has been affected by scholarly skepticism, thanks in large measure to its widespread dissemination through the media, can be seen in the way the Bible has come to be perceived in the Western world. "Boring and barbaric" is the way British authors John Barton of the University of Oxford and Julia Bowden of Guildford High School characterize most people's view of the Old

Testament (and most likely the New as well).[5] An expert in these authors' native country of Great Britain has predicted that "the Christian church in this country will be dead and buried within 40 years." It will vanish from the mainstream of British life, since only 0.5 percent of the population attends the Sunday services of any denomination.[6]

This phenomenon can be traced to an undermining of the Christian faith as a result of the previous centuries' attack on the Bible in the academic institutions and national life of Great Britain. Consequently, the kingdom that once sent more missionaries to the world than any other has become a mission field itself, and now ranks as one of the major international centers for occultism, which has rushed to fill the spiritual void left by a defection from true faith.

The Bible in American Culture

In the United States, a Barna Group poll comparing the moral and religious views of adults in their 20s and 30s with the views of adults over 40 reveals that young adults are rapidly abandoning the biblical faith.[7]

In addition, the entertainment world has mocked the Bible, regularly portraying members of the clergy as religious conspirators, money-hungry charlatans, and apocalyptic crazies—as well as Bible-believing Christians as unstable fanatics. Conversely, entertainment's "focus on the famous" has provided a positive image of celebrities (despite their stays at the rehab hotel—which only enhances their fame). Accordingly, sidewalk interviews reveal that the average person knows more about Jessica Simpson than any figure in the Bible. If we add to this the actual incidents of abuse by the clergy, sex scandals involving evangelical leaders, and religiously motivated school shootings, we can understand why the view of the Bible has sunk to an all-time low.

However, the cultural disintegration we are now seeing is not, as some would have us believe, the result of a narrow-minded Bible-believing fundamentalist. Rather, it is the social outcome of abandoning the Bible as a moral standard for Western civilization, which Chuck Colson has well described:

> We live in a *new dark age*. Having elevated the individual as the measure of all things, modern men and women are guided solely by their own dark passions; they have nothing above themselves

to respect or obey, no principles to live or die for. Personal advancement, personal feeling, and personal autonomy are the only shrines at which they worship.

The reigning god of relativism and the rampant egoism it fosters, coarsen character, destroy any notion of community, weaken civility, promote intolerance, and threaten the disintegration of those very institutions necessary to the survival and success of ordered liberty.[8]

Relativism Tips the Scales

In past generations the downward slide was slowed, and even reversed at times, by a return to the Scriptures. Preachers preached and people practiced the objective truths of the text, providing a counterbalance to that generation's collective weight of sin.

For our generation, however, that counterbalance is not the same. Having embraced relativistic standards (of which postmodernism is the current manifestation), higher education has now transferred its guiding principles of relativism and individualization to the Bible. In what is known as "reader-centered interpretation," it no longer matters what the author (human or divine) actually intended by what he wrote. Rather, what the reader "feels" a particular text "means to him/her" is what is important.

As far back as 1968, Roland Barthes argued for this method in an essay entitled "The Death of the Author," in which he stated that the *origin* of the text is not the important thing, only its *destination*—the reader. When the reader is allowed to invent new meanings, Barthas believed, the text is freed from the "tyranny" of the author's single intended meaning.

Following this method of self-centered interpretation when reading the Bible means that the reader has no reason to assume its words mean the same thing today as they did when it was written. Postmodern literary methodology achieves this through what is known as "deconstruction": reading a text to ferret out its hidden or multiple meanings. Context no longer matters, history is no longer necessary, the original meanings of Hebrew and Greek terms are unimportant. The only thing of importance in this method is the reader's context and culture, only how he/she uses and understands language, and only how the text fits his/her life situation.

On this subjective basis, the Word of God disappears. Only the imagination of man is left to make the Bible say whatever one wants— even the *opposite* of what its author intended it to say! The postmodern literary approach to the Bible can never inform the reader of what *God* thinks of the reader's world, and therefore can never effect a change in that world. And ironically, the very method of deconstruction that allows for the subjective search for hidden meanings in the text has also opened the minds of the present generation to old heresies of the past such as Gnosticism, and its secret Gospels and writings filled with invitations to hidden meanings that only the self-actuated interpreter can discover.

Lack of Balance in the Church

At the same time our country is struggling with moral relativism and the postmodern way of interpreting the world, the church is being seduced along similar lines to distance itself from the doctrines of Scripture, which are its only sure defense. Gary Johnson explains this assault of experientialism and anti-intellectualism in the modern American church:

> There is a prevalent conviction that the faith the church has confessed in the past is not adequate for a post-Enlightenment culture; the idea that the faith must be accommodated to culture has undermined the teaching of the church's faith. Popular evangelical faith has developed a bias against theology (not to mention the intellect) and has elevated the bias to the level of a virtue, defending it as vigorously as democracy. This is reflected more and more in the pulpits of professing evangelical churches. Doctrine...is purposely avoided....[9]
>
> They focus on practical matters, such as family concerns and personal growth, not doctrine, sometimes mixing psychotherapeutic concepts with biblical teaching. They often emphasize religious experience. They seek to feel God's love, not understand church theology, a theme that plays well with the decreasing importance of denominational doctrine among baby boomers.[10]

This trend is characteristic of the pendulum swing between emotionalism and intellectualism that has been evidenced throughout church history. In the second century AD, Montanism was a move to experience over doctrine, while Gnosticism in the second to third centuries was a move in the other direction, toward a heretical rationalism. In the third through tenth centuries, monasticism swung the pendulum back to the emotional with its focus on contemplation; then there was again a swing back toward the intellect with Scholasticism, in the eleventh to fourteenth centuries.

In reaction, the fourteenth to fifteenth centuries experienced the advent of mysticism, rebounding back to the intellectual with the Reformation in the sixteenth to seventeenth centuries. Out of the Reformation came Pietism and Methodism in the seventeenth and eighteenth centuries, swinging the pendulum back toward an emotional focus. The nineteenth and twentieth centuries then saw a move again to intellectualism, as German rationalism spawned higher criticism and produced liberalism and a passionless orthodoxy in mainline churches. In response to this, the pendulum swung back to an emotional focus with the twentieth-century advent of the Pentecostal and Charismatic movements.

Are the Scriptures Subjective?

At the beginning of the twenty-first century, the church remains in a crisis with an experientially oriented evangelicalism and a postmodern and spiritually skeptical scholarship. However, a "spiritual" postmodernism has begun to take over in Christian scholarship. It has made its way into the pews through pastors who have fled from rationalism and returned to "tradition" to recover a mystic experience with Christ (such as some branches of the Emergent Church Movement).

Therefore, the historic debates over such issues as the inspiration and inerrancy of the Scriptures no longer matter. So long as we have the "living Word" (Christ), the accuracy or historicity of the written words is not a primary concern.

However, does not our understanding of who the "Living Word" is depend on the written Word? Summit Ministries Executive Director, philosopher David Noebel, argues in favor of the traditional approach—that words, and especially the words of the Scripture, do matter:

Most importantly, God chose to communicate the Truth about Himself and His world by words contained in the Scriptures and the language of the heavens (Psalm 19). God's words do not depend upon a reader's interpretation. Instead, the reader is to interpret the Bible according to God's intention. The Apostle Peter is clear when he writes, "Above all, you must understand that no prophecy of Scripture came about by the prophet's own interpretation. For prophecy never had its origin in the will of man, but men spoke from God as they were carried along by the Holy Spirit" (2 Peter 1:19-21).

To correctly understand the meaning of any text of Scripture, we should heed Paul's advice to Timothy: "Do your best to present yourself to God as one approved, a workman who does not need to be ashamed and who correctly handles the word of truth" (2 Timothy 2:15). By acknowledging that God has communicated in language Truth about the real world, and by diligently studying the Bible, you can know the Truth that sets you free (John 8:32).[11]

For the postmodern and mystic, though, words are only symbols for a subjective interpretation of and experience with the "Living Word." This view has therefore led, and is leading, thousands in churches around the world to downplay the need to approach the Scriptures as objective truth and instead follow their feelings and trust their experience.

The Fear for the Future

Furthering the assault against objective biblical interpretation are the recent claims made about newly discovered ancient documents, like the Gospel of Judas. Its secret revelation (exclusive to Judas) and hidden message contradict the New Testament's historical portrayal of the relationship between Judas and Jesus, making the former the hero of the story. Likewise, the visual "recreation" of the Judas fiction on television by a venerable institution like the National Geographic Society has challenged the objective reality, as well as the historicity, of the New Testament Gospel accounts.

Further hastening the erosion of faith for the average person, as well as for postmodern Christians, has been the publication of several popular-market books such as *The Orthodox Corruption of Scripture; Lost Christianities, Lost Scriptures;* and *Misquoting Jesus*—all by lapsed evangelical and agnostic Bart Ehrman. He and a host of other scholars, who teach in our universities and seminaries and influence future pastors and teachers of the church, contend there is no "true Christianity"—and that the esoteric wisdom found in the lost Gnostic Gospels is as legitimate an expression of the words of Jesus as the content of the biblical Gospels.

What would happen to the modern church if it adopted such books as the Gospel of Thomas and the Gospel of Judas? For one thing, Gnostic ethics, or the lack of them, could supplant the traditional Christian values that have been a vibrant witness of the saving power of Christ. In regard to this alternate moral ethic, Edwin Yamauchi, former professor of the history of Christian origins, observes of Gnosticism,

> Since salvation was not dependent upon faith or works but upon the knowledge of one's nature, some Gnostics indulged deliberately in licentious behavior. Carpocrates [active c. 130 to c. 150 AD], for example, urged his followers to participate in all sins; his son Epiphanes taught that promiscuity was God's law.[12]

Rewriting History

There is today a concerted effort to change church history and conform it to the theories of the new school. New Testament textual critic Bart Ehrman published his book *Misquoting Jesus: The Story Behind Who Changed the Bible and Why* in 2005. Within three months more than 100,000 copies were sold, and the book had made it to the New York Times bestseller list.[13] As we will see, the thesis of this book is that the words of Jesus, in particular, have been so corrupted by orthodox Christianity that we cannot trust the copies of manuscripts behind our translation of the Gospels to portray an accurate historical image. This, in part, is the same kind of accusation made in *The Da Vinci Code*, but instead of coming from an author of fiction it comes from a top-rated scholar.

If such views as Ehrman's, and a host of even more radical speculations, are successful to any degree in influencing the public, the way the average Christian, as well as future scholars, will view their Christian heritage will be radically changed. If attacks on the integrity of the biblical texts continue to erode their longstanding status as Scripture, they will discredit the Bible's authority for the general population, including the majority of the Christian community. And if, subsequently, the heretical doctrines and values of an alternate Christianity are accepted, the untimate result could be the collapse of Western culture, which has been built upon the Scripture. However, this would be followed not by a lack of religion, but by a new dominance of other religions—those that have been waiting in the wings, such as Islam, which has long claimed that the Bible has been corrupted and that the only original revelation is that of the Qur'an.

Why This Book Was Written

Every average person has been affected in some way by the current attack on biblical credibility. Many Christians, too, have suffered doubts, and have needed answers to the things the critics are saying about the text.

Few Christians have understood that the Original Bible, the one that left the pens of the prophets and apostles, no longer exists. Instead, all we have are copies (manuscripts) in which there are thousands of variants (errors), so much so that no two copies are alike. It is from these that our Bibles have been translated.

Could then our Bible be filled with errors and be untrustworthy? Could it be so far removed from the original that its message is meaningless? Are there other books—some now coming to light—that *should* have been part of the Bible and might give it *new* meaning?

In past generations these questions could be largely disregarded because there still existed sufficient faith in the church that the Bible alone was true. But times have changed, and if those who share the faith do not address these issues in this generation, this will certainly be done by those who oppose that faith.

In the chapters that follow we will address such claims and challenge them based on the facts at hand. I invite you to come on this journey into the past where we will investigate the origin of the Bible, examine the methods of those who have passed the biblical text on to us, and consider the conclusions of textual scholars who are familiar with the thousands of ancient manuscript copies and translations of the Bible. If you have been convinced in this chapter that such a search does matter, I promise that you will find your quest for truth well rewarded.

Chapter 2

What Do We Mean
by the "Original Bible"?

Textual critics have recently been examining the question as
to what we mean by recovering "the original text" or whether
there is even such a thing as a single autograph and whether
it is recoverable....In some cases it is extremely difficult and
problematic to define what exactly an autograph is.

—JOHN J. BROGAN, *FROM EVANGELICALS AND SCRIPTURE*

Three women—one Jewish and two Christian (one Protestant, the other
Roman Catholic)—enter a bookstore, each to buy a Bible for their
daughter. Thus begins a story told by Jaroslav Pelikan, Sterling Professor
Emeritus of History at Yale University. The dilemma facing each woman,
and the store clerk as well, is which Bible to buy, for each needs a different
Bible to suit her particular faith.

Aside from the fact that each will have to choose from dozens of translations, the Jewish woman's search will be for a *Tanach,** which contains
only what Christians call the Old Testament. The Protestant will seek a
Bible containing a New Testament in addition to the Old Testament. And
the Roman Catholic will want a Bible that further adds the Apocrypha.
Each buyer, Pelikan asserts, has the right to expect "the Bible, the whole
Bible, and nothing but the Bible." Yet, it is clear from examining the table
of contents of each woman's purchase that their Bibles significantly differ
from one another. With issues of authority and faith at stake, who wants
less than "the whole Bible"?

---

* The acronym *TaNaK* (or *Tanach*) is taken from the first letters of the terms for the three divisions of
the Hebrew Bible: T=*Torah* (Pentateuch), N=*Nevi'im* ("Prophets"), and K=*Ketuvim* ("Writings").

For Pelikan, the question arising from the story was "Whose Bible is it?" (also the title of his book containing the story).[1] For our purpose, it might be phrased differently, as "Whose was the 'Original Bible'?" That question then brings us directly to the topic of this chapter, "What do we mean by the 'Original Bible'?"

This is not simply an academic issue, but one that deeply concerns the Christian who believes the Bible to be the Word of God. If it is to be the guide for this life and hold a promise of the life to come, which Bible is the original—"the whole Bible" that contains "the whole truth"? To begin to answer this most important question we must first briefly consider how the Bible has come to us.

The Coming of the Bible

"God, after He spoke long ago to the fathers in the prophets in many portions and in many ways, in these last days has spoken to us in His Son" (Hebrews 1:1-2a). With these words the author of the book of Hebrews summed up the means and method by which the Word of God—as the Old and New Testaments—came to the world.

The words "long ago" and "in these last days" refer to a transmission history of some 1050 years—1000 for the Old Testament and 50 years for the New Testament. The *means* was "God speaking" (the divine source) to "the prophets" (the human instrument). These people, chosen from all walks of life, were given a divine message to give to mankind. The *method* was "in many portions" (the various genres of sacred Scripture), and "in many ways" (the various processes by which this supernatural communication was received and recorded in the natural order).

The end result in literary terms of this divine and human cooperation is the written Word, the *Bible,* a term derived from the Greek *biblion,* "book." This word in turn came from the term *byblos,* a name for papyrus, the plant material used to create scrolls (papyrus sheets made to form a roll) and books (papyrus sheets folded and stitched to form a *codex*—a handwritten book). As such, *Bible* is an appropriate term to convey one message in two testaments, especially with respect to its original form: the Old Testament as scrolls, and the New Testament as *codices* (plural of *codex*), the first literature known to exist in this form.

Most people reading the Bible may never take thought of its original form, written over the millennia in Hebrew, Aramaic, and Greek on stone, papyrus, and parchment. Their thought, as it should be, is centered on the meaning of the message and how its ancient words apply to modern life. Yet, as noted in chapter 1, our modern lives have been challenged by skeptics and critics who attack the integrity of the message by claiming that the original texts we have today are not what they had then. These critics have disturbed the faith of many by contending that the words we moderns seek to apply for spiritual gain have been altered in the past for political gain.

Our first task, then, must be to take thought of those pristine documents that comprised the Original Bible and understand what has happened to them over time.

What Is the *Original Bible?*

The common understanding of something that is *original* is of something that is a first production, in contrast to subsequent reproductions which are *copies*. Just as an *autograph* is the handwritten signature of an individual, in the same way, documents "written by the hand of the author" (Greek *autograph*, Latin *manuscript*) are literary *autographs* (or *manuscripts*). *Autograph* is the accepted term for the original edition of a particular work, written or dictated by the author. It is the *earliest* copy, from which the *apographs* (all later copies) are ultimately descended. Ancient documents were written and copied by hand until the printing press came into widespread use because of the innovations of Johannes Gutenberg in the mid-1400s.

In the case of the Bible, the texts written by the biblical authors in their initial stage of composition are considered the *autographs* or *original manuscripts*. In both testaments, the biblical text records the production of these original writings. For example, in the Old Testament it is stated, "Moses *wrote down* all the words of the LORD" (Exodus 24:4). Likewise, in the New Testament we read, "I, Paul, write this greeting *with my own hand*" (Colossians 4:18), and "See with what large letters I am writing to you *with my own hand*" (Galatians 6:11). However, this definition also includes the production of manuscripts through the use of a personal scribe or *amanuensis* ("secretary") who received the text directly through dictation from the biblical author. Both the prophet Jeremiah (Jeremiah 36:4,6,17-18) and the apostle Paul (Romans 16:22), as well as others (1 Peter 5:12) had their communications recorded in this manner.

Although neither the Hebrew nor the Greek original manuscripts ever existed in a form resembling our present Bible, and in some cases they were edited by others before assuming the form known today, their collective existence as original manuscripts constitutes the *autographa*, or the "Original Bible."

The Importance of the Term Original Bible

Not only do both testaments make a point of stating that an author (or his scribe) wrote an original manuscript, they also record that this writing was done through divine instrumentality. When David communicated to his son Solomon the pattern for constructing the Temple, he declared, "All this...the LORD made me understand in writing *by His hand upon me*" (1 Chronicles 28:19). Likewise, when Paul describes the nature of the biblical authors' writings he states, "All Scripture is *inspired by God* [Greek *theopneustos*, "God-breathed"] and profitable for teaching, for reproof, for correction, for training in righteousness" (2 Timothy 3:16).

The apostle Peter recognized that this inspiration extended to the writings of the New Testament authors as well, stating with regard to Paul, "Just as also our beloved brother Paul, *according to the wisdom given him*, wrote to you...which the untaught and unstable distort, *as they do also the rest of the Scriptures*, to their own destruction" (2 Peter 3:15-16). Therefore, the words of the Original Bible were "inspired" by God in a way that cannot be said of the copies of them produced by others down through time.

For this reason the term *Original Bible* or *original manuscripts* is a convenient term to help convey the concepts of *verbal plenary inspiration* (*plenary* meaning "complete in every respect; unqualified") and biblical *inerrancy* (meaning that the Bible is without error in whatever it teaches). These characteristics are said to apply only to the creation of the original manuscripts, and they define the basis of biblical authority (see chapter 14 for more extensive discussion). For example, an evangelical declaration of the inerrancy of the autographs can be found in the Chicago Statement on Biblical Inerrancy:

We affirm that the whole of Scripture and all its parts, down to the very words of the original, were given by divine inspiration (Article VI)....

We affirm that inspiration, strictly speaking, *applies only to the autographic text of Scripture,* which in the providence of God can be ascertained from available manuscripts with great accuracy. We further affirm that copies and translations of Scripture are the Word of God to the extent that they faithfully represent the original (Article X, emphasis added).

As can be seen from this careful wording, the concept of inspiration and inerrancy "applies only to the autographic text of Scripture" and extends to copies and translations only insofar as they "faithfully represent the original." Therefore, it is the words of the Original Bible, and these words alone, that embody the authoritative text and serve as the standard of accuracy for every copy or translation.

Inspired Editions?

Some scholars hold the view that inspiration and therefore inerrancy should be applied to an "original edition" (rather than an *Original Bible)* that existed in its final canonical form only after centuries of editorial revision and acceptance by the community of faith—whether by Jewish sages or the early church fathers.

On the basis of tradition, Jewish sages believed the Masoretic Text of the Torah to be the exact words (and letters) given by God to Moses on Mt. Sinai. In like manner, the ante-Nicene Church Fathers (and the Eastern Church to this day) regarded the Septuagint (the Greek translation of the Old Testament made c. 250 BC) as inspired. On similar grounds, some Western Christians have claimed the Majority Text is closer to the original because it gained status as a "received text." (See page 207 for more discussion.)

However, the Scriptures do not extend infallibility beyond the original autographs, and for this reason, our definition of *Original Bible* should be confined to those autographs.

At this point, it will be helpful to consider the purpose for which the original texts were written and the method by which they were produced and transmitted in antiquity. Let us begin by considering the original Old Testament.

The Origin of the Old Testament

The "Original Bible" of Jesus, the apostles, and the early church was the Old Testament. Although Jesus and the apostles used the Hebrew text and even Aramaic Targums, the predominant text, expecially for the early church, seems to have been the Greek translation of the Hebrew Bible known as the Septuagint (see chapter 5). From it they preached the gospel, defended their faith in Jesus as the Messiah, and gained instruction for their lives as Christians. The foundational text of the church therefore was the Old Testament and, surprisingly, early Christians did not see a New Testament (as we know it) for some 400 years!

The writing of the Old Testament spans a historical period from the time of Moses in the beginning of the fifteenth century BC to the last of the writing prophets at the middle of the fifth century BC. (Although some critical scholars seek to place the book of the prophet Daniel in the second century BC, when Jewish apocalyptic writing was flourishing, conservative critics have made convincing arguments that it should remain dated to the time it describes—the late Neo-Babylonian and early Persian period.[2])

The Old Testament was composed with a national purpose—to define and direct the nation of Israel in its covenant relationship with God. However, certain portions (the psalms and wisdom literature) were composed for instructional purposes—to distinguish and develop Israel as a community of faith. Therefore these sections have a more universal application.

It is critical to understand that this literature was variously produced by scribes, scholars, and statesmen as well as by slaves, shepherds, and seers. These writings, in turn, were further edited by others before taking the fixed form, sometime in the first century BC, that stands behind the traditional text (the Masoretic Text, produced in the tenth century AD) from which our present Old Testament has been translated.

Original Documents

The Torah (the first five books of the Old Testament) was said to be for "all Israel" (Deuteronomy 5:1)—divine instruction for the Israelite nation to enable them to keep covenant with God (Exodus 24:8; 34:27; Deuteronomy 4:13; 12:28).

The Ten Commandments contained within this Torah (and according to Jewish tradition, the entire Torah itself—but see Exodus 34:28; Deuteronomy 9:10) were unique because the words were written directly by God:

> These words the LORD spoke to all your assembly at the mountain from the midst of the fire, of the cloud and of the thick gloom, with a great voice, and He added no more. *He wrote them on two tablets of stone and gave them to me* (Deuteronomy 5:22).

These words are said to have been "engraved" on the stone tablets (Exodus 32:16b) and "written on both sides...on one side and the other" (32:15b).

They are further described as being "written by the finger of God" (31:18), and as "God's work," "God's writing" (32:16a).

Even though this first set of tablets was broken at the foot of Mt. Sinai in response to Israel's having broken the commandments through the idolatrous act of worshipping the golden calf (Exodus 32:19; Deuteronomy 9:17), a second set, also written by God, was restored to Moses for the repentant nation (Exodus 34:1,4,28). Because of their special divine status, these tablets were placed inside

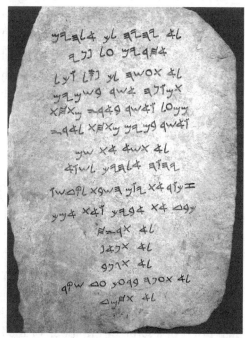

Replica of stone tablet containing the Ten Commandments (written in paleo-Hebrew script).

the Ark of the Covenant (Deuteronomy 10:5), in the Tabernacle's (and later Temple's) Holy of Holies.

Also written on tablets by Moses were "the words of the covenant, the Ten Commandments" (Exodus 34:28b). He further wrote "the words of this Law in a book" (Deuteronomy 31:24), words that were communicated directly from God while Moses was on Mt. Sinai for 40 days and nights (Exodus 20:22; 24:4a; 34:28a). This must refer to the five books of the Torah, which were also to be preserved "beside" the Ark of the Covenant:

> Moses wrote this law and gave it to the priests, the sons of Levi who carried the Ark of the Covenant of the LORD, and to all the elders of Israel...saying..."Take this book of the law and place it beside the Ark of the Covenant of the LORD your God, that it may remain there as a witness against you" (Deuteronomy 31:9,26).

This place of preservation was distinct from that of the tablets, which alone were kept *within* the Holy Ark, as later descriptions of the Ark's contents confirm (1 Kings 8:9; 2 Chronicles 5:10). Nevertheless, the books of the Torah were intended to be part of Israel's heritage and were preserved accordingly. Therefore, so long as the Holy Ark remained in the care of Israel, the original Mosaic Torah seems to have continued in existence.

Preservation of the Originals

Works that chronicled national events during the period of the monarchy, such as the books of Samuel, Kings, and Chronicles, may have been considered state documents and therefore may have had archival significance (see 1 Chronicles 9:11; 29:29; 2 Chronicles 16:11; 1 Kings 14:19; among others). Thus they may have been stored within the royal archive or the Temple library (depending on their intended use). If some were intended to have an official function they may have been inscribed on clay tablets, although most would have been produced in the form of scrolls (see Isaiah 30:8). This seems to be indicated by the report by the high priest of a scroll of the "book of the law" ("book of the covenant") that had been deposited in the Temple and discovered during renovations under King Josiah (2 Kings 22:8; 2 Chronicles 34:15—see pages 42–43).

For example, Moses had deposited the Torah as a "finished" work (Deuteronomy 31:24) in the Ark, and it remained unaltered at the time of Josiah 770 years later. This refutes the idea that the Torah was composed progressively by editors, or not until after the Exile. (For more about such theories, see pages 93–97.) Ezra, who headed the return from Exile, presents his credentials as a scribe already "skilled in the law of Moses... learned in the words of the commandments of the LORD and His statutes to Israel" (Ezra 7:6,11-12).

Moreover, writers from the time of Joshua onward refer to the "law of Moses" as though it were a standard for the Israelite nation, and all of Israel's kings are evaluated according to its statutes and ordinances (see 2 Kings 21:8). This would require that the Mosaic legislation (added to only by Joshua, Moses' appointed successor—Joshua 24:26) be unified and recognized as complete, and not something priestly editors substantially added to at a much later time. Jesus, too, believed in Mosaic authorship of the Torah (Luke 24:44; John 7:19), declaring that those who refuse to believe Moses' words cannot accept His own either (John 5:47).

How the Old Testament Developed

Beyond what is discussed above, there is very little internal or historical information on how the rest of the Old Testament came together or developed into the form we now know it. Some of the following can shed light on the matter:

The historical books. The prophet Samuel is said to have written "the ordinances of the kingdom" in "the book," and like Moses' autograph, it was "placed before the Lord" (1 Samuel 10:25)—that is, beside the Ark. Samuel may have arranged the historical material in one of the two books attributed to him up to the point where his death is recorded (1 Samuel 25:1). By the time of the Exile, the chronicler records that everything concerning David's career "from first to last" was written in "the chronicles of Samuel the seer, in the chronicles of Nathan the prophet, and in the chronicles of Gad the seer" (1 Chronicles 29:29). This may imply that the rest of Samuel (1 Samuel 25:1–2 Samuel 24) was compiled by Nathan and Gad, but it is not clear who compiled the material in the books of Kings and Chronicles.

The Proverbs. Another mention of compilers of biblical texts is the "men of Hezekiah king of Judah" (Proverbs 25:1), who are said to have "transcribed" Solomon's proverbs. This means that under King Hezekiah a committee selected proverbs (1:1–9:18; 10:1–22:16; 25:1–29:27) for the "Book of Proverbs" from among the 3000 in the larger Solomonic collection (1 Kings 4:32).

It can only be supposed that they also gathered the "sayings of the wise" (Proverbs 22:17–24:22-24), the "sayings of Agur" (Proverbs 30), and the "sayings of King Lemuel" (Proverbs 31), but there is no statement concerning this. However, since this selecting (at least of Solomonic proverbs) occurred some 250 years after they were originally written, there is the implication that the basic collection begun in the time of Solomon was expanded over time and then edited at the time of Hezekiah.

With the words of Agur in Proverbs 30:4-6 there is also evidence of later writers citing or incorporating earlier material from those recognized as divinely inspired authors. Agur admits in verses 2 to 3 that he has not "learned wisdom" nor does he have "the knowledge of the Holy One." However, in verses 5 to 6 he reveals that his source for both comes from the Scriptures, for his words in these verses are taken from David (Psalm 18:30 in verse 5) and Moses (Deuteronomy 4:2 in verse 6).

The Psalms and Pentateuch. Just as the "men of Hezekiah" arranged the collection of Proverbs, so others must have arranged the Psalms, the Pentateuch, and the other historical books (including those known as the former prophets). There is a difference, of course, in saying Moses wrote the Pentateuch and saying that his words were arranged by others to fit an orderly design with other books. This order can be observed in deliberately linked introductions and conclusions, which are seen in repetitions and overlaps of material from Deuteronomy 34 through 2 Kings 17.[3] Similarly, the book of Psalms was compiled and arranged from the psalms of David, Solomon, and others (many anonymous) into a five-part hymnbook (note the ending verses concluding each "book").

The book of Jeremiah perhaps fits in this time of collection and arrangement. Its shorter and longer versions have presented a challenge to scholars in understanding the transmission history of the Hebrew text. The shorter form exists in the Septuagint and in one of the Dead Sea

Book 1: **Psalms 1–41**	Davidic (1000 BC)
Book 2: **Psalms 42–72**	Davidic
Book 3: **Psalms 73–89**	Exilic (586–516 BC); Psalm 86 is Davidic
Book 4: **Psalms 90–106**	Postexilic (515 BC–); Psalms 101 and 103 are Davidic
Book 5: **Psalms 107–150**	Postexilic; Psalms 108–110, 122, 124, 131, 133, and 138–145 are Davidic; Psalm 127 is Solomonic (950 BC)

Scrolls, while the longer form is in the Masoretic Text. It may be that two editions of the book of Jeremiah existed, as implied by Jeremiah 36:32 and the statement that after King Jehoiakim had burned the scroll of Jeremiah's prophecies, Jeremiah's scribe Baruch wrote another scroll of prophecies and "added many similar things to them." Since the Septuagint was translated in Egypt, where Jeremiah had been taken captive, perhaps the shorter version had remained in circulation there, while the longer version had been taken back to Israel with those returning after the Exile.[4]

The prophets. The end of the period of divine inspiration and biblical composition comes in the fifth century BC with the writing prophets. Already in Daniel we find a reference to "the books" (Daniel 9:2), which must refer to those of the prophets, since he cites his contemporary Jeremiah as an authoritative source. However, Daniel is also viewing Jeremiah's prophecy (Jeremiah 25:11-12) as "inspired Scripture," since it is the basis for his prayer for the fulfillment of God's promise (Daniel 9:3-19) and his own revelation of the "seventy weeks" (verses 20-27). These prophets, both before and after the Babylonian Exile, addressed the calamities that had befallen the Jewish nation as a result of covenant disobedience, as well as the question of the harsh conditions upon their return and the lack of physical and spiritual restoration on the scale predicted by the earlier prophets.

Some of the literature of this period also includes official court records of the Persian administrations (Ezra 6:1-12; 7:11-28); lists of returned

Temple treasures and genealogies (2 Chronicles 36:22-23; Ezra 1–2; 8:1-14; Nehemiah 7:5-73), the latter being important for national census taking; and lists of priests and Levites (Ezra 8:15-20; Nehemiah 12:1-26).

Ezra was responsible for re-educating the returnees and interpreting the Mosaic legislation for them (Nehemiah 1:1-8), while Nehemiah may have established an archive in the Temple of all of the books known to be Scripture: "He founded a library, gathered together the books about the kings and prophets, and the books of David, and the letters of kings about sacred gifts" (2 Maccabees 2:13). Because of their administrative and scribal role in this formative period, Nehemiah and Ezra have been credited with the creation of the postexilic Jewish community in Israel and are viewed as two of the greatest figures in Jewish history.

Although the origin of the Old Testament is complicated and still uncertain, there should be no doubt that the Holy Spirit who inspired the writing of the sacred texts also superintended their collection and arrangement into what Jews know as the Hebrew Bible and Christians call the Old Testament. As a final note, it should be observed that some of the works were produced to endure as part of Israel's covenantal heritage, whereas others were intended for a particular audience in a particular place at a particular time and only continued as part of the Hebrew canon (see chapter 8) because they were recognized as having prophetic authority and relevance for the Jewish people. These differences in reasons for the texts' composition may have implications for the degree of preservation of the original manuscripts.

The Origin of the New Testament

Unlike the Old Testament, the New Testament has a much shorter period of composition, ranging from shortly after the formation of the church in the 30s AD to just before the end of the first century (a little more than 20 years after the close of the Second Temple period). Here the authors were primarily the apostles, some of whom had also been the disciples of Jesus, and others like Paul, who had a unique calling to the Gentiles. Luke, who wrote the Gospel that bears his name and the book of Acts, was a historical researcher and chronicler as well as an eyewitness who accompanied the apostle Paul and others on the missionary journeys.

The purpose of these compositions was much the same—to communicate to the believing Christian community 1) the events that fulfilled the prophecy of the Christ's coming, 2) the sayings of Jesus, 3) doctrinal instruction for the maintenance of the church (individually and collectively), and 4) the promise of Christ's second coming.

This early instruction, for perhaps the first decade of the church, was oral. In the beginning the apostles met regularly with the growing community of believers in Jerusalem to instruct them in the Old Testament (Acts 1:14-20) as well as teach them concerning the words and works of Jesus (Acts 2:42), as the Lord had promised (John 14:26; 16:13-15). This oral instruction was passed on to "faithful men," who in turn would pass it on to others who would teach future generations (2 Timothy 2:2). From Jerusalem, the apostles' teaching then spread to the wider region of Judea, then to the northern area of Samaria, and finally to Asia Minor and beyond (Acts 1:8).

The move from oral instruction to written instruction followed the needs of the church:

- information on historical matters concerning Christ and the Christian faith from eyewitness accounts (for example, Luke 1:1-4; Acts 1:1)

- addressing problematic situations in local churches and answering specific doctrinal questions (for example, 1 Corinthians 1:10-11; 5:1-13; 7:1,25; 8:1; 12:1; 15:2; 16:1)

- continuing instruction from afar or when imprisoned (for example, 2 Corinthians 13:10; the prison epistles)

- clarifying in writing previous oral instruction (for example, 2 Thessalonians 2:5)

- reaching the wider audience that would exist beyond the lifetime of the apostles (for example, Acts 20:29-32; Romans 16:25-27)

Initially, some of these writings were not regarded as Scripture, although they were deemed authoritative. In the case of Paul, even the question of authority had to sometimes be defended (for example, 1 Corinthians 4:9; 2 Corinthians 3:1; 10:8-18; 11:5; 12:11-13), while the matter of his writings as Scripture was defended by others (2 Peter 3:16).

The autographs that met these needs were written on materials in keeping with the particular circumstances that required them (imprisonment, swift reply, and so on). These materials, therefore, could not be expected to preserve their contents indefinitely. For example, when Jesus gave His revelation of the future to the apostle John, He ordered him to write it down immediately and deliver it to local churches in Asia Minor: "Write in a book what you see, and send it to the seven churches" (Revelation 1:11). It has been debated whether John (or his amanuensis) wrote *one* copy and distributed it around to the seven churches or made *seven* copies and sent one to each of the churches (though the stronger case is made for the latter position). Whatever the case, the recipients of the "book of Revelation" regarded it as "inspired Scripture" and must have thereafter circulated it through handwritten copies to other communities and churches who requested it.

From what has been said in this chapter, it could seem that every copy made of biblical texts has had the originals as a reference, and that the variety of translations that exist today reflect only stylistic or interpretive options of the translators. However, the facts are that *none* of the autographs are known to have survived anywhere in the world. How this situation came about, and what its importance is, will form the discussion in the next chapter.

Chapter 3

What Happened to the Original Bible?

Only in such conditions as are provided by the dry sands of Egypt and the volcanic ash of Herculaneum have papyrus documents been preserved; in humid climates they soon rotted away. So, while we can read the original inscriptions of Assyrian and Babylonian kings [written on clay bricks]...the autographs of the Hebrew prophets who were their contemporaries have disappeared long ago, as also have the autographs of all the other Biblical writers....But these autographs were copied before they perished, and throughout the intervening centuries they have been copied and re-copied continually.

—F.F. Bruce

According to the historical record, none of the autographs of the Original Bible have existed since ancient times. The original manuscripts of the Old Testament disappeared between the destruction of the First Temple and the time of Christ, and those of the New Testament shortly after the time of the apostles (and in some cases, even before the death of the last of the apostles).

This condition also exists for the early copies made of both the Old and New Testaments. Every translation of the Old Testament made today is made from the Masoretic Text, the standard Hebrew text codified in the tenth century AD. Those who produced the Masoretic Text mention earlier manuscripts, such as a "Codex Mugah," as well as a "Codex Hilleli," said to have been written c. 600 by Rabbi Hillel ben Moses ben Hillel, but both have vanished.

In the case of the New Testament, there seems to have been no special concern to preserve the originals over the copies made of them. Given the care we exert to protect and preserve original documents today, the lack of preservation of originals of the Bible, or at least the words of Jesus, seems to us astounding. The earliest complete manuscripts that lie behind our modern translations of the New Testament, such as Codex Sinaiticus and Codex Vaticanus, are both from the fourth to fifth centuries AD, their exemplars (manuscript copies from which they were copied) having also disappeared.

Since the autographs of the Bible are no longer to be found, and even the earliest copies of the autographs have disappeared, it is reasonable to ask what might have happened to them. There is no doubt that the originals of the Old Testament were held in high esteem (as we have seen from the deposition of the original Pentateuch with the Ark of the Covenant), and we may wonder how such valuable documents could have simply vanished. The answers are varied, but it must be remembered at the outset that though we no longer possess the originals, we do not possess any less of the Bible. Therefore, we also want to draw some conclusions concerning the copies that have been left to us as we consider the historical data about the disappearance of the originals.

Storage or Concealment by Priests

There are numerous accounts of old documents being found during the repairs of temples from both Egypt and Mesopotamia. Ancient scrolls have been found in the masonry of buildings in Egypt, and the famous Nag Hammadi texts (which include the so-called "Lost Gospels") were discovered in a cave (or tomb) in a monastery located in this Egyptian city. The Egyptian pharaoh Shabaka (c. 700 BC) is reported to have found a lost theological text concerning Ptah's creation of the world on a badly damaged ancient papyrus. Deposits of cuneiform tablets including royal inscriptions and dedicatory stelae* have often been unearthed in Mesopotamia. Nabonidus, the last king of Babylon, who reigned from 556–539 BC, was known for his search for such ancient documents buried in buildings.

In keeping with these examples from the ancient Near East, the "book of the law" found during repairs to the Temple's structure (see 2 Kings 22:8-20; 2 Chronicles 34:14-33) could have been preserved in a foundation

---

*A *stela* (plural, *stelae*) is a "carved or inscribed stone slab or pillar used for commemorative purposes."

box in the Temple, concealed in its walls, or stored within in its archives. It had apparently been hidden by loyal priests to protect it from the religious defection under the Judean King Manasseh that had violated even the sanctity of the Temple itself (2 Kings 21:2-9, especially verse 7). Similarly, according to Jewish tradition, the Ark of the Covenant was hidden in a secret chamber within the Temple before the Babylonian invasion. Even if the tablets of the Ten Commandments and the original Torah written by Moses had remained with the Ark (Deuteronomy 31:26), they were still lost to postexilic Judaism and all generations of Jews thereafter. (This raises an intriguing question. Would Judaism "revise" its present Torah, which is considered inspired and authoritative, if the Ark and the original Torah were discovered?) Our discussion at this point leads us to two necessary conclusions concerning hidden documents.

1. While some of the originals have been lost, their loss might not be permanent because they may have been purposefully stored in order to preserve them for future use. Perhaps such acts would have been influenced by Scripture itself, since Isaiah 30:8 states concerning one of this prophet's messages, "Now go, write it on a tablet before them and inscribe it on a scroll, that it may serve in the time to come as a witness *forever*." This leaves open the possibility that originals could be recovered someday by archaeologists (see chapter 11).

2. More important for our general discussion was that the *copy* of Scripture found hidden in the Temple was regarded as *Scripture*. This was apparently the motive for its hiding, and it was confirmed by Huldah the prophetess, who said, "Thus says the Lord, 'Behold, I bring evil on this place and on its inhabitants, even *all the words of the book* which the king of Judah has read' " (2 Kings 22:16). Here God Himself confirms that what was in the copy was His word.

Loss Through Deterioration

Although passages of the Old Testament were on special occasion recorded on stone,* it is clear from other references to writing with "pen

---

*Exodus 24:12; Deuteronomy 27:2-3; Isaiah 8:1; 30:8a.

and ink" on "scrolls" or "books" in both testaments that the materials normally used were either papyrus or parchment.*

Such perishable materials rapidly deteriorate in humid conditions and only on rare occasions have been preserved—in arid climates such as in caves in Upper Egypt and the Judean desert.

Adding to this was the wear suffered by constant use. When an Old Testament biblical text became old and worn from long use (or became defective in some way) it was consigned to a special storage area known as a *genizah*. Because the texts contained the name of God, the scrolls could not be disposed of; it would have been unthinkable to destroy the name of God! The very act of consignment to a *genizah* rendered them "lost," in the practical sense that they could no longer be read in the synagogue service.

However, the ancients expected their scrolls to deteriorate, and for this reason scribes made new copies to preserve their contents for continued use. This way of thinking made new and perfect scrolls preferable to old and imperfect scrolls, since they were freer from defect or damage. In this way earlier copies passed out of use, a practice that contributed to their ultimate disappearance.

Intentional Destruction by Enemies

As a natural land bridge for foreign armies on the march, the land of Israel was frequently invaded and occupied, with its capital city of Jerusalem suffering the brunt of the violence. The Torah, as the basis for Jewish legal and ritual observance, often conflicted with the lifestyles observed (or imposed) by other nations that ruled Israel. Pagan authorities, when outlawing Jewish practice, also sought to destroy the source that commanded it. For example, the first-century Jewish historian Flavius Josephus records in his *Wars of the Jews* (published c. AD 75) how the Syrian-Greek ruler Antiochus IV Epiphanes abolished Jewish practice by persecution:

> The king...came upon the Jews with a great army, and took their city by force, and slew a great multitude of those that favored Ptolemy, and sent out his soldiers to plunder them without mercy. He also spoiled the temple, and put a stop to the constant

---

*Numbers 5:23; Deuteronomy 17:18; Isaiah 30:8b; Jeremiah 30:2; 36:2,4,14,18,28; Ezekiel 2:9; 3:1-3; Ezra 6:2; 2; Zechariah 5:1-2; 2 Corinthians 3:3; 2 John 12; 3 John 13; Revelation 1:11.

practice of offering a daily sacrifice of expiation for three years and six months…Now Antiochus was not satisfied either with his unexpected taking the city, or with its pillage, or with the great slaughter he had made there; but being overcome with his violent passions, and remembering what he had suffered during the siege, he compelled the Jews to dissolve the laws of their country, and to keep their infants uncircumcised, and to sacrifice swine's flesh upon the altar; against which they all opposed themselves, and the most approved among them were put to death…and tormented the worthiest of the inhabitants, man by man, and threatened their city every day with open destruction (*Wars* 1.1, 2).

The historical account of this "spoiling of the Temple" in the book of 1 Maccabees reveals a forced cessation of the sacrificial system brought about by the erection of an idol of Zeus Olympias beside the Bronze Altar and indicates a complete pagan usurpation of the Temple complex— including any place original biblical manuscripts might have been stored.

On another occasion, an Israelite king who opposed the political position of a biblical prophet destroyed the original manuscript the prophet had written. Before the Babylonian invasion of Judah, the prophet Jeremiah declared that the southern kingdom of Judah would fall to the Babylonians as a divine judgment against the spiritual defection of the royal court and the priesthood. Jeremiah had this prophetic message (the original book of Jeremiah) written on a scroll by his scribe Baruch and then read publicly in the Temple precincts.

Shortly thereafter, the Judean King Jehoiakim ordered that the scroll be read to him. The account in Jeremiah 36:23 records what happened next: "And it came about, when Jehudi had read three or four columns, the king cut it with a scribe's knife and threw it into the fire that was in the brazier, until all the scroll was consumed in the fire that was in the brazier." Although a second "original" was composed in the same manner as the first, it was an expansion that included "additional words" (Jeremiah 36:32). Even so, this incident revealed that original manuscripts were wantonly destroyed within Israel.

When the Babylonians invaded Judah (605–589 BC) and finally burnt the city and the Temple (586 BC), the royal archives and the First Temple's library, where sacred documents would have been stored, suffered destruction. Such a calamity struck Jerusalem again in AD 70, when the Roman 10th Legion invaded and burnt the Second Temple. These violent devastations of the city of Jerusalem, where any originals of the Old Testament books would have been stored, argue against the preservation of these manuscripts (unless the priests were able to remove them before the attack).

Evidence of this is also seen at Qumran, which the Romans invaded and burned in AD 68, and at Masada where in AD 73 the Romans attacked fleeing Jewish rebels and burned their buildings, including a synagogue,

where the remains of biblical texts were later found. Priests escaping during these wars with items vital to perpetuating Jewish religious practice would most likely have taken with them the best copies of these texts that were easily accessible and legal for use. These may have been hidden away, such as were the Dead Sea Scrolls, with the hope of recovering them in better times.

Both the Old and New Testaments declare that these destructions of the Temple were from God (2 Kings 23:27; 24:13; Luke 19:43-45).

Author in genizah of the Jewish synagogue at Masada (destroyed in AD 73).

And from a theological perspective, if God allowed the destruction of the originals of His Word, it was because He recognized the copies of His Word as sufficient.

The Situation During the Time of the Early Church

Possible mentions of the original manuscripts of the New Testament (or at least early copies) may be found in comments made by some of the early Church Fathers. Tertullian, who was born shortly after the middle of the second century and who wrote extensively against the various enemies of the church that had arisen, seems to make specific mention of the continued existence in his day of the original apostolic manuscripts. In one treatise against heretics he writes,

> Come now, you who would indulge a better curiosity, if you would apply it to the business of your salvation, run over the apostolic churches, in which the very thrones of the apostles are still pre-eminent in their places, in which *their own authentic writings* are read, uttering the voice and representing the face of each of them severally (*On Prescription Against Heretics* XXXVI, emphasis added).[1]

Tertullian's defense seeks to make an indisputable claim that the orthodox church can trace its sources to the apostles. He appears to assert that the autographs were still in the possession of the local churches to which they were addressed.

However, scholars debate the intended reference of Tertullian's Latin term *authenticae* ("authentic"). Tertullian offered as evidence the apostolic writings being read in the orthodox churches and indicated that they faithfully represented the apostles' original doctrines. But did he have in mind the Greek originals of the apostles in contrast to the Latin translations—or complete and accurate copies of the originals in contrast to the incomplete and errant copies used by the heretics? In support of his reference being to the autographs is the context. In the previous paragraph Tertullian had made appeal to the doctrinal system of the orthodox church "being earlier than all," and "evidence of that truth which everywhere occupies the first place" (*On Prescription Against Heretics* XXXV).

These statements appeal to an original and unbroken connection with apostolic teaching that appears to have as its support the evidence of the original writings mentioned in the following paragraph. However, such a claim could still be made if Tertullian's reference was to copies, correct because they were made from the original—in contrast to those of the heretics, which had been compiled from other sources and altered to fit their own views. However, even if he meant the autographs, it is unclear whether they actually existed; the majority of scholars believe that Tertullian's statement was simply rhetorical since, as historian Robert Grant observed, "He touched upon nothing which he did not exaggerate."

Even if the second generation of church leaders (the postapostolic fathers) did not have access to the autographs, this does not appear to have affected their use of the copies in the church for faith and practice. Interestingly, there are some references to first-generation church leaders, when the apostle John was still alive, consulting him for clarification of what he had written. The implication is not that the meaning of his words was in doubt, but that there was a dispute about which actual words he had written. This indicates that even in the apostolic age the originals may have disappeared, or that the church only had access to copies. Nevertheless, these copies were what they considered the Word of God and what they used to defend the faith against heretics, who claimed for their false Gospels inspiration and authority as legitimate Scripture.

We do know from the way different text types or families of text types developed in different localities (Caesarea in Israel, Alexandria in Egypt, Byzantium in Asia Minor, and Rome) that the originals in those places were replaced by copies, which inherited the traits common to the scribes in these city centers. It must be remembered that until Constantine in the fourth century, the Christian community was persecuted because its religion was illegal (or more precisely, as a late religion it had unprotected status) in the eyes of the Roman authorities. Its books could not be legally circulated and were often confiscated and destroyed. Too, the evidence of the *palimpsests* reveals that older texts were not considered as valuable as newer ones and therefore could be discarded or reused.* Thus it is possible that the autographs of the early church suffered destruction.

We have seen that the originals of the biblical texts

- were written in many cases (certainly true of the New Testament) on perishable materials such as papyrus

---

* A *palimpsest* (from the Greek, "to rub again") is a manuscript from which the original text has been erased and a different text written on top of the original writing. Various methods, such as ultraviolet light and new digital-imaging techniques, can expose the original text with extreme accuracy. Palimpsests that survive bear witness to what happened to many of the early uncials, the remnants of which, having been erased and re-used to copy sermons or liturgical texts, would then have been destroyed or discarded once their texts were no longer deemed valuable.

- were written in some cases for a limited audience and not for continued publication and distribution on a wide scale
- suffered conditions natural and accidental that contributed to their destruction or loss

It should be further noted that copies of the originals were subject to the same conditions that led to the loss of the autographs. However, as Michelle P. Brown, Curator of Illuminated Manuscripts in the British Library, London, explains, some of those conditions have also preserved the copies for future recovery:

> Some have remained in ancient monastic libraries or cathedral treasuries since they were written; others have languished, concealed in desert caves, sealed up in long-forgotten rooms, or buried to await resurrection by archaeologists from the ground itself; many have passed from hand to hand down the centuries and are now preserved in great public libraries, museums, and private collections.[2]

Since the autographs no longer exist (God having deemed them not necessary for the continuation of His Word) and nothing remains to us but manuscripts (copies) and versions (translations), what then are these documents that have been preserved against time and carry on a witness to the Original Bible? In our next two chapters we will take a tour of these ancient texts.

Chapter 4

Witnesses to the Original Old Testament

Even copyists make mistakes, as every proofreader knows. So we will never be able to claim certain knowledge of exactly what the original text of any biblical writing was.

—ROBERT FUNK, ROY W. HOOVER,
AND THE JESUS SEMINAR, *THE FIVE GOSPELS*

A good friend of mine is a black preacher, and I have had the opportunity of speaking with him in churches where the congregation is used to being actively involved in the preaching service. When my friend wants to emphasize a crucial point in his message he says, "Can I get a witness?" And the audience passionately responds with either a wave of the hand or a shout of affirmation! In the last chapter the crucial point was made that the original texts of the Old and New Testaments no longer exist, but this has in no way altered the message that God gave. Therefore, in this chapter we will ask, "Can I get a witness?" In other words, if the Original Bible has vanished from the stage of history, what remains in the present day to testify to it? Fortunately, the response is a good one, for abundant manuscripts (copies) and versions (translations) that witness to the original have been left to us.

Even though the original words that God gave and men wrote no longer exist in the form of the same paper and ink, they were committed to faithful witnesses who would be able to teach others. These witnesses are the textual materials used by textual critics (see chapter 13) to recover the wording of the original text. Let us first survey the ancient documents that continue the word to us in our own day from the Original Old Testament.

Primary Witnesses to the Hebrew Bible

The original text of the Hebrew Bible is witnessed to by both primary and secondary sources. In the first category are the copies (ancient Hebrew manuscripts), and in the second category are the versions (ancient translations in other languages). There is also a third category that includes paraphrases of the Hebrew text, and even a fourth category that includes quotations of Hebrew texts (usually in Greek or Latin).

Witnesses to the Text of the Hebrew Bible

Primary sources (Hebrew manuscripts)	Secondary sources
Silver amulet	Samaritan Pentateuch
Nash Papyrus	Greek versions or recensions*
Dead Sea Scrolls (202 manuscripts)	Septuagint
Psalms (36 manuscripts) [Psalms Scroll]	Aquila
Deuteronomy (29 manuscripts)	Symmachus the Ebionite
Isaiah (21 manuscripts) [Isaiah Scroll]	Kaige-Theodotion
Habakkuk Commentary	Origen's Hexapla
Tefillin and mezuzoth from Judean Desert	Hesychius
Severus Scroll (R. Meir's Torah)	Lucian
About 3000 Masoretic Text manuscripts	Post-Hexaplaric revisions
	Aramaic targums
	Syriac versions
	Peshitta Syro-Hexapla
	Latin versions
	Old Latin Latin Vulgate
	Coptic versions
	Sahidic Akhmimic
	Bohairic
	Ethiopic version
	Armenian version
	Arabic versions

* A *recension* is "1: a critical revision of a text; 2: a text established by critical revision." The word comes from the Latin *recensere*, "to review."

The copies and versions reveal the text of the Hebrew Bible in various stages of its transmission. Even though we may have a later *copy* of a text, the *text itself* reflects an earlier date of composition. By comparing these witnesses through the science of textual criticism we are able to determine which readings bring us closest to how the original must have read (see chapter 13).

Although our modern Old Testaments are translated from the tenth-century Masoretic Text, most translations also take into account the witness of the ancient versions (translations). Since the Masoretic Text is itself a witness to the original (although not without comparison to other Hebrew texts and the versions), let us begin with it and progress in descending order of importance to discover the identity and importance of the various manuscripts and versions.

The Masoretic Text

We begin with the Masoretic Text because it is the traditional text of the present Hebrew Bible and that from which all of our English translations of the Old Testament have been made. The Masoretic Text represents a group of closely related ancient Hebrew manuscripts called the *Masorah* (because of the textual apparatus attached to it—see sidebar). It reached its final, fixed form in the tenth century AD. Its name is derived from the scribal school called *Masoretes* (possibly from the Hebrew term *masar,* "to hand down"), whose primary activity from AD 500 to 1100 was to copy, edit, and preserve the textual traditions passed down to them. Therefore, the Masoretic Text is based on hundreds of medieval manuscripts now lost to us.

The Masoretic "Textual Apparatus"

The Masorah, which refers to the transmission of "tradition," is a collection of scribal notations (apparatus) on everything from alternate readings to grammatical forms designed to preserve the accuracy of the transmission of the text, also continued as part of the Masoretic Text. One such type of scribal notation that was included to indicate corrections to the unchangeable consonantal text was called *Kethiv-Qere* ("what is written"—"what is read"). Since the scribes did not want to alter the text, even though they believed it obviously was incorrect, they left "what was written" in place while adding in the margin "what is [to be] read" in place of what is written.

Two scribal schools were involved in the production of the Masoretic Text: the Eastern, or Babylonian, school; and the Western, or Palestinian, school. The Palestinian school had two branches: the families of Aaron ben Moses ben Asher and the ben Naphtali in Tiberias (northern Israel). Although these two families upheld two separate textual traditions, between them there were only eight small differences in the consonantal text—and in fact, their traditions actually represented one text with minor variations. In about AD 925 ben Asher produced the first complete Hebrew Bible. This Bible is known as the Aleppo Codex, because Aleppo, Syria, was the home of the Jewish community that kept this text for centuries, which is today at the Hebrew University in Jerusalem.

Page of Aleppo Codex (British Library)

The Masoretic Text, accepted as the authorized text, is the starting point for textual critics in their attempts to reconstruct the original text, and the standard text to which all other ancient Hebrew manuscripts (such as the biblical manuscripts of the Dead Sea Scrolls) are compared. Even though the Masoretic Text (actually made up of a group of texts) was not the only text circulating in ancient Judaism, when compared with the other witnesses it is usually recognized to be closest to the original. The development under the Masoretes included the addition of vowel indicators (a vocalization system) and diacritical marks (cantillation marks, accents) to the consonantal Hebrew text to enable correct pronunciation and interpretation.

This text served as the basis for the scholarly standard edition of the Hebrew Bible, Kittel's *Biblia Hebraica,* and serves as well for translation of the Old Testament in any language. For many decades a new critical edition of the Masoretic Text has been in preparation at the Hebrew University in Jerusalem (the effort is known as the Hebrew University Bible Project).

The most important surviving manuscripts of the Masoretic Text all come from the ben Asher family. The earliest, providing our best examples of the Masoretic tradition are

1. *Codex Cairensis* (AD 895), containing only the Former and Latter Prophets

2. *Aleppo Codex* (AD 930), once a complete copy, but one-fourth destroyed in a fire

3. *Oriental 4445* (AD 950, 1540), containing most of the Pentateuch (Genesis 39:20–Deuteronomy 1:33)

4. *Codex Leningradensis,* or *Leningrad B19a* (AD 1008–1009), a complete text of the Old Testament that served as the source for the most current critical editions of the Hebrew text: *Biblia Hebraica,* ed. Rudolf Kittel (1973), and *Biblia Hebraica Stuttgartensia,* eds. Karl Ellinger and Wilhelm Stuttgart (1984)

5. *Leningrad (Petersburg) Codex of the Prophets* (AD 916), containing only the Latter Prophets

6. *Damascus Pentateuch* (late ninth or tenth century AD), containing most of the Pentateuch

7. *Codex Reuchlinianus of the Prophets* (AD 1105), containing an editorial revision of the ben Naphtali text

8. *Erfurtensis Codex* (AD 1000–1300), consisting of three manuscripts, all containing the entire Old Testament

Since the Hebrew text (Codex Leningradensis) on which almost all of our present translations of the Old Testament are based is not a critical, or reconstructed, text (which the standard critical editions of the Greek New Testament are), modern translators feel it may need to be corrected on the basis of other Hebrew manuscripts, giving priority to those that are earliest (the biblical manuscripts found among the Dead Sea Scrolls—see below), and the earlier versions.

Page of Codex Leningradensis (National Library of Russia, St. Petersburg)

The Nash Papyrus

Before the discovery of the Dead Sea Scrolls, the earliest example of a Hebrew biblical text written on papyrus was the Nash Papyrus. (There exists a silver amulet with the oldest Hebrew biblical inscription, which is mentioned in chapter 6.) The Society of Biblical Archaeology in England, whose secretary was W.L. Nash, acquired the papyrus fragment in 1902 from an Egyptian dealer and subsequently donated it to the Cambridge University library. Its paleographic date, determined by the style of the script, is the Hasmonean period (169–37 BC), although some have dated it to the end of the Second Temple period (before AD 70) based on internal evidence.

Nash Papyrus (University of Cambridge Library)

The text is made up of a combination of biblical passages from Exodus 20:2-17 (the Ten Commandments) and Deuteronomy 6:4 (the *Shema:* "Hear O Israel…") It was a portion of a collection of passages used for some devotional or liturgical purpose. However, what is of interest is the variants that are found even in these two brief passages. The Exodus passage appears to have a text that borrowed terms from Deuteronomy 5:6-21 (a parallel passage), and it has reversed the order of the sixth and seventh commandments. The Deuteronomy 6:4 passage begins with a word supported only by the Septuagint.

Therefore, even in such a small text it can be seen that scribal variation occurred. Or perhaps the Nash Papyrus reflects an earlier copy that contained these variants.

The Dead Sea Scrolls

The Dead Sea Scrolls were first revealed to the world in 1948. Discovered in jars or buried in the floors of caves lining the cliffs along the western shore of the Dead Sea in Israel, these documents produced by

Jewish scribes represent our oldest copies of the Hebrew Bible. The text is written in columns in the languages of Hebrew, Aramaic, and Greek, on leather parchment and papyrus. The number of biblical manuscripts is about 230,[1] including in whole or fragmentary form every book of the Hebrew Bible except the book of Esther; biblical

Author in Dead Sea Scroll Cave 4 at Qumran

texts in other forms, such as Targums (Aramaic free translations of the Bible), Tefillin, and Mezuzot (biblical passages from Exodus and Deuteronomy), and numerous interpretive commentaries on the biblical text (largely written from a prophetic perspective).

Designating the Scrolls

The Dead Sea Scrolls were discovered in 11 different caves in a chronological order. Thus they were originally designated by a number that reflected this. For example, 1QIsa = Isaiah Scroll from Cave 1; 4QpaleoEx = Exodus Scroll (written in paleo-Hebrew script) from Cave 4; 11QTemple = Temple Scroll from Cave 11.

Biblical Manuscripts of the Dead Sea Scrolls

Canonical division (according to the Hebrew Bible)	Old Testament book	Number of Qumran and other manuscripts
Pentateuch (Torah)	Genesis	24
	Exodus	18
	Leviticus	18
	Numbers	11
	Deuteronomy	33
Prophets (Nevi'im)	Joshua	2
	Judges	3
Former prophets	1 & 2 Samuel	4
	1 & 2 Kings	3
Latter prophets	Isaiah	22
	Jeremiah	6
	Ezekiel	6
	Twelve (Minor) Prophets	10
Writings (Ketuvim)	Psalms	39
	Proverbs	2
	Job	6
	The Five Scrolls:	4
	Song of Songs	4
	Ruth	4
	Lamentations	3
	Ecclesiastes	0
	Esther	8
	Daniel	1
	Ezra–Nehemiah	1
	1 & 2 Chronicles	
		231 total
		223* adjusted total

* The total has been adjusted to read 8 less, since 6 scrolls from Qumran contain portions of two books (counted 2 times), and 1 scroll from Wadi Murabba'at contains portions of 3 books (counted 3 times).

Paleographic analysis (dating by the style of a manuscript's script), carbon-14 testing on the scrolls' outer wrappings, and association with datable material finds in the caves (such as coins and oil lamps) have supported a range of dates for the biblical manuscripts from 225 BC to AD 68. For this reason, most scholars believe they were composed during the Hasmonean period (152–63 BC) and during the Early Roman period (63 BC–AD 68). Although finds from other caves (see below) have yielded dates much older (Wadi el-Daliyeh, 352 BC) and much later (Wadi Murabba'at, AD 69–136, and Khirbet Mird, AD 744), the general range for the biblical material has remained the same.

Muhammad Hammad al-Ubiayt, one of the Bedouin who discovered the Dead Sea Scrolls, throws a rock into Cave 1 at Qumran.

The Scrolls' Witness to the Hebrew Bible

The most significant single contribution of the scrolls has been their witness to the earliest known text of the Hebrew Bible. In the case of the latest Minor Prophets, the Dead Sea manuscripts witness to a text within only a couple of generations of the original text itself, a situation comparable to the earliest (second-century) papyri of the New Testament.

Before the discovery of the scrolls the oldest Hebrew text was the tenth-century Aleppo Codex, which contained the Masoretic Text. Despite its antiquity, it was still 1300 years removed from the latest book composed by a biblical writer (c. 425 BC). The problem for biblical critics was that with so much distance in time between the originals and the Masoretic Text, it was possible that transmission mistakes by generations of scribes had multiplied themselves in the medieval text. Comparisons with other ancient versions such as the Greek Septuagint, Latin Vulgate, and Samaritan Pentateuch seemed to confirm this and call into question the integrity and reliability of the traditional Hebrew text.

However, all doubts were laid to rest with the discovery in Cave 1 of a copy of the entire book of Isaiah (1QIsa^a) dated to 125 BC, *1000 years earlier* than the Aleppo Codex. This scroll, itself a many-generational copy, proved to be identical to the Masoretic Text of Isaiah in more than 95 percent of the text. The 5 percent variation consisted primarily of obvious slips of the pen and spelling alterations. This also proved to be the case for all of the other biblical scrolls among the Dead Sea Scrolls. In fact, about 60 percent of these biblical texts reflect the same text as that in the Masoretic Text. Although interesting deviations and additions do appear and are of great value in understanding the history of the transmission of the biblical text, on the whole the scrolls testify to the exceptional preservation of the biblical text through the centuries and validate the traditional text as the closest witness we have to the original.

The understanding of the original composition of the Hebrew text of the Old Testament is also illuminated by comparison with both the biblical and nonbiblical Dead Sea texts. These comparisons reveal that there is agreement with the Masoretic Text 80 percent of the time,[2] with the remaining 20 percent divided between agreement with the Septuagint

Biblical Dead Sea Scroll (Psalm scroll) from Cave 11

(5 percent), the Samaritan Pentateuch (5 percent), and mixed texts from several traditions (10 percent). Hebrew University professor Emanuel Tov explains the minor changes that make up most of these variations from the Masoretic Text:

> If we compare our knowledge prior to the finding of the Qumran Scrolls—that is, of the Masoretic text—to the Qumran Scrolls we find hundreds or thousands of differences and these differences are in small details and in large details. Small details will pertain to a letter here or a letter there, irregular spellings. The large differences could involve a singular word; they could also involve a whole phrase or a sentence or sometimes even a paragraph.[3]

The textual diversity that appears in the scrolls may be a reflection of the geographical diversity of local text types (Egyptian, Babylonian, Palestinian), as one theory goes; or perhaps it indicates that scribes considered the biblical text still open to scribal activity, as another theory explains. Whatever theory is accepted, the scrolls have revealed different versions of the Hebrew text upon which the Septuagint, Samaritan Pentateuch, and the Masoretic Text all depended (though most agree with a proto-Masoretic Text).

Textual Alignment of the Dead Sea Scrolls with the Masoretic Text

Distribution of the biblical manuscripts in the Qumran caves		Alignment of biblical manuscripts found at Qumran with other biblical versions	
Cave 1	17	Proto-Masoretic texts	60%
Cave 2	18	Qumran-style texts	20%
Cave 3	3	Nonaligned texts	10%
Cave 4	137	Septuagintal-type texts	5%
Cave 5	7	Proto-Samaritan	
Cave 6	7	(Pentateuch) texts	5%
Cave 7	1		
Cave 8	2		
Cave 9	0		
Cave 10	0		
Cave 11	10		

Other Dead Sea Manuscripts

Along the western shores of the Dead Sea, but south of the Dead Sea Scroll caves, other scroll discoveries were made in the 1950s and 1960s, though one came as late as 2005. These texts are often treated separately from the Dead Sea Scrolls because they come from different time periods and therefore were produced by a group of Jews distinct from the sect that produced the Dead Sea Scrolls.

The earliest discoveries (1951–1952) were made in caves at Wadi Murabba'at, where a number of biblical texts had been deposited during the time of the Bar Kokhba Revolt (AD 132–135). These include fragmentary texts from the Torah (Genesis, Exodus, Numbers, Deuteronomy) and a copy of the Latter Prophets (Mur. 88) that contained ten of the twelve Minor Prophets. These texts showed an almost complete affinity with the Masoretic Text, with only three meaningful variants appearing in the text of the Latter Prophets. The significance of this is that it reveals that the proto-Masoretic Text was already stabilized at this point, confirming the belief that the stabilization had been completed by the end of the Second Temple period.

At the same time as the discovery at Wadi Murabba'at, caves in the area of Nahal Hever and Nahal Seelim yielded other scrolls, also from the Bar Kokhba period. From Nahal Hever came fragments of Genesis, Numbers, Deuteronomy, and Psalms, and the most complete text of the Latter Prophets (8 HevXIIgr). Unlike the other scrolls, which were written in Hebrew, this text of the Prophets was in Greek, except for the name of God (YHWH), which was written in the paleo-Hebrew script. Like the manuscripts from Wadi Murabba'at, these texts were also almost identical to the Masoretic Text.

From Nahal Seelim came two phylactery* texts of Exodus 13:2-16, and a portion of Leviticus (purchased in 2005). Then, from 1963 to 1965, excavations were conducted at Masada, a mountain fortress of Herod the Great also located on the shores of the Dead Sea and destroyed by a Roman siege in AD 73. Inside the remains of a synagogue at the site was discovered a genizah, a storage place for manuscripts retired from use (see photo on

---

* A *phylactery* is "either of two small square leather boxes containing slips inscribed with scriptural passages and traditionally worn on the left arm and on the head by observant Jewish men and especially adherents of Orthodox Judaism during morning weekday prayers."

p. 50). From this came 14 scrolls, which included fragments of sectarian, apocryphal, and biblical texts (Genesis, Leviticus, Deuteronomy, Psalms, and Ezekiel).[4]

Secondary Witnesses to the Hebrew Bible

Not only do the ancient biblical manuscripts testify to the Original Old Testament, but ancient versions (translations) do as well.

The Septuagint

The Septuagint (Latin for "seventy"), also given the designation LXX ("seventy" in Roman numerals), is the most important of the versions. It was used extensively by the authors of the New Testament (most of their quotations of the Old Testament are from this source), and it served the early church as its authoritative biblical text. Jewish writers such as Flavius Josephus and Philo also used the Septuagint (the latter more than the former). The *Letter of Aristeas* records a highly stylized and probably legendary account of the production of the Septuagint. According to the story it tells, a request was made by Ptolemy II of Egypt (285–246 BC) to the High Priest Eleazar for 6 elders from each of the 12 tribes (a rough total of "seventy," hence the name of the document) to make a translation in Greek of the Hebrew Bible for the library at Alexandria.

Although the *Letter of Aristeas* claimed the Septuagint was translated uniformly by equally skilled translators under divine inspiration and with

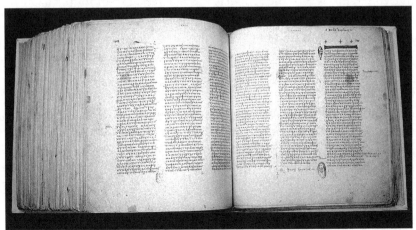

Septuagint, Codex Vaticanus (Vatican Library)

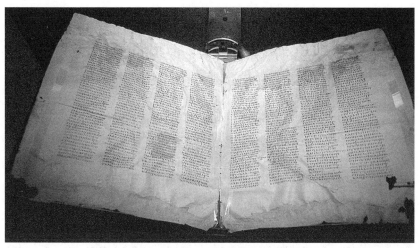

Septuagint, Codex Sinaiticus (British Library)

an accuracy that implied inerrancy, the historical facts reveal otherwise.[5] The translation is not a uniform and consistent translation; it was done by many different hands whose skill, and even philosophy, of translating varied considerably. The Pentateuch (Torah) was first translated (probably in the third century BC, as the legend states), and is therefore referred to as the Old Greek text. The only church Father on record to point this out was Jerome.[6] The rest was completed over the next few centuries, with the whole being constantly revised for an equal period of time.

The value of the Septuagint is that it is a witness to a proto-Masoretic Hebrew text that is different from that in the Masoretic Text itself. These differences include the addition of words to create longer versions of some texts, most notably parts of the book of Jeremiah, and variants that were the result of misunderstanding or misinterpreting a Hebrew word or phrase. In addition, the interpretations reflected in the text by the various authors, translations, and versions of the Septuagint are indicative of Diaspora Judaism (Jews who lived outside the land of Israel). For this reason, and because of the fact that Greek had become the international language of the day, the Septuagint became the Bible of Diaspora Judaism and of Hellenistic Jews in the Land of Israel.[7]

However, in comparison with the Masoretic Text, the latter appears intrinsically more reliable than the Septuagint, although in some cases the Septuagint preserves a reading that is to be preferred when it is in agreement with a Hebrew manuscript (such as the biblical manuscripts of the Dead Sea Scrolls).

The most important manuscripts of the Septuagint are

1. The *Chester Beatty Papyri* (second to fourth centuries AD), containing various parts of the Old Testament

2. The *Oxyrhynchus Papyri* (first to ninth centuries AD), containing the Pentateuch through Ruth, the Psalms and the Prophets

3. The *Rylands Papyri* (second century BC to fifth century AD), containing Genesis, Deuteronomy, Chronicles, Job, and Isaiah

4. *Codex Vaticanus* (fourth century AD), a major uncial manuscript containing (originally) the entire Old Testament and Apocrypha

5. *Codex Sinaiticus* (late fourth to early fifth century AD), a major uncial manuscript containing portions of the Old Testament and the Apocrypha

6. *Codex Alexandrinus* (mid-fifth century AD), a major uncial manuscript containing (originally) all of the Old Testament

7. *Codex Ephraemi* (fifth to sixth centuries AD), a major uncial manuscript that is a palimpsest. Its text was erased in the twelfth century and written over with a sermon (about 50 of the New Testament manuscripts are palimpsests). It originally contained a complete Old Testament, but now has only portions of Proverbs–Song of Solomon, Job, and part of the Apocrypha.

*Page of Codex Alexandrinus
(British Library)*

8. The *Amherst Collection* fragment (early fourth century AD), containing Genesis 1:1-15.

The Samaritan Pentateuch

The Samaritan Pentateuch is a Hebrew version of the Torah, written in consonantal pre-Exilic paleo-Hebrew script. There are some 6000 variants from the Masoretic Text; however, some 1600 agree with the Septuagint. Bruce K. Waltke, after studying manuscripts of the Samaritan Pentateuch from the thirteenth to sixteenth centuries, concluded that the text is "a uniform tradition drifting away from the Masoretic Text through scribal error," although most of these "errors" are simply differences in spelling.[8] It is a smoothed-over, modernized, and expanded text as compared with the Masoretic Text.

The scroll is limited to the Torah because, as the biblical text implies (see sidebar on page 72), the Samaritans were only taught the Mosaic legislation. Moreover, since their existence came about during the Assyrian exile, they had no relation to the Jews to whom the pre-Babylonian Exile prophets were sent, nor to those Jews who returned to Judah and their postexilic prophets. For this reason the Samaritans never adopted the square script for writing Hebrew that arose from the Jews' experience with the Aramaic language.

Samaritan priests with Samaritan Pentateuch (Mt. Gerizim, Shechem)

Samaritans vs. Jews

The modern Samaritan sect claims to be the descendants of the tribes of Ephraim, Manasseh, and Levi, and to represent faithful Israelite worship from the time of the Assyrian conquest. However, this is disputed by the facts of their history as recorded in the book of Kings:

> The king of Assyria brought men from Babylon and from Cuthah and from Avva and from Hamath and Sepharvaim, and settled them in the cities of Samaria in place of the sons of Israel...They spoke to the king of Assyria, saying, "The nations whom you have carried away into exile in the cities of Samaria do not know the custom of the god of the land; so he has sent lions among them, and behold, they kill them because they do not know the custom of the god of the land."
>
> Then the king of Assyria commanded, saying, "Take there one of the priests whom you carried away into exile, and let him go and live there; and let him teach them the custom of the god of the land." So one of the priests whom they had carried away into exile from Samaria came and lived at Bethel, and taught them how they should fear the Lord.
>
> But every nation still made gods of its own and put them in the houses of the high places which the people of Samaria had made, every nation in their cities in which they lived (2 Kings 17:24,26-29).

Because of this record, the Jews regarded the Samaritans as half-pagan syncretists whose substitution of Mt. Gerizim in Shechem for the legitimate Temple in Jerusalem denied their claim to be true worshippers of God. This rejection is evidenced in the Gospels (for example, John 4:9) and is affirmed by Josephus (*Antiquities* 9.288). However, this Samaritan distinctive was included in the Samaritan Pentateuch, so that worship on Mt. Gerizim became the "tenth commandment"!

Despite the appearance of antiquity from the use of the paleo-Hebrew script, the actual composition date of the Samaritan Pentateuch is between the fifth and second century BC, with most scholars opting for the later date (after the destruction of the Samaritan temple on Mt. Gerizim by the Jewish leader John Hyrcanus in 128 BC). The later composition date does not preclude the possibility that the text was based on an earlier text, especially a pre-Samaritan text. However, we already have such a text, preserved in some of the biblical manuscripts of the Dead Sea Scrolls, which reveal that the Samaritan Pentateuch has been reworked and that this editing could not have occurred earlier than the second century BC. Even so, the oldest and most complete version extant of the Samaritan Pentateuch (the Abisha Scroll of the Samaritan community in Nablus) is dated to 1150 AD.

The value of the Samaritan Pentateuch lies not so much in its agreement with the Masoretic Text or the Dead Sea Scroll text, but in its explanatory notes and glosses (synonyms or brief definitions written above a word or in the margin of a text) that give a more expanded form of what is found in the Masoretic Text. Once sectarian tendencies are factored out, these differences help textual critics (see chapter 13) better understand how the text has been transmitted over time, and they aid in restoring the text to a state closer to the original.

Aramaic Targum

The pervasive influence of the Babylonian empire on the Near East raised its language, Aramaic, to the level of an international language. Living in a world dominated by this influence, as well as spending 70 years in captivity in Babylon, the Jewish people adopted Aramaic and used it alongside Hebrew in their daily discourses and written works.

One of these works was a translation of the Hebrew Bible into Aramaic, called the Targum (singular) with its Targumim (plural), meaning "explanations" or "commentary." This Aramaic translation used to accompany the reading in the synagogue (and still does in Yemenite synagogues). Outside the synagogue, it acquired significant literary additions. Therefore, while some Targumim have a fixed text with a uniform transmission, all have (as their name implies) the characteristic of adding something in their translation, namely a paraphrase (similar to *The Living Bible*).

However, in some cases the Targumim add significantly more, inserting commentary and explanatory notes as well as entire legends.

The Targumim include almost every book of the Hebrew Bible except Ezra–Nehemiah and Daniel. Some of the most significant are those on the Pentateuch:

- *Neofiti I* (text third to fourth centuries AD, extant copy 1504)
- *Targum Onkelos* (second to fifth centuries AD)
- *Targum Jerusalem I* (seventh to eighth centuries AD)
- *The Targum on the Prophets* by Jonathan ben Uziel (c. AD 270–333)

The Dead Sea Scrolls also contain numerous Targumim. One of the most important is a *Targum of Job* (late second century AD) that has a literal translation of a Hebrew text similar to the Masoretic Text, though deviating in some places from the other textual witnesses.

The Targumim are useful in helping scholars understand how early texts were read and the interpretation given to them, especially in the case of difficult passages. The oldest extant Targum is the Palestinian Targum from the second century AD.

Syriac Peshitta

The Peshitta Old Testament originated in the first-second centuries AD either in Jewish or Christian circles as a translation into Old Syriac, an Aramaic language, from the Hebrew text. Since the fifth century AD it has served as the official Bible (along with the New Testament Peshitta) for the Syriac Church. (The word *Peshitta* is part of a phrase meaning "simple" or "common version.") The Hebrew text that served as its exemplar (master copy) for the translation was similar to the Masoretic Text, although it is certain the translators (different people at different times in different places) compared their work to the Septuagint.

Because of the varied nature of its translation the Peshitta is not always a literal translation; it also contains paraphrase. It is useful as a comparative text, especially with the Dead Sea Scroll of Isaiah (1QIsa^a), with which it has numerous affinities. The oldest complete copy of the Old Testament Peshitta is from the seventh century AD, although an incomplete copy exists from the fifth century AD. The early Syriac version of the Old Testament (and New Testament with the four Gospels) is called the *Old Syriac (Vetus Syra)* version.

Syriac Peshitta, AD 622 (British Library)

Other Secondary Witnesses

Other significant witnesses to pre-Masoretic texts are, first, quotations from the Old Testament by the Hellenistic Jewish philosopher Philo Judaeus (c. 20/15 BC–AD 50). Philo's quotations are taken from an old Greek version close to, but different from, the Septuagint, which in some places is similar to the Hebrew text. Second among this group is the Latin Vulgate. It goes back to the fourth century AD because it is a translation in Latin from both Greek and Hebrew texts by the church Father Jerome (c. 347–419). Although his translation method was not literal (word for word) but only sought the general sense of the passage, Jerome studied Hebrew and the Hebrew text with local rabbis in Israel (he made his translation in Bethlehem), and some of this understanding is reflected in his translation.

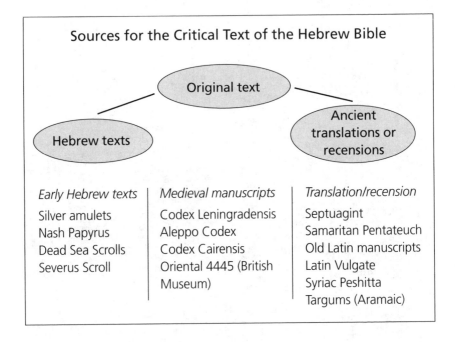

Early Hebrew texts	Medieval manuscripts	Translation/recension
Silver amulets	Codex Leningradensis	Septuagint
Nash Papyrus	Aleppo Codex	Samaritan Pentateuch
Dead Sea Scrolls	Codex Cairensis	Old Latin manuscripts
Severus Scroll	Oriental 4445 (British Museum)	Latin Vulgate
		Syriac Peshitta
		Targums (Aramaic)

Chapter 5

Witnesses to the Original New Testament

We who live at the [beginning of the twenty-first] century have an advantage over the early Christians with respect to the number of manuscripts...that are available to us for ascertaining the original wording of the New Testament text....These discoveries have brought us much closer to the original text of the Greek New Testament.

—PHILIP WESLEY COMFORT, *EARLY MANUSCRIPTS AND MODERN TRANSLATIONS OF THE NEW TESTAMENT*

The kinds of witnesses to the New Testament are the same as those for the Old Testament (manuscripts, versions, and quotations), although the material is far more abundant. Some of the Greek versions of the Old Testament that were described in chapter 4 also contain the New Testament, and so they will be only mentioned by name and in brief descriptions.

Greek Manuscripts

The most important documents for recovering the original wording of the New Testament are the Greek manuscripts. These are a total of 5745 manuscripts (to date), divided into four classes according to the materials from which they are made or their particular style of writing. (The number after the name of the class is the number of copies that presently exist.)

1. *Papyri* (118). Manuscripts written in the second to sixth centuries AD on paper made from the papyrus plant into scrolls and written on with ink.

2. *Uncials* (317). Manuscripts written in the fourth to tenth centuries AD in large elegant "capital" letters that are disconnected from one

another, although words were not separated and no punctuation was used. These are written on parchment (sheepskins or goatskins) or vellum (treated calfskin) with ink.

3. *Minuscules* (2877). Manuscripts written in the ninth to sixteenth centuries AD in smaller cursive script, in which the letters are connected to one another (written with a running hand).

4. *Lectionaries* (2433). Manuscripts in which the books of the New Testament are arranged for daily study and meditation, and not according to the canonical order.

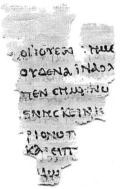

Reproduction of earliest portion of Gospel of John (AD 125), Rylands Papyrus ($\mathfrak{P}^{52}$), recto

The earliest manuscripts are those written on papyrus. These are the most significant for the early history and restoration of the original text. The earliest of these is a fragment of John 18 known as Papyrus 52 ($\mathfrak{P}^{52}$) that dates to about AD 125. There is also a collection of five papyri manuscripts from Oxford University that brings the number of the earliest manuscripts (early as second century AD) to 15.

Several of the important early manuscripts dating to around AD 200 contain portions of the Gospels and the epistles:

• One group is enumerated as $\mathfrak{P}^{32}$ (Titus), $\mathfrak{P}^{64,67}$ (Matthew 3; 5; 26), $\mathfrak{P}^{46}$ (Romans 5ff.; Hebrews, 1 and 2 Corinthians, Ephesians, Galatians, Philippians, Colossians, 1 Thessalonians), $\mathfrak{P}^{66}$ (John), and $\mathfrak{P}^{75}$ (most of Luke and more than half of John).

Portion of Gospel of John (AD 200), Papyrus Bodmer II ($\mathfrak{P}^{66}$)

- The Chester Beatty Papyri ($\mathfrak{P}^{45,46,47}$) contain fragments of all of the books of the New Testament (including the oldest copy of Luke, $\mathfrak{P}^{45}$).

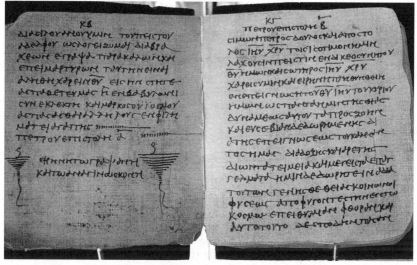

Earliest copy of Jude and 1 and 2 Peter (AD 200 to 300),
Papyrus Bodmer VII-VIII ($\mathfrak{P}^{72}$)

- The Bodmer Papyri ($\mathfrak{P}^{66,72,74,75}$), dated c. AD 175–200, contain portions of John, Acts, 1–3 John, and the oldest copies of Jude and 1 and 2 Peter.

The uncial manuscripts were produced in the fourth century AD, the period in which manuscripts were first bound in book form (codex). The most important of these are

- Codex Alexandrinus (designated in manuscript shorthand as **A**)
- Codex Sinaiticus (designated with the Hebrew letter aleph **א**)
- Codex Vaticanus (designated **B**)

Codex Alexandrinus is a fifth century AD manuscript that contains most of the New Testament, though it is missing most of Matthew and some of John and 2 Corinthians. Its text of Revelation (along with $\mathfrak{P}^{47}$) is one of the best early copies of this book. Sinaiticus and Vaticanus contain the earliest complete copies of the New Testament. Even though these

Codex Vaticanus, close-up of John 1:1-14

two manuscripts come from the same time period, there are thousands of variants between them, but where they agree they appear to represent a text that goes back to the second century AD. Interesting variants in both Sinaiticus and Vaticanus are the absence of the longer ending of the Gospel of Mark (16:9-19) and of the Adultery pericope* (John 7:53–8:11).

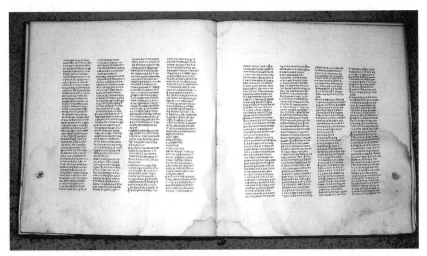

Codex Sinaiticus (British Library)

---

* A *pericope* is "a section of a book."

A Manuscript Saved

There is an interesting story connected with the discovery of Codex Sinaiticus. It was found in May 1844 by German scholar Konstantin von Tischendorf. Tischendorf had traveled to the

Orthodox Greek monastery of St. Catherine at the foot of the traditional location of Mt. Sinai (today in Egypt). His purpose was to study ancient manuscripts (the monastery still houses one of the greatest libraries of ancient documents in the world).

He was lodging in one of the typically sparse quarters at the site, where the only source of heat was a small stove. The fuel for the fire, Tischendorf

*Konstantin von Tischendorf
(1815-1874)*

discovered to both his delight and dismay, was baskets of old scrolls! Warming his mind rather than his body, he studied some of the manuscript leaves in the basket, obtained more, and found they together comprised what we now call Codex Sinaiticus.

Without showing too much excitement, which might spoil his plans, Tischendorf sought permission to "borrow" the manuscript and take it with him to his country for further study. Every time I visit the monastery, I make it a point to stop by Tischendorf's letter promising to return the manuscript—which is still prominently displayed on a wall! The Codex was first published in 1862 at the expense of the Tsar of Russia, and today it is exhibited in two volumes in the British Library in London.

*Greek Orthodox monks with codex at
St. Catherine's Monastery (Mt. Sinai)*

New Testament Versions

Early translations into various languages are the next most important source for textual criticism of the New Testament. These were not simply translations between languages (for example, from English to Spanish), but translations directly from the original Greek into another language.

These translations exist in the languages of Old Latin, Coptic, Old Syriac, Armenian, Ethiopic, Persian, Gothic, Georgian, Old Slavonic, and Arabic. Because they are translated from the original Greek, they are useful in cases of disputed readings (such as in the omission or addition of passages) in revealing what words were in the text from which they were translated. Also, because once these translations were completed they did not again resort to the Greek text, when a version consistently has one reading in its copies, that reading must go back to the version's origin.

By comparing the text forms of these various versions with textual quotations from the church Fathers, it is possible to arrive at a composition date for these versions. However, there are always difficulties with translations for the very reason that they are in a different language than the original. For example, Greek has a well-developed use of the definite article (*the* being the main such article in English), but Latin has no definite article and is therefore useless in critical questions where a textual problem depends on such usage.

The most important of the versions are those that are earliest (Latin, Coptic, and Syriac), and therefore closest to the earliest copies of the Greek New Testament. The *Latin* manuscripts are the most important. First, some of their dates are early (third to sixteenth centuries AD, but the texts from which they were translated may go back to the second century); second, they number more than 10,000 (mostly of the Latin Vulgate), almost double the number of the Greek ones.

The *Coptic* manuscripts (which exist in different dialects, Bohairic and Sahidic being the most important) number about 1000, although not all have been catalogued. They come from Egypt, Coptic being a form of the old Egyptian hieroglyphic language. They range in date from the third to fifth centuries AD.

With respect to *Syriac*, we have already discussed the Old Testament of the Syriac Peshitta, but the New Testament is also part of this document. The Syriac Peshitta (fifth century AD) was first translated no later than the third century AD (the church in Syria goes back to the second century AD). Although they are not completely catalogued, it is estimated that the number of Old Syriac New Testament manuscripts may be in the thousands.

If we add the other early versions, this brings the number of extant manuscripts in this category of sources to between 15,000 and 20,000. The dates for these others range from the fourth century AD for the Gothic; the early fifth to sixth centuries AD for the Armenian, Georgian, and Ethiopic; to the eighth to ninth centuries AD for Arabic and Old Slavonic.

Patristic Citations

The final category of textual evidence is drawn from citations of the New Testament in the sermons, commentaries, and correspondence of the church Fathers (known as Patristic literature). This material dates as early as the first century AD and as late as the thirteenth century, and the number of citations exceed one million. These are useful because for the most part they are datable and provide information of their provenance (geographical location, which is important in understanding textual families—see chapter 13). Further, sometimes a church Father wrote concerning a disputed reading in a text and thus provides valuable information about the variants as they existed in the texts of his time.

Having said this, Patristic quotations must be carefully evaluated (subjected to text-critical analysis) since their accuracy is difficult to determine. The author may be citing a text directly (but which text—since they may have used many?) or loosely from memory, in which case a type of paraphrased text might result. Even so, those quotations provide invaluable information that is available from no other source.

Additional Discoveries

The discovery of new ancient manuscripts is continuing. For instance, as the new millennium dawned, word came of 17 New Testament papyri from Oxyrhynchus (an archaeological site about 100 miles south of Cairo, Egpt). These papyri date from the second to sixth centuries AD and contain portions of Matthew, Luke, John, Acts, Romans, Hebrews, James, and Revelation.[1] In 2003 what are now the Cambridge Private Collection Greek manuscripts 1 through 7 surfaced. These are fragments of Greek vellum manuscripts of the Gospels (Mark, Luke, John) and Paul's epistle to the Romans, dated fourth to eighth centuries AD.[2] No doubt eager Bedouin, Egyptian scavengers, private collectors, and legitimate archaeologists will continue to add to our store of such materials in the years to come.

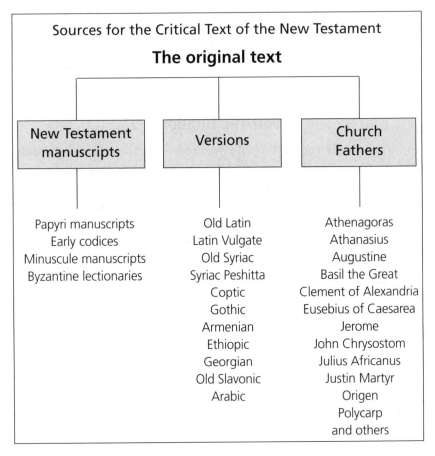

Sources for the Critical Text of the New Testament

The original text

New Testament manuscripts	Versions	Church Fathers
Papyri manuscripts	Old Latin	Athenagoras
Early codices	Latin Vulgate	Athanasius
Minuscule manuscripts	Old Syriac	Augustine
Byzantine lectionaries	Syriac Peshitta	Basil the Great
	Coptic	Clement of Alexandria
	Gothic	Eusebius of Caesarea
	Armenian	Jerome
	Ethiopic	John Chrysostom
	Georgian	Julius Africanus
	Old Slavonic	Justin Martyr
	Arabic	Origen
		Polycarp
		and others

Having seen the witnesses to the texts of both the Old and New Testament, we now must move in the next two chapters to apply this knowledge and consider the histories of the composition of each testament. This will tell us more of how our Bible came to be what it is today and help us answer questions concerning how reliable and trustworthy it may be after more than 2000 years of textual transmission.

PART TWO

Searching for
THE RELIABILITY OF
THE
Original
Bible

Chapter 6

Can We Trust the Text of the Old Testament?

We have given practical proof of our reverence for our Scriptures. For although such long ages have now passed, no one has ventured to add, or to remove, or to alter a syllable; and it is an instinct with every Jew, from the day of his birth, to regard them as decrees of God, to abide by them, and if need be, cheerfully to die for them.

—JOSEPHUS FLAVIUS, *CONTRA APIONEM* 1:42

When the Jewish historian and apologist Josephus Flavius penned these words between AD 94 and 100, he reflected the traditional belief (assumed by rabbis and church Fathers alike) that the Jewish people possessed an unchanged and unchangeable Hebrew text, the *Hebraica veritas*. Today, Orthodox Jews could repeat these words concerning their "immutable" Masoretic Text, the canonical Hebrew text in use by Jews since the tenth century AD and by most Christians since the Reformation.

However, is it accurate to say that the Hebrew Bible (Tanach*)—or the Old Testament, as it is known in the Christian community—has remained unchanged? Or, as Josephus contended, nothing has been added, removed, or altered since its inception? In other words, do we have the same Hebrew text that Josephus knew—and if not, can we truly trust the text of the Old Testament? The gravity of this matter has been well expressed by Old Testament scholar Walter C. Kaiser Jr.:

---

* The acronym *TaNaK* (or *Tanach*), as previously noted, is taken from the first letters of the terms for the three divisions of the Hebrew Bible: T=*Torah* (Pentateuch), N=*Nevi'im* ("Prophets"), and K=*Ketuvim* ("Writings").

How well was the original text of the Old Testament preserved for us today? Can the present text be trusted as an authentic transmission of the words that came from the pens of those prophets, poets and sages who were authorized by God to record them? What assurance do we have that all our efforts to understand the Bible before us are not in vain? If key points on which we base our theology and our eternal destiny turn out to be based on insecure readings or texts that are not true to the original wording given by the author who stood in the council of God, how can they be considered reliable?[1]

In order to answer the overall question that is the title of this chapter—"Can we trust the text of the Old Testament?"—we must progress through several crucial subordinate questions:

1. What is the origin of the Old Testament?
2. Was the Old Testament edited or rewritten?
3. How was the Hebrew text transmitted in order to reach its present fixed form?
4. Can we have confidence in the Masoretic Text (the standard Hebrew text today)?

By addressing these issues, we will better grasp the complex subject of the text as it stands today.

What Is the Origin of the Old Testament?

The Jewish Bible (Old Testament) maintains it is of divine origin. Our first task is to examine the internal and external evidence that bears on this issue. The Jewish Bible came into being progressively from the time of Moses to the time period whose events are recorded in the books of Chronicles. The Mosaic authorship of the Torah, or Pentateuch, is the internal testimony of the Old Testament, and this testimony is joined by the witness of the New Testament.[2]

Moses and the Hebrew Language

Some Old Testament scholars have questioned the text's assertion because the Hebrew language of the first millennium BC (as we know it from the Hebrew Bible) did not yet exist in Moses' time—the second millennium BC.[3] However, as Richard Averbeck has pointed out,

> Just because Moses did *not* write in *exactly* the same *script* or exactly the same *form* of the *language* as we find it in the first millennium, does not mean that he could not have written the Pentateuch in the Hebrew language.[4]

Evidence from Ancient Writing Systems

Our information concerning the development of the Semitic language in the second millennium BC is based on inscriptional material, which is sparse. However, we know from the Ebla tablets that in the third millennium BC, Semites had adapted the logographic system of writing invented by the Sumerians and had used it in their own literature for centuries,* even though their spoken language was different.[5] We also know from the amount of Ugaritic cuneiform alphabetic writing that has survived from the mid-1000s BC because it was written on clay tablets that there was second millennium literature written in the proto-Semitic linear alphabet. However, these writings are now lost because they were on perishable materials.

In support of this, researcher William Shea has recently published proto-Semitic alphabetic rock inscriptions from Wadi el-Hol in Egypt (near the Valley of the Kings by ancient Thebes) dating to 1800 BC or earlier.[6] According to the wording of the inscription, it was written by and refers to a Semite in Egypt. This would make it quite plausible that nearly 400 years later (c. 1440 BC) a Semite in Egypt—named Moses—could write the Pentateuch.

Furthermore, there is no reason Moses could not have written the Pentateuch in biblical Hebrew, which is merely a Canaanite dialect—a form of Old Canaanite.[7] Moses' ancestors lived in Canaan for several generations,

---

* In a logographic system of writing, "a letter, symbol, or sign is used to represent an entire word."

and of course learned its language, before moving to Egypt. During the 40 years Moses was in Egypt he was not only "educated in all the learning of the Egyptians" (Acts 7:22), which would have included the scribal craft, but would naturally have learned the language of his own people. And he would have perfected yet other dialects during the 40 years he later sojourned in Midian (Exodus 2:15-22; Acts 7:29-30).

The primary part of Moses' record is divine revelation he received directly from God on Mt. Sinai. The core of this revelation is the Decalogue, or Ten Commandments (Exodus 20:1-17). This material came directly from the "hand of God," engraved on stone tablets (31:18). These tablets were then shattered by Moses at the foot of the mountain in response to the sin of the people with the golden calf (32:19). However, a second set was made by the Lord in the same manner (34:1-4), which was then deposited as a national document in the Ark of the Covenant (Deuteronomy 10:1-5).

Moses also received a supplemental revelation on Mt. Sinai, which contained legal instruction for the formation and regulation of the nation (Exodus 20:22–23:19). This material, known as "the Book of the Covenant" (24:7), was not written by God but by Moses, although it came in the form of divine dictation (24:4). It contained the laws that amplified the Decalogue to uniquely guide Israel in being distinctly a priestly nation.

Sources and Additions

In addition, the Torah includes historical material that recounts the origin of mankind from the Creation (Genesis 1–11), the beginnings of the Jewish people at the time of the patriarchs (Genesis 12–50), and the wanderings of Israel in the wilderness before entering the land of Canaan (the book of Numbers). Since Moses lived long after the time of the patriarchs, it is possible that the patriarchal narratives had been transmitted in oral form among the Hebrews up to his day.[8]

It is also possible that Moses employed ancient sources and genealogical records in compiling the Pentateuch. He seems to reference such sources in Genesis, with introductory notations such as "this is the account of" (Genesis 2:4), "this is the book [literally, "scroll"] of the generations of" (5:1), and "these are the records of the generations of" (6:9; 10:1;

11:10,27; 25:12,19; 36:1,9; 37:2). This can also be inferred in Genesis 14, where ancient place names (toponyms) such as "Bela," "Valley of Siddim," "En-mishpat," and "Valley of Shaveh" are restated in contemporary terms: "Zoar," "Salt Sea" (Dead Sea), "Kadesh," and "Kings Valley" (verses 2-3,7-8,17). Compare this to the Chronicler, who includes some 75 sources in compiling his history of the Jewish monarchy.

Also within the historical material is an account detailing the nation's history from the defection at Mt. Sinai up to its entrance into the Promised Land (the books of Numbers and Deuteronomy). This account was originally penned by Moses (Numbers 33:2; Deuteronomy 31:22-24), but it was completed after his death by Joshua (Joshua 24:26)—unless Moses received the details of his death and burial, and of Joshua's succession (Deuteronomy 34:5-8), prophetically.

However, even here (verse 8), an epitaph of Moses hardly seems appropriate coming from his own hand (verses 10-12). This is even more the case in Numbers 12:3, where Moses is called "very humble, more than any man who was on the face of the earth." For Moses to speak of himself in such a manner would automatically disprove the assertion! Therefore, it would be more reasonable for this statement to have been made by Joshua, Moses' constant companion. When reviewing the repeated call to "humility" in this text, Joshua would have reverentially inserted his mentor as the epitome of this virtue. For this reason most translations indicate this as a parenthetical statement.

If we accept that Joshua made additions to the Mosaic account, how do we understand the exhortation of Deuteronomy 4:2: "You shall not add to the word which I am commanding you, nor take away from it, that you may keep the commandments of the LORD your God which I command you"? If we understand "the word" to be "the commandments" containing the covenantal blessings and cursings, then it is understandable that any attempt to increase God's blessing or diminish God's judgment by altering His words would usurp divine prerogative.

However, Joshua's "additions" did no such thing. Rather, they enhanced Moses' authority, and therefore its divine Source. Moreover, Joshua's completion of the final part of this account was under the direction of the same Holy Spirit who superintended the whole. Consequently, there is no problem accepting that Moses finished a complete Book of the

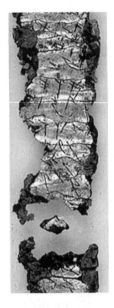

Law (see Exodus 17:4; 24:4; 34:27), and that it was so regarded by Israel when it was placed beside the Ark of the Covenant (Deuteronomy 31:24-26).

There would be a problem if parts, if not the whole, of the book of Deuteronomy (and some would say the entire Torah) were composed in the postexilic period (almost 1000 years after Moses), as some critical scholars assert! Yet, the discovery of the text of Numbers 6:24-26 (the high-priestly benediction) inscribed on a silver amulet from a tomb at Ketef Hinnom in Jerusalem and dated to the seventh century BC (long before the return from the Exile) argues against such an assumption.

Silver amulet inscribed with the oldest text of the Hebrew Bible, from Numbers 6:24-26.

Divine Superintendence

Because the Torah contained the divine legislation that defined and directed Israel's existence, as well as having an abiding role as "a witness" against Israel (Deuteronomy 31:26), it was revered as "the Law" by every king, priest, and prophet. (No doubt this all-consuming importance lay behind the words being inscribed on the silver amulet mentioned above.) This conferred upon the Torah an accepted status that was never in dispute. It was this preeminent position that distinguished it as a "canon within the canon" during the postexilic Second Temple period, when a multifaceted Judaism was ascertaining the Hebrew Bible's final form.

The same divine superintendence that Moses experienced is seen in King David's reception and transmission of the word of the Lord. In 2 Samuel 23:2-3 we find David's own explanation in his "last words":

> David the son of Jesse declares, the man who was raised on high declares, the anointed of the God of Jacob, and the sweet psalmist of Israel, "the Spirit of the Lord spoke by me, and His word was on my tongue."

Here David testifies that although human instrumentality was the indirect means for the psalms, the direct means—the words themselves—was wholly divine.

This superintendence extended also to David's narrative. For example, in 1 Chronicles 28:10-18, David told his son Solomon that God had chosen him to build the Temple. David then gave to Solomon the complete structural plans for its buildings, rooms, and storehouses, including instructions for the organization and work of the priests and Levites and for the manufacture of the primary and secondary vessels that would be used by them in the sacred service.

Following the list of these details in verse 19 is David's explanation of how he received this information: "All this...the LORD made me understand in writing by His hand upon me, all the details of this *pattern*." The final word in this sentence, the Hebrew word *tabnit* ("plan, pattern"), links the revelation given to David with that previously given to Moses in Exodus 25:8-40. Note especially the words of verses 9 and 40:

> According to all that I am going to show you, as the *pattern* of the tabernacle and the *pattern* of all its furniture, just so you shall construct it...See that you make them after the *pattern* for them, which was shown to you on the mountain.

Texts such as these enable us to see that over the millennium that separates Moses' completed Torah and the completion of the book of Chronicles, there remained the belief that the origin of the Bible, despite the length of time and process of composition, was the result of divine revelation. In other words, regardless of how the text was transmitted over time, it retained the value of being a text given by God. This belief is affirmed countless times throughout the poetic and prophetic material that are evidence of both indirect and direct revelation.

Was the Old Testament Edited or Rewritten?

One matter that relates to the origin of the Bible, and may make some question its accuracy, is the matter of the editing of the biblical texts from isolated historical records, individual prophecies, and collections of psalms and songs, into the canonical form we are familiar with today.

The Challenge of Historical Criticism

The historical critical method of biblical interpretation (or historical criticism), since the seventeenth century at least, has embraced the concept of an "editor" or "editors" who rewrote the Bible, usually in the postexilic Persian or Greek period. This view holds that the Bible as we know it today is the product of successive editing from its earliest stages of composition through to its "canonical" textual form. (One such idea is the old J.E.D.P. theory.*)

The idea of the historical critic is to try to ascertain the "literal sense" of the text as it existed in its original historical context. The problem, as the critic sees it, is removing all of the "outside controls" that have been placed upon the text, including God as a divine agent.

As such critics imagine the process of textual development, a narrative (story) was orally transmitted for hundreds, even thousands of years, with all kinds of myth and legend becoming interwoven with (and indistinguishable from) the original historical events. The author wrote down this "history," including the elements that had become a part of the story in his day. Later, an editor (or editors) rewrote the story to meet the social and religious needs of a different audience in a different time and setting. Beyond this the critics add the influence of ecclesiastical tradition, which has affected the interpretation of the text, particularly in translation. Therefore, the reader of the Bible is actually faced with a multilayered text that needs to have its compositional strata analyzed and separated—even demythologized in some cases—so the literal sense of the text can be validly understood.

However, there are crucial problems with this method for those who have held to a high view of Scripture, and in particular for evangelicals who hold to "verbal plenary inspiration and total inerrancy" in its strictest definition (see pages 34–35):

1. It is impossible to interpret ancient history, especially the history of Israel, without understanding that God has directed that history and is an inseparable part of it.

---

* This abbreviation stands for the terms J=*Jahwist*, E=*Elohist*, D=*Deuteronomist*, P=*Priestly Writer*, which were put forward in the source-critical theories of higher criticism. They were developed on the basis of "perceived differences" in the use of the names of God in the Pentateuch and were therefore given to different authors and editors (redactors) of the material over time. Usually a much later time was proposed, after the return from the Babylonian Captivity. This theory has been refuted by many conservative scholars since it was first proposed in the nineteenth century by Julius Wellhausen. One of the standard refutations is that by the late professor of Bible at the Hebrew University of Jerusalem, Umberto Cassuto, *The Documentary Hypothesis* (Jerusalem: Shalem Press, 2006).

2. In addition, not only God has been removed as an agent of history, but the text has been continually revised by "creative editors" who produced numerous different "editions" (recensions*) of biblical books in response to "new religious situations," then the concept of the literal historical fulfillment of prophecy, such as messianic prophecy, is rendered meaningless.

Answering the Historical Critics

John Van Seters, though himself a historical critic, has challenged the notion of "editors" and "editions," especially of the scribes and their work in this capacity:

> I have concluded from this study that there never was in antiquity anything like "editions" of literary works that were the result of an "editorial" process, the work of editors or redactors.† It is a figment of scholarly imagination that had its origins in an anachronistic analogy based on the supposition that the scribes and scholars of antiquity were engaged in the same kind of activity that occupied European scholars of the Renaissance... Consequently, all talk of "redactors" and "redactions" should be scrupulously avoided in biblical studies...[Bible critics] have populated their imaginary biblical world with myriads of text-corrupting editors, who virtually replace the actual authors of the text. These editors are given great religious authority to shape the text as they wish until the form of the text is declared canonical. It is time to rid biblical scholarship of this great fantasy and to attempt to reconstruct historically the development of the biblical text as the basis of its interpretation and exegesis.[9]

Having said this, Van Seters did not mean to deny that there were additions and interpolations made to various parts of the "original" text—only that these should not be attributed to "editors." Rather, they occurred

---

* As noted previously, a *recension* is "1: a critical revision of a text; 2: a text established by critical revision." The word comes from the Latin *recensere,* "to review."

† To *redact* is "to select or adapt (as by obscuring or removing sensitive information) for publication or release; broadly: *edit.*"

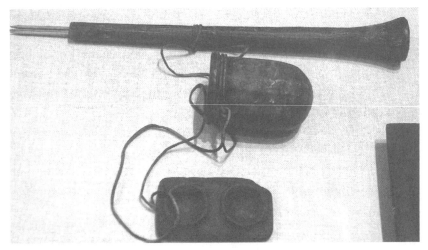

Tools of the scribe: stylus, inkwell.

through the process of scribal transmission. The aim of this kind of "editing" is the faithful reproduction of the originals—an attempt to express as accurately as possible the words and intentions of the author. If Van Seters is correct, the school of redaction criticism (which has already declined in the field of classical literary criticism) would be forced to abandon the redaction theory and return to giving priority to the style of the original authors.

Presenting a different view of this issue is Old Testament scholar David Noel Freedman. He believes "an authoritative and quasi-canonical 'Bible' was already functioning by the middle of the sixth century BC as the product of both priestly and scribal activity and community use."[10]

He contends that this early Hebrew Bible grew to its present form due to the changed circumstances after the Exile, which required the postexilic prophets to write new prophetic works to guide and instruct the Jewish community. However, he finds no such revisions or additions being made to the already existing historical and prophetic books, which must have already been "fixed" in their form.

Therefore, he concludes, the postexilic books were added to a pre-exilic Bible consisting of the "Primary History": Torah and Former Prophets (Joshua–2 Kings) plus the prophetic works (what we call the Major Prophets, though Freedman would see Isaiah 40–66 as a postexilic addition).

In sum, everything in the "Primary History" must be dated before 560 BC, with the latest possible publication dates for prophetic books also within the mid-sixth century BC, such as Jeremiah (581 BC) and Ezekiel (571–568 BC). While Freedman believes there was "intense editorial activity" during this post-exilic period, it "took place in a relatively brief interval and the work was carried out in accordance with a general plan."[11]

How Was the Hebrew Text Transmitted?

If we are searching for the original text of the Hebrew Bible, it is necessary to trace the Masoretic Text back to its source. This, however, has been one of the most formidable tasks in the textual study of the Old Testament. Until the mid-twentieth century our knowledge of the Hebrew text, apart from some important inscriptions (such as the Gezer calendar) or papyri fragments (such as the Nash Papyrus—see pages 61-62), was limited to copies of the tenth century AD Masoretic Text. The discovery of the Dead Sea Scrolls offered significant help in understanding how the Hebrew Bible was transmitted, but only back to the third to fourth century BC. As a result, scholars have formulated a number of theories of textual transmission both before and after the Dead Sea Scrolls:

- In the nineteenth century Paul de Lagarde theorized *there was one original or archetype* (the direct descendant of the autograph textual critics wish to reconstruct), designated by him as the *Urtext,* that served as the source for the Masoretic Text.

- In the twentieth century, the theory of Paul Kahle argued it was useless to try to go back to an original source when it appeared that the source for the medieval Masoretic Text was more common (vulgar) intermediate texts. Therefore, *our single Masoretic Text had come from a plurality of earlier texts.*

- In 1955 William F. Albright and Frank M. Cross presented another theory—that all of the textual witnesses (proto-Masoretic Text, Septuagint, Samaritan Pentateuch) could be *grouped into families and traced back to their geographical points of origination.* The lack of contact between these centers explained the differences between the texts.

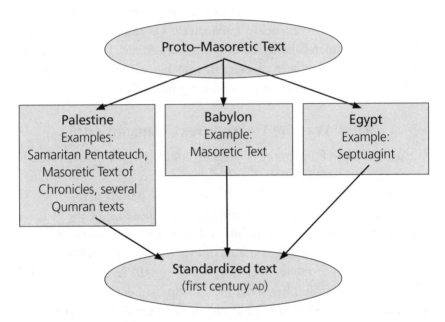

Local Text Family Theory

Multiple Text Types

When the Dead Sea Scrolls were discovered it became apparent that Kahle's idea of a plurality of texts extended back into the Second Temple period. Even though the proto-Masoretic Text type was predominant, the scrolls revealed that in earlier periods a number of different text types had circulated concurrently and within the same community. One major example is the Qumran biblical text of Jeremiah. Six copies of Jeremiah have the longer form of the text, in agree-

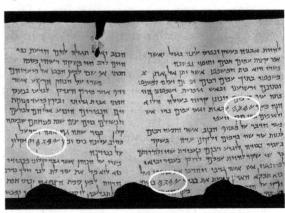

Name of God (YHWH) written in paleo-Hebrew square Aramaic script in Hebrew Dead Sea Scroll biblical manuscript.

ment with the Masoretic Text, but two (4QJer^(b,d)) have the shorter, in agreement with the Septuagint.[12] The latter also lack words, names, and sentences, and exhibits a different sequence in some places.

Before the discovery of these copies there was no evidence for the existence of a shorter Hebrew variant behind the Septuagint. Emanuel Tov, Editor-in-Chief of the Dead Sea Scrolls Publication Committee, and an expert in the textual criticism of the Bible, explains the importance of discovering these different text types:

> In Cave 4, fragments of the text of Jeremiah (designated a, b, c, and d) were discovered right alongside some other representations of Jeremiah. These fragments represent a type of text which more resembles the text of the Septuagint than that of the Masoretic Text (the Septuagint [text of Jeremiah] being about 15 percent shorter than the Masoretic Text).
>
> This was quite a surprise to scholars. For hundreds of years they had considered the text of the Septuagint inferior because they had no idea what Hebrew text it represented. The scrolls have revealed for the first time evidence of a Hebrew text type represented by the Septuagint. Circulating in that time (third to first century BC), it was probably used by a large part of the Jewish communities, just as other text types were. This helps us to understand that the final text of a book developed over a period of time and that God used a number of different writers or editors (whatever you want to call them) to bring a book to its present or to several final forms.[13]

Since these different versions all appeared to have been produced in Israel, Tov felt this disproved Albright's local text theory. He also believed that the shorter version of Jeremiah provided evidence that the Septuagint reflects an earlier Hebrew *Vorlage* (German, "a copy [used as a source]") than does the Masoretic Text, and thus brings us closer to the original of that book.

However, how could any of the previous theories account for two different versions of the same book developing side by side in the same place? Were both originals? Should both be considered inspired auto-graphs? For Tov, the existence of two versions meant that we should not seek to recover the original *autograph*, but the original *edition*. This is based on the belief that different authors or editors worked on the text at an early stage.

Does this mean that we need to revisit what we mean by "original autographs" or expand our doctrine of inerrancy to include editorial editions?[14] Evangelical Old Testament scholar Bruce K. Waltke suggested as much when he stated that "the idea of 'original autographs' may have to be modified to accommodate the possibility of two equally inspired editions of the same biblical book or pericope [section of a book]."[15] However, this may be a premature assesment based on the available evidence (see sidebar, page 101).

Scribal Enhancement

The Dead Sea Scrolls also provide evidence that scribes exercised a "controlled freedom" in the process of transmission. When the biblical writers cited other Scripture they used a variety of methods, including introductory formulas ("as it is written..."), allusions by means of key words, phrases, or ideas,[16] and sometimes paraphrase or loose quotation.

Previously scholars believed that such paraphrases or quotations were made for one reason: They were drawn exclusively from the writer's memory because he did not have ready access to the text. The scrolls have now shown that paraphrase was a normal practice, necessary on the one hand to convert older and potentially misunderstandable idioms into the common vernacular; and on the other, to adapt the quoted text to the writer's intention in expression (that is, to compose their thoughts scripturally). This method was also commonplace for the scribes, as Tov observes:

> People approached the text of the Bible quite freely. We think about the scribes of the Bible as pious men who copied every word precisely and didn't allow for any changes. But that was in a different period. The farther back in time one goes, the more freedom the scribe appears to have had—and the closer one comes to our times, the less we find such differences.
>
> Yet, even when those major and minor differences were inserted in the biblical text, the scribes approached the text with reverence and considered it to be sacred. However, their view of sacredness did not imply that changes could not take place.

The Unique Situation of the Book of Jeremiah

In my opinion, the case of Jeremiah is unique, even though the Dead Sea Scrolls have other less significant variations (such as a longer version of the opening verses of 1 Samuel 11, already known from the Septuagint and Josephus). If Jeremiah dictated both versions at different times to his scribe Baruch, then each would be an original and inspired autograph. On this basis, a scribe would have had to respect both versions, and thus each text could have developed on its own through the process of transmission.

However, this is a special situation that does not require a new textual theory or a modification of the existing definitions of *autograph* or *inerrancy*. The circumstances that produced this situation can be understood from the book of Jeremiah itself with 1) the existence of an earlier shorter and a later longer autograph of the book (chapter 36); 2) the removal of Jeremiah from Jerusalem to Egypt (chapter 43); and 3) the dispersion of the Jewish community from Jerusalem to Babylon (chapter 52), which accounts for the distribution of the two versions.

There are, however, other possibilities. Jack R. Lundbom, for example, argued that the Septuagint's Jeremiah resulted from the translation of a flawed Hebrew text (such as appeared at Qumran) that contained more than 300 cases of *haplography* (the copying error of omission of words by accidental oversight). This would account for 64 percent of its word loss.[17] Therefore, it is not necessary to conclude from the existence of two copies of Jeremiah that two "editors" created two authoritative "editions" of Jeremiah, and that evangelicals therefore have to extend the notion of inspiration beyond the original author. Nevertheless, until more textual evidence from the pre-exilic period is discovered, the debate over theories of textual transmission will continue, in all probability, without resolution.

> The biblical scrolls from Qumran reveal many interesting features [changes, insertions] which we might call scribal.[18]

The controls over this "freedom" to change the text can be seen in the fact that the scope of variation within all of the textual traditions is relatively restricted. Retired Hebrew University professor and scroll scholar Shemaryahu Talmon has stated,

> Major divergences which affect the sense are extremely rare... the conclusion [is] that the ancient authors, compilers, tridents, and scribes enjoyed what might be termed a controlled freedom from textual variation.[19]

The reason for this "freedom" was not to change the sense or meaning of the text, but to enhance it. Almost all of these variants make no difference in sense or meaning, but even if every alternate reading from the Masoretic Text were adopted, the reader would not be left with a different impression.

This can be demonstrated today by a reading of *The Dead Sea Scrolls Bible* (see Recommended Reading), which is an English translation of all of the biblical scrolls from Qumran, arranged in canonical order. This can also be seen in those English translations of the Old Testament that have employed the variants from the scrolls, and whose meaning has been unaffected.[20] Those translations lend support to, rather than emend, those versions that rely upon the Masoretic Text. Therefore, as Bruce K. Waltke has affirmed,

> Over 90 percent of the Old Testament is textually sound and uniformly witnessed to by major exemplars. Of the remaining 10% of the text that exhibits any type of variation, extremely few are of such significance that they would involve any major doctrinal issues.[21]

The scrolls further demonstrate that the Hebrew text was a stable text. The scroll labeled *MurExod* confirms this. It runs for 144 words and is identical in every detail to the traditional Hebrew Bible. The late date of this scroll—the early second century AD—gives evidence for an established Hebrew text by the end of the first century.

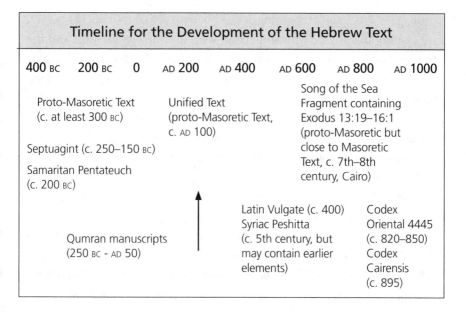

Can We Have Confidence in the Masoretic Text?

As we have seen, the standard text for all translations of the Old Testament is the Masoretic Text. As a late text, it has been judged on the basis of the biblical scrolls from Qumran to be a text with a stable and reliable history of transmission. However, since we do not have earlier examples of texts closer to the time of their composition, how confident can we be of the accuracy of the message?

The problem this has presented can be seen by the fact that, as modern theories of textual development have placed the final form of the text ever later in time—for some as late as the Hellenistic period—scholars have tended to devalue the Hebrew Bible.

The basis for this has come from the presupposition that what is "late" has less historical value. For this reason some scholarly schools (such as those represented by scholars from Copenhagen) no longer find any validity in using the Bible in historical research, such as in the field of archaeology. Since the Bible comes late in time with respect to the events it describes, it must be untrustworthy and unreliable with respect to real history. How could a text from the hands of storytellers far removed from the historical reality, and most likely promoting religious and political propaganda, help an archaeologist dealing with actual remains? However, we can say that, based on comparison with the various versions and the transmission history of the text, there is no warrant for assuming that the final form of the Masoretic Text is substantially different from earlier forms.

In addition, the place of oral transmission should be recognized and respected, since the Hebrew Bible to some extent may have been based on oral tradition. Some have asked how long an oral tradition can be and still be considered reliable in its rendering of past events. In other words, how soon does historical information have to be written down in order to preserve it accurately?

In answer, there is no reason to doubt the accuracy of the oral tradition that preserved and passed on the biblical text.* As one Copenhagen scholar, Poul Hoffmann, has pointed out, "Not granting the generations of a thousand years [ago] the ability to understand anything about themselves on the basis of their own reality is [not] worth calling wisdom."[22] Although our society depends on recorded information for knowledge, for most of history, and particularly in the Middle East, less-literate cultures depended on oral transmission of knowledge. They were able to manage huge bodies of text.[23] Even today, Muslim clerics and Eastern Orthodox clergy still memorize hundreds of pages of sacred texts. In regard to the Hebrew Scriptures, however, Jens Bruun Kofoed, another Copenhagen scholar, has demonstrated, at least in the case of the books of Kings, that there was not a prolonged oral tradition before they were written down.[24]

Outside the field of biblical studies, critical scholars have taken a different view of lateness in dating for the earliest extant manuscripts of a literary work. They have never assumed this means the work was composed at the time of the manuscript, or that its distance in time from its setting in, or record of, an earlier period rendered it historically unreliable. For example, no classical scholar would reject the histories of Herodotus or Thucydides as unreliable witnesses, even though their earliest extant manuscripts were composed in the Middle Ages.

---

*For more information on oral transmission, see page 268, note 1.

Nonetheless, members of the Copenhagen School such as N.P. Lemche hold that the biblical material was written down only in the Persian period—hundreds of years after most of the events. They deny there could have been an Israelite monarchy ruled over by a King David or a King Solomon because they believe that the late evidence of the biblical narrative of Samuel through Kings is historically unreliable. The sparse archaeological evidence is therefore interpreted independent of the biblical text and then used against the biblical text to show its history is unreliable. However, based on his own study of the historiography of the book of Kings and the reliability of its historical information, Jens Bruun Kofoed concludes,

> Writing was possible at a relatively early time, and it is likely that written texts existed and were copied; what, then, is the possibility that a written tradition was handed down from, say, the ninth century to the fifth century BCE, thus providing the author(s) of the books of Kings with reliable historical information on early Israel's history?…
>
> It is certainly possible to argue for a historical connection between the late, extant text of the books of Kings and the society of Iron Age Syria–Palestine. Though we have not *disproved* Lemche's claim that the ordinary man in the street of Persian Period Palestine, on the basis of either oral or written transmission, could not have known anything about what happened in his country more than three hundred years before, we have nevertheless presented evidence to question seriously his *grounds* for saying so.[25]

Therefore, we may say that the lateness of the final, fixed form of the biblical text does not affect the question of its historicity or the quality of its historical information.

Not only was oral transmission able to accurately preserve oral traditions; it is also possible the history could have been written close to the time of the actual events. The mention of such earlier written sources in the historical books of Samuel, Kings, and Chronicles documents this fact and should be considered ancient testimony to the care given by the biblical authors to their transmission of history.

Is the Bible a Scribal Invention?

A more radical interpretation of the origin of the Bible and its transmission history has been proposed by Karel van der Toorn, President of the University of Amsterdam.[26] He contends that the entire Bible is the product of the priestly-scribal workshop in the Second Temple period (500–200 BC). He makes the assumption that Israelite scribes were simply the counterparts of scribes in Egypt and Mesopotamia, and thus he believes that scribes attached to the Temple were responsible for authoring (crafting as artisans) the various genres of Scripture to create an authoritative body of instruction that would in turn be communicated by other scribes.

Following this reasoning, the Bible is a scribal invention (though it doesn't explicitly acknowledge this). It compiles memories and oral chronicles joined by myths, prayers, and ritual prescriptions of the past in literary form and gives them authority by attributing them to legendary Israelite figures. The issue for the ancient scribe, van der Toorn claims, is not authenticity, but *textual authority*. Therefore, "the legendary founder of the nation," Moses, is made the author of the Torah to serve as a model for and precursor of the elite scribal class.

Likewise, a "scribalization" of prophecy took place. The unrecorded oracles of prophets were recorded and expanded by scribes so that the prophetic authority became a scriptural authority. In this regard, the scribe transformed the concept of *revelation* (oracles that were the result of an interaction between God and a prophet) into a *scribal construct* in which God alone is the author and the scribe is legitimized as mediator. Accordingly, the construction of the canon is said to be the final triumph of scribal culture, in that this professional class officially put an end the prophetic period (allowing no new revelation) and turned their own written traditions into a national library.

While the main points made by John Van Seters (see pages 95–96) answer the thesis of van der Toorn, it is difficult for those having a high view of original scriptural composition to deal with a hypothesis that assumes such a low view of biblical origins. One could argue that books of the Bible already were accepted as authoritative before the scribal workshop began their task, such as the account in 2 Kings 22 (2 Chronicles 34) where the scribe Shaphan (c. 622 BC) was surprised to find a copy of the Book of the Law (Deuteronomy) hidden in the Temple (verses 8-10), which then became the authoritative basis for religious and political reform by King Josiah. However, van der Toorn contends that the story of the Book of the Law's "spectacular discovery in the temple is an invention designed to convey a false aura of antiquity."[27] (He bases this on a parallel with the Babylonian *Enuma Elish.*)

In sum, once one has accepted the radical view that the whole of Scripture is a product of the scribes, every individual text must be reinterpreted as implicitly revealing scribal activity. As van der Toorn puts it,

> The notions of antiquity and revelation reinforce each other. In reality, Deuteronomy is a recent text and the notion of revelation it promotes is a scribal construct formulated in the early sixth century B.C.E. [BC].[28]

The practical application of such a theory is a radical shift—from viewing the Bible as a divine message that controls the life of the believer to seeing it as the literary fiction of a professional class in the ancient world, a book that commands no authority at all.

Reviewing the complex history of the origin of the Old Testament has revealed that our present state of knowledge concerning the "original text" of the Hebrew Bible is lacking. We do know, based on the evidence from the earliest texts we possess, that we have multiple families or types of texts, composed and completed at different places and times. If we accept this as the state of the original texts, then we could hold that the Holy Spirit inspired the initial authors to communicate divine messages (sometimes using independent sources) to specific audiences. Then that same Spirit later directed others to complete these messages, expanding them in some cases for another audience and collating them to present the unified message God wanted the nation of Israel, and the nations, to understand.

However, all of the texts that evidence diversity come to us from no earlier than the third to first centuries BC. Granted, they are our earliest witnesses—but they are not necessarily correct ones. Just because they reveal that the text at their stage of history was pluriform (having multiple text traditions), this does not disprove the theory that there earlier existed one single text, the *Urtext*. The diversity witnessed in late Second Temple Judaism had followed periods of geographical segregation and sectarian rivalries. These and other influences could account for these diversities.

In conclusion, it is important to note the following:

- While the analysis by Masorete Moshe ben Asher of the medieval texts available to him in the tenth century was not perfect, it resulted in a text that has been found to closely reflect the readings of earlier scrolls (such as the Dead Sea Scrolls) and in most places to be superior to them.[29]

- It also appears that by the first century AD (perhaps even the first century BC), the final "canonical" form of the text was fixed. And the lateness of a final form for a text does not mean that the text is in any way unreliable as a witness to the history it contains.

- Throughout the process of bringing the text to a state of completion, the Holy Spirit must be acknowledged as having superintended the text, since it was unreservedly recognized as "the word of the Lord" throughout the transmission period.

- The composition of the text by its original authors was held as authoritative and its transmission carefully preserved through the work of professional scribes. This text was then the basis of the Masoretic scribes' edition of the tenth century AD that has since been accepted as the received, or traditional, text—and therefore as authoritative by Judaism and the Western Church, as well as by Reformed and Protestant Christianity.[30]

In sum, we can trust the text of the Old Testament because it has proved itself to be trustworthy. For the Christian world, however, this is only part of the picture. For this reason we need to examine the credentials of the New Testament text in the next chapter.

Chapter 7

Can We Trust the Text of the New Testament?

> What was from the beginning, what we have heard, what we have seen with our eyes, what we have looked at and touched with our hands, concerning the Word of Life—and the life was manifested, and we have seen and testify and proclaim to you the eternal life, which was with the Father and was manifested to us—what we have seen and heard we proclaim to you.
>
> —1 John 1:1-3a

Jesus never left a written autobiography, a book of sermons, or even a collection of sayings. In keeping with the method of oral transmission common to the day and verified to be extremely accurate,[1] He committed His words and works to eyewitnesses, who in turn passed this teaching on to the church and the apostle Paul.* The early church historian Eusebius noted this:

> Guided by the Holy Spirit and endowed with a miraculous power, the apostles carried everywhere the proclamation of the kingdom of God, caring very little about committing it to writing, because they had to fulfill a ministry more elevated and exceeding human strength (*Ecclesiastical History* 3.24).

While this may have been true of the beginning of the church, within two decades, as the church increased, the apostles realized the need to preserve and circulate the teachings. The Gospels were written along with

---

*See, respectively, in regard to *eyewitnesses:* Luke 1:1-2; John 20:30; 1 John 1:1-3. The *church:* Luke 1:3-4; John 21:24-25. *The apostle Paul:* 1 Corinthians 11:23.

the epistles to add needed instruction and resolve problems that arose in the local congregations of believers.*

The accuracy of transmission in the move from oral history to written history has been questioned by form critics, who doubt that a genuine history was preserved by the theologians of the church. Richard Bauckham,[†] who has written an important critique of the school of form criticism, argues against such a view:

> Certainly something happened when the traditions were appropriated by the writers of the Gospels, but it could not have been so discontinuous with the attitude of the oral traditions themselves. The nature of the traditions—as soon as we consider them outside the perspective the form critics have brought to them—shows that they made reference to the real past history of Jesus.[2]

This conservative assessment, despite its abundant scholarship, has been rejected by the new-school critics. It should be noted that these critics' distrust of the transmission of the text is biased by their view that the existence of textual variants has, as we have seen earlier, rendered every text unreliable and made reconstruction of the original impossible. For example, in his New York Times bestseller *Misquoting Jesus,* author and Princeton-educated New Testament scholar Bart Ehrman gives his assessment of the early transmission of the text of the New Testament and the degree to which it faithfully represented the original:

> Not only do we not have the originals, we don't have the first copies of the originals. We don't even have copies of the copies of the originals, or copies of the copies of the copies of the originals. What we have are copies made later—much later. In most instances, they are copies made many *centuries* later. And these copies all differ from one another, in many thousands of places...
>
> These copies differ from one another in so many places that we don't even know how many differences there are. Possibly

---

*See 1 Corinthians 14:37; 2 Corinthians 1:13; 1 Timothy 3:15; Jude 3.

† Richard Bauckham, PhD, wrote the important work *Jesus and the Eyewitnesses: The Gospels as Eyewitness Testimony.* He has published widely in theology, historical theology, and New Testament studies, and is Professor of New Testament Studies at St. Andrews College, St. Andrews, Scotland.

it is easiest to put it in comparative terms: there are more differences among our manuscripts than there are words in the New Testament.[3]

Despite Ehrman's statement that the variants are incalculable, he elsewhere makes the attempt, saying he estimates there may be as many as 400,000 variants attested in the New Testament manuscript tradition. His concern expressed above over the loss of the originals and the present state of our text is twofold:

1. There is a significant distance in time between the original and our earliest copy. This suggests that the lateness of the text as received makes it unreliable with respect to the historical events it records. (This supposition was countered in the previous chapter concerning the Old Testament.)

2. The vast number of variants in the text makes it impossible to recover the original text. (We will address this question later in this chapter and in chapter 13.)

Given such conclusions from a world-renowned expert concerning the Original Bible vs. the state of the text of our modern Bibles, is it possible any longer to trust the text of the New Testament?

As with the attacks leveled against the text of the Old Testament, we will see that there are answers to the questions raised by New Testament critics and good reasons to argue for the trustworthiness of the text.

An Abundance of External Textual Evidence

Pastor Dr. Mark Minnick has summed up the question in most Christians' minds and also proposed a positive answer:

> Doesn't the existence of those variants undermine our confidence that we have the very words that God inspired? No! The fact is that because we know of them and are careful to preserve the readings of every one of them, *not one word of God's Word has been lost to us.*[4]

The text of the New Testament is witnessed to by thousands of manuscripts and versions, and more than one million Patristic citations

(see also page 83). The number of Patristic citations—quotations of
the New Testament by the church Fathers—is so great that it has been
estimated that if we had lost all of the ancient manuscripts and versions
it would still be possible to reconstruct almost all of the New Testament
simply from the writings of the early Church!

In a word, it is important to understand the exceptional wealth of
documentary evidence that is available to scholars who help recover the
ancient text of the New Testament. Having this understanding of the
external evidence for the text will prepare us for understanding the nature
of the argument concerning the internal evidence (the textual variants
the witnesses contain). The following chart gives a glimpse of the external
evidence for the text.

External Evidence for the New Testament Text		
Type of witness	Number of copies extant	Dating of copies
Uncial manuscripts	274	second–eleventh centuries AD
Minuscule manuscripts	2555	ninth–sixteenth centuries AD
Lectionary manuscripts	2280	fourth–sixteenth centuries AD
Versions (translations)	10,000	c. mid-second–ninth centuries AD
Latin (Vulgate)	(8000)	c. mid-second–fifth centuries AD
Syriac (Diatessaron, Peshitta)		c. second–fifth centuries AD
Coptic (Sahidic, Bohairic)		c. third–fifth centuries AD
Gothic fourth (primary, Byzantine text)		c. fourth century AD
Armenian (secondary translation)		c. early fifth century AD
Georgian (tertiary translation)		c. mid-fifth century AD
Ethiopic (primary and secondary translation)		c. fifth–sixth centuries AD
Arabic (multiple versional influence)		c. eighth century AD
Old Slavonic (primary translation, Byzantine text)		c. ninth century AD
Patristic (early church Fathers)	1,000,000+	c. early second–fifth centuries AD

In addition, the provenance (geographical origin) of these manuscripts is from different parts of the ancient world (Israel, Syria, Egypt, Turkey, Greece, and Rome), which indicates they represent *distinct* witnesses to the original text. Had they been from one provenance only, or had they been collated into a unified text, we would not have the necessary evidence to recover the original text through the science of textual criticism.

This abundance of textual evidence (what one scholar has called "an embarrassment of riches") puts the New Testament in a class by itself, distinguishing it as having the most and the earliest manuscripts of any literary document from the ancient world. For example, the John Rylands Papyrus (found in Egypt) has been dated to AD 125, and other papyri (discovered in 1935), which contain the four Gospels, have been dated to AD 150. The Papyrus Bodmer II (discovered in 1956) contains the first 14 chapters and portions of the last 7 chapters of John's Gospel and has been dated to AD 200. The Chester Beatty Papyri (discovered in 1931) contain the Gospels, Acts, Paul's epistles, and Revelation, and have been dated to AD 200 to 250.* A timeline view of these dates and primary manuscripts follows.

Dates of the Earliest New Testament Manuscripts					
C. AD	200	250	300	350	450
Matthew		$\mathfrak{p}^{45}$	Vaticanus	Sinaiticus	
Mark		$\mathfrak{p}^{45}$	Vaticanus	Sinaiticus	Alexandrinus
Luke		$\mathfrak{p}^{4}$, $\mathfrak{p}^{45}$, $\mathfrak{p}^{75}$	Vaticanus	Sinaiticus	Alexandrinus
John	$\mathfrak{p}^{66}$	$\mathfrak{p}^{45}$, $\mathfrak{p}^{75}$	Vaticanus	Sinaiticus	Alexandrinus
Acts		$\mathfrak{p}^{45}$	Vaticanus	Sinaiticus	Alexandrinus
Romans–Hebrews	$\mathfrak{p}^{46}$		Vaticanus	Sinaiticus	Alexandrinus
James–Jude		$\mathfrak{p}^{72}$,	Vaticanus	Sinaiticus	Alexandrinus
Revelation		$\mathfrak{p}^{47}$		Sinaiticus	Alexandrinus

---

*For photographs and comments on many of these witnesses, see chapter 5.

The textual material base as of the fourth century is adequate for establishing the text of the Greek New Testament. Sinaiticus, Alexandrinus, and Vaticanus represent nearly complete parchment manuscripts, which have been found to be quite consistent based on comparison with the earlier papyrus manuscripts.

In particular, the many points of agreement between Vaticanus and Sinaiticus indicate they both go back to a common ancestor text of the second century AD. Thus they provide evidence of the earliest form of the text, and they, together with the 118 papyri manuscripts available today, serve to demonstrate a fairly stable transmission of the text from the earliest period to the later (the fourth and fifth centuries). Thus we have in these manuscripts a reliable witness to the original text of the New Testament.

Incomparable Textual Evidence

The number of New Testament manuscripts is overwhelming compared to other famous and trusted ancient historical writings, such as, for example, Caesar's *Gallic Wars,* the *Annals* of Tacitus, the writings of Livy, and those of Plato.

Manuscript Evidence for Ancient Writings

Author	Approx. date written	Earliest copy	Time span	Number of extant manuscripts
Caesar	100–44 BC	AD 900	1000 years	10
Livy	59 BC–AD 17	AD 350	400 years	27
Plato	42–347 BC	AD 900	1200 years	7
Thucydides	46–400 BC	AD 900*	1300 years	20
Tacitus	AD 5–120	AD 1100	1000 years	3
Suetonius	AD 6–140	AD 950	800 years	200+
Herodotus	484–425 BC	AD 1st cent.	400 years	75
Homer (Iliad)	900 BC	400 BC	500 years	643
New Testament	AD 40–95	AD 100–150	25–50 years	5700

*Two fragments exist from the first century AD, but the most complete copy is from the tenth.

Dating the New Testament

The letters of the Patristic (early Christian) writers date to the second century, which makes it certain that the portions of the New Testament they cite came from the first century. Evidence for a first-century date also can be gathered from the internal witness of the text. For example, the book of Acts ends with Paul in prison, awaiting trial (Acts 28:30-31). If the book had been composed after Paul had been tried and executed by Emperor Nero (c. AD 63), then it surely would have included this historical fact in its conclusion. Therefore, it can be deduced that Luke wrote both Acts and its companion Gospel during the first 30 years of the church—when the eyewitnesses they describe were still alive.

In like manner, the greatest historical juncture for Judaism and the Church, the destruction of Jerusalem in AD 70, does not receive mention. Since Jesus had predicted this pivotal event (Matthew 24:1-2; Mark 13:1-2; Luke 19:41-44; 21:5-6,20-24), it is inconceivable that the writers of the New Testament, in giving evidence for Jesus' identity as the Messiah, would fail to include His prophecy's fulfillment in history.

Overall, so strong is the evidence for a first-century date that Nelson Glueck, renowned Israeli archaeologist of the last century, stated, "In my opinion, every book of the New Testament was written between the forties and eighties of the first century AD."

What About "Errors" in the Manuscripts?

The claim of the critics is that the many thousands of manuscripts, each with its own variants, have produced so many discrepancies in the New Testament text that it is impossible to reconstruct the original. Therefore, we cannot really know what was written, let alone what happened, in the first century. Indeed, the 400,000-some variants estimated by Bart Ehrman appear to be a significant number of "errors."

However, one key fact is that from the earliest copies to the latest copies (about 1400 years later) the New Testament increased only 2 percent (about 2500 words) in size. Since the earliest texts essentially agree with the latest texts, this indicates not only a small amount of growth but also an exceptionally stable process of transmission.

Along with these additions, though, we must also include subtractions of words and other differences. Now, if all we look at is the *quantity* of the variants, the critics' position seems justified. But what is the *quality* of the variants; that is, how many are really significant enough to be *viable* (change the text's meaning in translation)? Consider the following:

- The vast majority of the variants—some 75 percent of the total—are simply *nonsense readings or differences in spelling* (which was never standardized).

- The next 24 percent of variants are *meaningful, but not viable,* differences. They do not affect the translation or the *sense* in translation. Such instances include 1) harmonizations in parallel passages in the Gospels; 2) problems with grammatical subtleties (for example, misinterpreting tense); 3) transposing word order (substituting "Jesus Christ" for "Christ Jesus", for example); 4) substituting "Christ" for "God" (for example, 1 Thessalonians 2:9) and the like. If we recognize that in Mark's Gospel, as an example for some 89 verses (Mark 6:31–8:26), Jesus is identified only by pronouns, we can understand why a scribe would want to add the obvious. Therefore, we find the name "Jesus" added to Mark 6:34, 7:27, 8:1, and 8:17 in the majority of later manuscripts.

- Then there is the last 1 percent—variants that are *both meaningful and viable* (affect the translation). However, "even here the situation can be overstated," says Daniel B. Wallace, Executive Director of the Center for the Study of New Testament Manuscripts: "By 'meaningful' we mean that the variant changes the meaning of the text to some degree. It may not be terribly significant, but if the variant affects our understanding of the passage, that is meaningful." He concludes, "To argue for large-scale skepticism because we cannot be certain about a very small portion of the text is careless overstatement."[5]

Resolving Discrepancies

Most of the discrepancies in the 1 percent of meaningful and viable variants can be resolved by the internal evidence (see chapter 13). However, there is still a small number that are unresolved and therefore problematic.

These are occasions where words may have either been added or omitted, and a few cases where verses appear in later manuscripts but not in earlier.

Examples of these are the account of the woman caught in adultery (John 7:53–8:11), the stirring of the waters (John 5:3b-4), and the ending of the Gospel of Mark (16:9-20). Whether these verses are authentic—in the original—or not, they do not affect any cardinal doctrine of the Scripture (unless we include drinking poison and snake handling in this category!). Most translations either retain the verses or indicate the textual options in a note so the reader can make his own decision about genuineness based on the manuscript evidence. Nevertheless, despite these unresolved discrepancies, there is very little disagreement. The New Testament manuscripts agree in 99.5 percent of the text, a greater percentage by far than for any other ancient literary work.

All this said, the new school critics still argue that most of these variants entered into the text during the earliest period of textual transmission, for which we have very little documentation. They claim that the earliest text we know was already extensively corrupted by free-thinking scribes. This forces us to then ask, How stable was the process of transmission in the early church?

How Stable Was the Transmission of the New Testament Text?

In denying the possibility of recovering the original text, Bart Ehrman and other scholars, such as Harvard professor Helmut Koester and professor William L. Petersen, argue that the New Testament does not even represent the original text. This, they assert, is because during the first and early second centuries AD, when the original was being copied, the text was not established but was in a "state of flux." In other words, they believe that the scribes who transmitted the text altered the original words of Jesus and the apostles.

The new school's basis for this bold assertion is drawn from a comparison with the way the apostolic fathers cited the text—which was quite freely (see more on pages 120–123)—and the way their scribal contemporaries copied the text. According to the new school, the early Christians "took liberties," introducing "free expansions" and performing "endless tinkering" with the text in order to promote their own doctrinal views (such as the deity of Christ) and to address social issues (such as the role of women in the church).[6]

An Islamic Argument Against the Scriptures

The issue of textual corruption is at the forefront of the Islamic argument against the Jewish and Christian Bible. For example, Islamic apologists cite a note in the New International Version of the Bible concerning Mark 16:9-20:

> Serious doubt exists as to whether these verses belong to the Gospel of Mark. They are absent from important early manuscripts and display certain peculiarities of vocabulary, style and theological content that are unlike the rest of Mark. His Gospel probably ended at 16:8, *or its original ending has been lost.*[1]

In light of this comment one Islamic apologist concludes, "We can be absolutely certain now that the above quotes prove without a doubt that the Bible is doubtful. The quote 'or its original ending has been lost' proves that what we call today 'Gospels' were not written by their original authors such as Mark, John, Matthew, etc....It proves that the Gospel had been tampered with by man. Let alone considering it as the True Living Words of GOD Almighty."[2] According to the Islamic argument, if there is any uncertainty concerning the originality of a portion of a text, then the integrity of the whole text and of the Bible itself is cast into doubt.

However, when one examines the kind of changes introduced by the scribes, one does not find doctrinal ones as the critics claim. Nevertheless, it was on the basis of this claim that Ehrman entitled one of his books *The Orthodox Corruption of Scripture,* in order to make the point that the original text, after it was first distributed, was deliberately changed by orthodox Christianity. Therefore, according to these scholars, the text was still being reworked and revised long after the last of the apostles had died. The scribes, under the influence of the early church, added and deleted what the church wanted in order to make the text conform to its theological ideas.

Before responding to this view, it should be noted that when a scribal alteration occurs in a text, there can be a number of reasons, and sometimes determining the reason is subjective. This is especially so when the determination is based on internal evidence comparing the author's contextual appropriateness and use of grammar, vocabulary, and theology. Scribal variants due to spelling are easier to identify, while alterations made to reflect a scribe's theology are much harder to identify.[7] Therefore, a greater caution should be exercised in making the judgment that a variant is intentional, as other factors may offer a more plausible explanation; and this is even more necessary when a basic assumption exists that textual variants can alter cardinal doctrines. Consequently, in many of the examples Ehrman offers as evidence of textual tampering to produce theological change, he overstates his case.[8]

When the earliest manuscripts are examined with respect to the question of their texts exhibiting a "state of flux," a different picture is seen than the one expressed above. In their discussion, "The Text of the Early Period," Kurt and Barbara Aland, whose textbook on textual criticism is a standard reference, offer an explanation. It was once thought, on the basis of $\mathfrak{P}^{45}$ (AD 150), $\mathfrak{P}^{46}$ (AD 185), and $\mathfrak{P}^{66}$ that the second/third century text was irregular. But $\mathfrak{P}^{75}$ proved this wrong because of its similarities to Vaticanus (of which it was thought to possibly be the exemplar). This, they note, provides the key witness to the early history of the text:

> Even for later scribes, for example, the parallel passages of the Gospels were so familiar that they would adapt the text of one gospel to that of another. They also felt themselves free to make corrections in the text, improving it by their own standards of correctness, whether grammatically, stylistically, or more substantively. This was all the more true of the early period, when the text had not yet attained canonical status, especially in the earliest period when Christians considered themselves filled with the Spirit.

As a consequence the text of the early period was multi-faceted, and each manuscript had its own peculiar character. This can be observed in such papyri as $\mathfrak{P}^{45}$, $\mathfrak{P}^{46}$, $\mathfrak{P}^{66}$, and so forth. The fact that this was not the normative practice has been proved by $\mathfrak{P}^{75}$, which represents a strict text, just as $\mathfrak{P}^{52}$ of the period around AD 125 represents a normal text. It preserves the text of the original exemplar in a relatively faithful form (and is not alone in doing so).[9]

On the basis of the internal evidence, even though changes were made to the text during the second century AD, it appears to have remained stable. Moreover, as the Alands note, the dynamism experienced by the early church also did not affect the stability of the text itself. Eldon Jay Epp further notes this fact:

> It is of more than passing interest that the NT papyri contribute virtually no new substantial variants, suggesting not only that virtually all of the NT variants are preserved somewhere in our extant manuscript tradition, but also that representatives of virtually all textual complexions have been preserved for us in the papyri.[10]

This comment should be sufficient to answer assertions to the contrary, since it reflects the actual state of the text and not an inferred state of unstable scribal practice, based on a certain view of the external evidence supplied by the patristic "citations." Nevertheless, we can still learn much from examining and explaining the Church Fathers' apparent loose handling of citations from Jesus and from those texts recognized as the New Testament.

The Early Church and the Text of the New Testament

It is unclear how the early church of the late first century transmitted the text in the time immediately following the completion of the writing of the New Testament. The only surviving material from this period is from the Gospel of John ($\mathfrak{P}^{52}$—see page 78), dated to AD 125. However, it is too fragmentary to provide any clear information other than that the text was being circulated on papyrus.

Even so, there is nothing to suggest that the apostolic Fathers altered the original manuscripts in transmitting them to the church. The evidence for this can be found in the way the Fathers of the early second century handled the text. With respect to the Old Testament, they reveal they regarded it as a source of authority, at least in demonstrating that Jesus was the fulfillment of the messianic prophecies (although this use is extrapolated from later writers such as the second-century Greek apologist Justin Martyr—c. AD 100–165). Nevertheless, their citations of the text are extensive and exact.

By contrast, the Fathers' use of the New Testament consists of only brief allusions rather than formal citations. And even where citations are present, they do not appear to have used them to establish Christian truth (the same may be observed of the Old Testament). David Warren summarizes this point:

> Neither Clement of Rome nor Ignatius of Antioch ever makes any quotations from the New Testament…Ignatius only echoes or alludes to Paul's language. Like Clement, he never really quotes from Paul, and he never uses any introductory formula like "as it is written." He never attributes any statement to Paul. Polycarp follows the same basic pattern of use, except he does appear to quote Paul on four occasions…However, in none of these instances does Polycarp seem to be appealing to Paul for authority…None of the orthodox Christians before Irenaeus… cite the New Testament as an authority to prove Christian doctrine or truth.[11]

The reason for this does not seem to be a lack of appreciation for written tradition, but rather, a preference for oral tradition. At this early period (AD 100–150) the apostolic Fathers as well as the apologists believed they shared continuity with the original apostles through the continuation of the prophetic gifts and the inspiration of the Holy Spirit. David Warren sees this as a plausible explanation for both the scarceness of citations and the apparent impreciseness of citations when they are present:

> What has changed so that Irenaeus now must cite Jesus' words from a written gospel? What has changed has nothing to do with the authority of Jesus' words. The authority of his words has not

changed. But the authority base of the Christians in Irenaeus' community has...

> The gift of prophecy endowed Christians like Clement of Rome with such authority that they did not have to use a book when giving the words of Jesus or even the words of Paul...Even as late as Justin Martyr one finds in the orthodox church the same prophetic gift...
>
> But the situation changes dramatically in the time of Irenaeus. According to Irenaeus, the gift of prophecy is dying out in the church...Once the gift of prophecy ceased, the Christian leaders had to find a new authority base for their preaching and teaching. The New Testament writings now take center stage, and any appeal to them as authority in matters of Christian doctrine and truth shows a concern for exactness and precision in citation.[12]

Therefore, the informality in citations in the early church was not due to the text being in a state of flux. Rather, it reflects a penchant for a "living voice"—that is, a teacher with the gift of prophecy (which some of the apostolic fathers claimed[13]), who could speak by the inspiration of the Holy Spirit. A very similar preference was expressed by one of the church leaders living in the age of oral tradition—Papias, Bishop of Hierapolis (c. AD 70–160)—with respect to obtaining facts from eyewitnesses rather than from records: "For I did not think that information from books would profit me as much as information from a living and surviving voice" (Eusebius, *Ecclesiastical History* 3.39.3-4).

In a word, while the text of both the Old and the New Testament was considered authoritative, there was no *need* to appeal to Scripture as the sole authority. For example, Ignatius, the Bishop of Antioch (c. AD 50–107), makes many references and allusions to Paul's writings, but does not seem to treat them as the ultimate authority.[14] In his defense of Christian truth against heretics he relies mainly upon his own authority, and he appeals to his own writing as authoritative.

However, by AD 180 a shift has evidently occurred from an assumed personal authority to an appeal to the authority of Scripture. This was the time that the Montanist movement appeared. This heretical group gained a following when its leader Montanus claimed that the gift of prophecy had continued with him and his prophetesses. Before this time, when the gift of inspired speech was still active in the church, it was the heretics who had had to appeal to a written document for authority.[15] With the cessation of prophecy in the church, the appeal of heretics to the gift is understandable, as is the church's reliance upon the biblical text as its final authority.

If this explanation is accepted, then there is no ground for maintaining the early Fathers mishandled the text or for assuming that the scribes of this period did the same. Rather, there is sufficient evidence that, just as the apostles were eyewitnesses to the facts they recorded, so also were those who followed them and were responsible for the preservation of their writings have the ability to accurately transmit them to the next generation.

Did the Eyewitnesses to Jesus and the Church Fathers Have an "Agenda"?

There is one final area we must examine in which the new school critics are calling the trustworthiness of the New Testament into question. Bart Ehrman, among others, has argued that, because "each Gospel writer has an agenda—a point of view he wants to get across, an understanding of Jesus that he wants his readers to share,"[16] the Gospels have lost their objectivity and cannot be viewed as historical documents. Moreover, because the differences in the accounts—(the result of these different agendas)—are irreconcilable, the accounts are historically unreliable.

This argument has been put forward by countless critics and answered by countless others. Historians such as A.N. Sherwin-White and Michael Grant have repeatedly stated that documents written with a particular theology (agenda) in view are not necessarily untrustworthy.[17] Because accounts differ, this does not mean their message is distorted or discredited. The early church did not have a difficulty with these differences, and Christian apologists have adequately reconciled them to reasonable minds.

In addition, Richard Bauckham has successfully demonstrated that the four Gospels are the result of eyewitness accounts (and are therefore trustworthy accounts). He responds to the idea that, because the Gospel accounts were first transmitted orally, their message could have been altered in some way during the time period before they were written down. Commenting on the results of research concerning oral tradition as history by scholar J. Vansina, Bauckham writes,

> We need note here only that even when Vansina speaks of the comparatively small change that historical accounts undergo in oral tradition, the time span he envisages is longer than that between the events of Jesus' history and the Gospels. Nevertheless, what is important for our present purposes is that oral societies treat historical tales and historical accounts differently and in such a way that the latter are preserved more faithfully. In the latter case there is intention to preserve faithfully, which is lacking in the former.[18]

The Gospels, in fact, present themselves as historical accounts of Jesus' life—"about all that Jesus began to do and teach until the day he was taken up" (Acts 1:1-2, with reference to the Gospel of Luke). Although they are not, in the modern sense, biographies, because they do not give a complete chronological account, neither are they simply *sui generis* ("unique"), as old school critics, such as Rudolf Bultmann, wished to categorize them. Rather, they fit the style of the genre of the Greco-Roman biographies or "lives" (*bioi*).[19]

For this reason Richard Bauckham concludes,

> Reading the Gospels as eyewitness testimony differs therefore from attempts at historical reconstruction behind the texts. It takes the Gospels seriously as they are; it acknowledges the uniqueness of what we can know only in this testimonial form. It honors the form of historiography they are.
>
> From a historiographic perspective, radical suspicion of testimony is a kind of epistemological suicide.* It is no more practical in history than it is in ordinary life. Gospels scholarship must free itself from the grip of the skeptical paradigm that presumes the Gospels to be unreliable unless, in every particular case of story or saying, the historian succeeds in providing independent verification…But this approach is seriously faulty precisely as a historical method.[20]

---

* *Epistemology* is "the study or a theory of the nature and grounds of knowledge especially with reference to its limits and validity."

Some of the Church Fathers, who were the immediate heirs of the apostles in the transmission of the Gospel and New Testament accounts, could be said to have been secondary witnesses. One of the Fathers, Papias, claimed to be a personal disciple of the apostle John, and others claimed to know people who had been acquaintances of the apostles. John, the longest-living apostle, who had relations with the churches of Asia Minor and is believed to have lived his last days in Ephesus, is also mentioned as having been consulted by some of the early Fathers who had questions about the correct wording or interpretation of certain of his texts.

These Fathers were extremely careful to pass on through their writings the apostolic tradition, which included frequent citations and allusions to the New Testament. As a result, as we have already stated, most all of the New Testament could be reconstructed from the patristic writings alone. In fact, Sir David Dalrymple surveyed the Fathers of the second and third centuries in an attempt to discover just how much of the New Testament could be pieced together from their writings. His conclusion was that he found all of the New Testament except for 11 verses.[21]

Who Quoted What from the New Testament

Irenaeus, Bishop of Lyons (martyred around AD 180), was a student of Polycarp, the long-lived disciple of John himself. Extant quotes from Irenaeus' writings include those from Matthew, Mark, Luke, Acts, 1 Corinthians, 1 Peter, Hebrews, and Titus. Ignatius (AD 70–110) quoted from Matthew, John, Acts, Romans, 1 Corinthians, Ephesians, Philippians, Galatians, Colossians, James, 1 and 2 Thessalonians, 1 and 2 Timothy, and 1 Peter. Barnabas quoted from the New Testament around AD 70, Hermas around AD 95, and Tatian, AD 170. Clement of Alexandria, who lived from AD 150–212, quoted from all but three books of the New Testament. Justin Martyr, in AD 133, quoted from the Gospels, Acts, Revelation, and both Pauline and the other epistles.[22]

The early patristic use of almost the whole of the New Testament reveals that it had an implied kind of canonicity at this early date and that its text was being handled with respect, even reverence. Again, doubts of accuracy in the early period of its transmission can be put to rest.

— — —

To sum up, we can take confidence in our New Testament text as an accurate reproduction of the Original Bible:

- In our abundant manuscripts and versions, as well as in other ancient literature citing the Scripture, we have preserved the textual variants. This means that we have today all of the original words of Scripture—they are not lost to us.

- The wealth of variant readings is actually a boon to translators and students of ancient interpretation, because how a text has been understood through the ages helps us make better interpretations of the text today.

- Textual critics have developed their science and art to enable them to weigh variant readings and separate those that are simple spelling variations, accidental mistakes in copying, and nonsense errors, as well as those that involve uses of the definite article, synonyms, transpositions, and the like, from those that are more meaningful. Those variants that actually affect a translation are less than 1 percent of the total.

- Even though the earliest period of transmission for the New Testament is largely unattested, the manuscripts still reveal a stable process, and our critical texts have presented to us a highly reliable text that is very close to the original.

- Lastly, it needs to be remembered again that no unsure reading (with respect to the original) has compromised one single truth of the Scripture or affected any doctrinal understanding, since those same truths are taught throughout the Bible.

However, what if there was more to the Original Bible than we have in our present-day Bible? The question of the canon of Scripture, and whether or not apocryphal books belong in our Bibles, is the subject of our next two chapters.

PART THREE

Searching for
THE TRUTH ABOUT
THE
Original
Bible

Chapter 8

Are Books Missing from Our Bible?
The Question of the Canon

In the canon of scripture we have the foundation documents of Christianity, the charter of the church, the title-deeds of faith. For no other literature can such a claim be made. And when the claim is made, it is made not merely for a collection of ancient writings. In the words of scripture the voice of the Spirit of God continues to be heard.

—F.F. Bruce

Remember the story in chapter 2 about the three women shopping for a gift Bible? One of them bought a Bible that had 39 books, the second bought one that had 66 books, and the third bought one that had 77 books. The question this chapter addresses is, should two of those women feel cheated since books were missing from their Bibles? The greater question, of course, is why Bibles differ—and an extended question, in light of newly discovered "lost Gospels," is whether such books must be considered "missing" from our Bibles?

Another way of stating this with respect to our study of the Original Bible is, If the wording of the original has not been lost, is it still possible that what we think is the original is in fact only a portion of it? In other words, is it possible that parts of the original, other books that were part of the divine revelation, have been lost and are today missing from our Bibles?

Have Books Been Lost from the Bible?

When we take a careful look at both the Old and New Testaments we find they make reference to a number of historical books, psalms, proverbs, prophetic oracles, and epistles (some written by authoritative figures in Israel and the church) that are no longer extant. For example, the Old Testament historical books refer to a number of books no longer known:

- the book of Jasher (Joshua 10:13; 2 Samuel 1:18)
- the book of the Wars of the Lord (Numbers 21:14)
- the book of the Acts of Solomon (1 Kings 11:41)
- the book of the Genealogies (Nehemiah 7:5)
- the Records of Nathan the Prophet
- the Prophecy of Ahijah the Shilonite
- the visions of Iddo the Seer (2 Chronicles 9:29)

In addition, 1 Kings 4:32 records of King Solomon that "he also spoke 3,000 proverbs, and his songs were 1,005." Yet, we have only a fraction of those proverbs (Proverbs 1:1–9:18; 10:1–22:16; 25:1–29:27) and only one of those songs (the Song of Songs).

Similarly, the New Testament also refers to books now apparently lost, such as

- the sorrowful letter of Paul to the Corinthians, written after his first epistle to this church but before his second (cf. 2 Corinthians 2:4).
- an epistle to the Laodiceans (Colossians 4:16). However, this may not be a lost letter, since the text says "the letter that is coming to you *from* Laodicea," which could refer to the epistle to the Ephesians that was in the process of being circulated around the churches of the region.

What are we to make of this missing material? First, it should be understood that this material was not included in the Bible because it was missing; rather, *it is most likely missing because it was not included in the Bible.* Bruce K. Waltke and Michael Patrick O'Connor make this point:

That no other Israelite writings, such as the Book of Jasher (for example, 2 Samuel 1:18) or the Diaries of the Kings (e.g., 2 Chronicles 16:11), survive from this period indirectly suggests the determination of the scribes to preserve the books that became canonical. The foes of Hebrew Scripture sometimes included audiences who sought to kill its authors and destroy their works (cf. Jeremiah 36). From the time of their composition, however, they captured the hearts, minds, and loyalties of the faithful in Israel, who kept them safe often at risk to themselves. Such people must have insisted on the accurate transmission of the text.[3]

In other words, the Divine Author never intended this material, even though written by such men as King Solomon and the apostle Paul, to be included in the sacred corpus we call Scripture. This should not surprise us, though—the apostle John makes it clear that even Jesus' words where excluded! He notes that his Gospel, like those we call the Synoptic Gospels, was selective in its inclusion of material:

> Many other signs therefore Jesus also performed in the presence of the disciples, which are not written in this book; but these have been written that you may believe that Jesus is the Christ, the Son of God; and that believing you may have life in His name...And there are also many other things which Jesus did, which if they were written in detail, I suppose that even the world itself would not contain the books that would be written (John 20:30-31; 21:25).

From John's perspective, Jesus said and did so much that no number of books could contain it all, but the essential was included: that which was necessary for faith in Jesus' divine nature and work as the Messiah.

In like manner, the apostle Paul wrote letters to many local churches, but only those deemed necessary by the Holy Spirit for the instruction of the universal church survived. Likewise, having additional historical details to those provided by the books of Kings and Chronicles, or extra psalms and proverbs, was unnecessary to the purpose already served by those selected by God for preservation.

In this chapter and the next three we will explore the question of books that in some quarters of Christianity are thought to have been part of the Original Bible. In this chapter and the next we will examine Jewish documents that were written during the latter part of the Second Temple period. They have always been known and have been included in some Bibles as part of the Old Testament. In chapters 10 and 11 we will consider ancient documents rediscovered in our modern era—documents some scholars claim are missing from, or should have been part of, the original New Testament.

The Rise of Extrabiblical Literature

Let us first take a look at the historical time period of the Jewish texts in order to understand something of the religious and political conflicts that produced them. The late Second Temple period witnessed a spate of extrabiblical books. This time has been called the Intertestamental Period by Christians because it spans some 400 years between the writing of the last book of the Old Testament and the writing of the New. It has also been termed "the silent years" because God ceased to speak through writing prophets during this period.

However, the time was anything but "silent" with respect to the political conditions—and the large body of Jewish literature produced in response, claiming that God *had* spoken. The political, religious, and social atmosphere in Israel and in the Diaspora changed significantly during this period and brought about sweeping changes throughout the ancient world.

These years began with the Jews under Persian control and the return of approximately 50,000 of them to Judah to rebuild Jerusalem and its Temple. Change began with the advent of Alexander the Great, who within the few years before his death in 323 BC conquered the vast Persian empire and introduced Hellenism into the social, political, and religious realms. This led to persecution of the Jewish population in the land of Israel, which in turn led to an overthrow of Greek (Seleucid) control with the Maccabean Revolt (began 166 BC) and some 100 years of Jewish independence.

The Maccabean period ended in 63 BC when the Roman general Pompey entered Jerusalem and placed the country under Rome's rule. Having lost independence and living in an oppressive pagan state, Jews suffered and even rebelled. The First Jewish Revolt (AD 66–73) resulted in the Roman destruction of the city of Jerusalem and its Jewish Temple (AD 70), with exile or severe restrictions imposed on the Jewish population thereafter.

During this time of turmoil and political upheaval (mainly between 185 BC and AD 100), a vast amount of Jewish literature was produced to address questions concerning Israel's prophetic expectations. Had the promises of restoration failed? What was the meaning of the continued occupation of the land and the oppression of the people? These writings, for the most part done under false names, testify to Jews who remained faithful to God in this time of trouble, and they encourage ethical behavior in the face of compromise. They are found among the Dead Sea Scrolls, the oldest collection of Jewish documents preserved by the Dead Sea sect, whose own sectarian documents also represent this genre.

The significance of the *apocryphal* and *pseudepigraphical* literature is in bringing us information about Jewish life and religious thought in the three centuries not recorded in the canonical Jewish and Protestant Scriptures. Understanding the theological development of Jewish sects during this period provides a background for many of the ideas—especially the apocalyptic ones—circulating in Judaism at the time of Jesus and the writers of the New Testament. The chart below gives an overview of this largely Jewish literature that fills the literary gap between the two testaments.

The value of this extrabiblical literature is that it opens a window on a period of Jewish history during which there were significant political, social, and religious developments. For one, the various Jewish sects trace their origins to this period. For another, this period also saw the development of apocalypticism (both in response to the political situation and because of the need to address religious expectations). The extrabiblical literature reveals myriad facets of all of these subjects, as well as showing how important the Hebrew Bible was to the Jewish community. Of course, it is also a rich resource for those who study the biblical text in terms of the development of terminology and religious ideas, and as a background to the Jewish context of the New Testament.

What Is the Apocrypha?

The *Apocrypha* (Greek, "concealed, hidden things")—or more precisely, the "Old Testament Apocrypha," in distinction from the "New Testament

Books of the Apocrypha

1 Esdras	Wisdom of Solomon
2 Esdras	Wisdom of Ben-Sira
Tobit	Baruch
Judith	Letter of Jeremiah
Additions to Esther	Prayer of Azariah

Books of the Pseudepigrapha
(includes some works of non-Jewish origin)

Apocalypse of Abraham	Eupolemus
Testament of Abraham	Pseudo-Eupolemus
Apocalypse of Adam	Apocryphon of Ezekiel
Testament of Adam	Ezekiel the Tragedian
Life of Adam and Eve	Greek Apocalypse of Ezra
Ahiqar	Questions of Ezra
Letter of Aristeas	Revelation of Ezra
Aristeas the Exegete	Vision of Ezra
Aristobulus	Fragments of Pseudo-Greek Poets
Artapanus	Pseudo-Hecataeus
2 Baruch	Hellenistic Synagogal Prayers
3 Baruch	Testament of Isaac
4 Baruch	Martyrdom and Ascension of Isaiah
Cleodemus Malchus	Ladder of Jacob
Apocalypse of Daniel	Prayer of Jacob
More Psalms of David	Testament of Jacob
Demetrius the Chronographer	Jannes and Jambres
Eldad and Modad	Testament of Job
Apocalypse of Elijah	Joseph and Asenath
1 Enoch	History of Joseph
2 Enoch	Prayer of Joseph
3 Enoch	Jubilees

Sectarian Documents of the Dead Sea Scrolls

Rule of the Community (1QS)

Damascus Document (4Q265-73. 5Q12, 6Q15)

Rule of the Congregation (1Q28a)

The Temple Scroll (1 1Q19, 20, 4Q365a)

MMT (Acts of the Law) (4Q394-9)

The Wicked and the Holy (4Q181)

Exhortation by the Master to the Sons of Dawn (4Q298)

Register of Rebukes (4Q477)

Remonstrances (4Q471)

The Hymns Scroll (1QH)

Songs for the Sabbath Holocaust (4Q400-407, 11Q17)

Poetic fragments on Jerusalem and King Jonathan (4Q448)

Calendars of Priestly Courses (4Q320-30)

Calendar Signs (4Q319)

Horoscopes (4Q186, 4Q534, 4Q561)

Phases of the Moon (4Q317)

Zodiacal Calendar with Brontologion (4Q318)

Order of the Divine Office (4Q334)

Words of the Heavenly Lights (4Q504-6)

Liturgical Prayer (1Q34)

Prayers for Festivals (4Q507-9)

Daily Prayers (4Q503)

Celebration of the Morning and Evening (4Q408)

Vision of Jacob (4Q537)

Ritual Purity Laws (4Q274)

Apocryphal Psalms (4Q88, 4Q448, 11Q5-6)

Blessings (lQ28b)

Confession Ritual (4Q393)

Purification Ritual (4Q512)

A Liturgical Work (4Q392)

The Seductress (4Q184)

Exhortation to Seek Wisdom (4Q185)

Parable of the Tree (4Q302a)

Sapiental works (4Q413, 4Q415-18, 423, 1Q26, 4Q420-21, 4Q424)

Bless, My Soul (4Q434-7)

Songs of the Sage (4Q510-11)

Beatitudes (4Q525)

The Divine Throne Chariot

The Book of Secrets (1Q27, 4Q299-301)

The Thanksgiving Psalms (lQHa)

The Parable of the Bountiful Tree (4Q302a)

A Baptismal Liturgy (4Q414)

The Coming of Melchizedek (11Q13)

Tongues of Fire (1Q29, 4Q376)

The Book of Giants (4Q203, 1Q23, 2Q26, 4Q530-532, 6Q8)

Reworked Pentateuch (4Q158)

Genesis Apocryphon: Exhortation based on the Flood (4Q370)

Apocrypha"—is a collection of 14 Jewish documents, written for the most part in Hebrew and Aramaic, and composed in Israel, Alexandria (Egypt), Antioch (Syria), and Persia between the late second century BC and the first century AD.

The Hebrew Bible did not include these books, but the final form of the Greek Septuagint and Latin Vulgate did. Because of the dominance of the Septuagint in the Eastern Church and the Vulgate as the standard translation of the Western Church for a thousand years, most people during this time never questioned that the Apocrypha was originally a part of the Old Testament Scriptures.

What Are the Pseudepigrapha?

The term *Pseudepigrapha* literally means "falsely entitled." It refers to a collection of some 65 documents written between 250 BC and AD 200 by Jews and Hellenistic Jews (some say Jewish Christians). Each book was written under a pseudonym (usually the name of a biblical person whose work was not part of the canonical Hebrew Bible), and on this basis it claimed inspiration.

J.H. Charlesworth, a specialist in Christian origins at Princeton Seminary, has explained the use of pseudonymity as a scribe's preference to attribute his work to someone who inspired him (or others), rather than himself. However, it is clear that the intent of such a scribe was to convince people that his was the work of a genuine and influential biblical personage so that it would be received as authoritative. Therefore, even if this false attribution was considered an acceptable practice in some ancient circles, it must be judged as deceptive and fraudulent according to the standard of Scripture (Deuteronomy 18:20-22; see 4:2; 12:32; Proverbs 30:6; Revelation 22:18).

There are over 100 texts and fragments that are considered Pseudepigrapha,[4] and they fall into four different genres: legendary (for example, Book of Jubilees, Testament of the Twelve Patriarchs), apocalyptic (for example, Enoch, Baruch, 2 Esdras), poetical (Psalms of Solomon), and didactic (Magical Book of Moses).

As with the apocryphal texts, no pseudepigraphal texts are referred to or explicitly cited in the New Testament. However, one allusion may appear in Jude 14-15, where wording similar to that in Enoch 1:9 concerns

Divisions of the Apocrypha

The material in the apocryphal documents may be put into four divisions:

1. *Historical:* 1 Esdras, 1 and 2 Maccabees
2. *Religious:* Tobit, Judith, Susanna, Additions to Esther, Bel and the Dragon
3. *Wisdom or ethical teaching:* Ecclesiasticus, Wisdom of Solomon, Wisdom of Ben Sira, Baruch, Prayer of Manasseh, Letter of Jeremiah, Prayer of Azariah
4. *Apocalyptic:* 2 Esdras

Based on these groupings, the Septuagint (which included these books) placed them with the canonical books of the same genre: 1 Esdras with Ezra–Nehemiah; 1 and 2 Maccabees after the Prophets; Additions to Esther with the Book of Esther, and Judith and Tobit after Esther; Bel and the Dragon with the Book of Daniel; Baruch and the Letter of Jeremiah after the Book of Jeremiah; and the Prayers of Manasseh and Azariah with the Psalms.

a prophecy of "Enoch, the seventh from Adam." If this statement concerning the biblical Enoch (Genesis 5:18-24) is indeed an allusion from the pseudepigraphical book of Enoch, it of course does not imply that Jude viewed the book of Enoch as being inspired or even true. It would only mean that in this particular instance, as deSilva says, Jude "regarded it as a valuable resource for the exhortation and edification of Christians, a suitable quotation from an ancient authority to advance his rhetorical goals."[5]

Likewise, the citations by the apostle Paul from the poet Epimenides in Acts 17:28 and Titus 1:12 do not imply that this poet's writings had any special authority. In fact, the citation used by Paul in Acts 17:28 appears in Jewish anthologies of proof texts useful for showing pagans the truth about God. Therefore, Paul either employed these citations in the same way, or else may have learned of them from just such a Jewish anthology.

Some scholars have suggested that the appearance of the book of Enoch among the collection of documents of the Dead Sea sect, as well as citations in their sectarian literature, implies that the Hebrew Bible at this time had a more flexible canon, which included Enoch. However, like Paul's use of Epimenides, this Jewish sect could have simply referred to Enoch as a recognized and influential pseudepigraphical work. If these works had authority in the Dead Sea community, it must have been a *limited* authority, supporting their specific doctrines and practices but not determining them, as did Scripture.

Unlike the Apocrypha, none of the Pseudepigrapha were included in the Septuagint or Vulgate. Therefore they were never considered by the church for inclusion in the canon.

The Church and Extrabiblical Books

Neither the Jewish religious authorities nor the church Fathers regarded the apocryphal books as heretical, but both agreed they were not to be treated the same as canonical Scripture. The early church in the West originally had a twofold distinction of books, as canonical or non-canonical. However, both the Roman Church and the Eastern Orthodox accepted some apocryphal books in their early list as Scripture, and eventually accepted the same 14 apocryphal books that became attached to the Septuagint (excluding 2 Esdras) and included them within their Bibles. Consequently, these churches do not use the term *apocrypha* to refer to this corpus of material (but reserve it only for the Pseudepigrapha).

The Roman Church prefers to think of the apocryphal books as "scripture" (with a little "s") and distinguishes them as a "second canon," or *deuterocanonical* (a term introduced in 1566 by Sixtus of Sienna), which indicates they are not equal in authority to the books of the "first canon" *(protocanonical)*. The Eastern Orthodox Church devised a different three-fold distinction: books that could be read in the church (canonical), books that could be read privately (Apocrypha), and books that could not be read (pseudepigrapha).

The Reformers, with the beginning of Protestant Christianity, severed any obligation to ecclesiastical tradition in this matter (such as the 1546 Council of Trent, which both canonized the Apocryphal books and anathematized the Reformers!). Therefore, they followed the example of the Hebrew Bible in omitting the Apocrypha from their Bibles (though the Anglican Church retained it in its early editions of the King James Bible).

Many Christians who reject the canonicity of the Apocrypha nevertheless see it as useful for historical information on the intertestamental period (1 and 2 Maccabees in particular). And some, following the recommendation of the church Fathers, find the books helpful as religious devotional material (for example, Ecclesiasticus, Wisdom of Solomon, Prayer of Manasseh). This, however, must be done with caution, as it is difficult to do this without emotionally confusing the literature with inspired Scripture.

The Need for Canonization

In response to the attack on Scripture by the Gnostics, who excluded the Old Testament and most of the apostolic writings and substituted Gospels of their own invention, the orthodox constituency of the church sought to hold to a Bible that was in continuity with the Jewish scriptures and recognized according to apostolic criteria. Thus, there was a need to *canonize* the existing texts in order to confirm them as authoritative Scripture.

The word *canon* derives, quite literally, from the Hebrew term *qaneh* ("reed" or "stalk"), which indicated a type of rod or stick used as a means of measurement (1 Kings 14:15; Job 40:21; Ezekiel 40:3). The Hebrew term was brought over into the Greek language as *kanon* with the same literal meaning of "[measuring] rod," but it was also used in a figurative sense as a "rule," "standard," or "guideline." According to John Van Seters,

> The term *canon* arose in Christianity out of Hellenism and Hellenistic Judaism, and in its primary meaning of "rule" or "standard" originally referred to a "rule of faith" as well as a mode of interpretation of Scripture that was in conformity with that rule.[6]

Secondarily the term came to designate a list of sacred texts recognized as authoritative.

Even so, the early Church did not appear to apply the notion of *canonicity* to any particular textual form of the books they recognized as authoritative. This is in harmony with the view that there were no editors or redactors involved in a "canonical process" in the history of the text. Instead, canonization was based on recognition of authoritative authorship and theological harmony, regardless of the text that preserved the author's written word. This is not to suggest there was not a final form of the text that was eventually "received" as authoritative. Rather, the early church in its canonization of the Christian Bible, initially did not consider textual form a priority.

In the final analysis, for the believer, the answer to the question "Are books missing from our Bible?" must rest with the character of God (Numbers 23:19). If God is sovereign with respect to the giving of His revelation (Hebrews 1:1; 2 Peter 1:21) and unchanging with respect to the nature of His word (Psalm 119:89; Titus 1:2), how could He lose books of the Bible?

Put another way, why would God allow books that He inspired to not be included in His Bible? If books have been "discovered" that should have been in the Bible, then the Bible for all of the history of the church has been incomplete. Moreover, if books were found thousands of years after the establishment of the Church—books that changed the defining doctrines of Christianity or argued in favor of an alternate Christianity—how could God be trusted? He would have either shortchanged or outright deceived all previous generations of the faithful.

However, the evidence as to who helped recognize what books should go into the Bible tends to confirm God's sovereign superintendence. This we will examine in the next chapter.

Chapter 9

Who Decided What Books Went into the Bible?

The Protestant Christian canon is a fallible collection of infallible books. This is because while the books themselves are understood to be inspired and inerrant scripture, mere men chose what books they thought should be a part of the canon. Nevertheless, these men did not believe they were creating the canon, rather, they were simply recognizing and submitting to the sacred truth inherent in the ancient texts while avoiding those considered errant and of questionable authorship.

—R.C. Sproul

What is truly God's Word belongs in God's Book,"[1] Howard Vos stated. This is a succinct understanding of the principle of canonicity. However, who decided what books were "truly God's Word," and what criteria were used for this determination? To answer this, let us look at the method of canonization—first for the Hebrew Bible (Old Testament), and then for the New Testament.

The Establishment of the Old Testament Canon

Because the concept of *canon* was first devised in a fourth century AD Christian context with respect to the New Testament, no equivalent Hebrew term was used with reference to those books recognized as inspired Scripture and made a part of the Hebrew Bible. The closest Hebrew term to *canonical* might be the expression "books that defile the hands" (books viewed as sacred rather than common, and therefore affect the ritual status of those handling them).

It should also be understood that in Rabbinic (Orthodox) Judaism, books could be *authoritative*, but not be considered *Scripture* (that is, canonical). This certainly applies to works like the Mishnah (c. AD 200) and the Talmud (Babylonian and Jerusalem versions, completed by the sixth century AD), which have always been accepted as authoritative, as well as writings and commentaries by leading rabbinic sages such as Rashi, Rambam, and Maimonides.

Nevertheless, Orthodox Judaism does have a *rabbinic canon*, which can be defined as "those books accepted [by the rabbis] for doctrine and religious practice and whose authority is binding upon the Jewish people of all generations."[2]

Arriving at the point at which a collection of books was decisively determined to be both authoritative and sacred was a process involving the application of several rules over a period of approximately 1000 years. Some scholars propose a fivefold process of *composition, circulation, revision, collection,* and *recognition* (canonization)—though some books were immediately recognized (see below), while the status of others came about progressively at different times and places.

Scholar John Miller has proposed a process of three distinct stages, identified according to the people who promulgated each collection and ordered it according to a theological purpose:[3]

1. A collection made during the reigns of Hezekiah (2 Kings 18–19) and Josiah (2 Kings 22–23) of the historical books of the Torah that emphasized the blessings of covenant obedience if kings were successful in their reforms.

2. Additions made at the time of the postexilic return to Jerusalem. Other books, including the Prophets, were added in chronological order, and the collection took on the threefold arrangement of *Torah/Prophets/Writings*. The purpose of this order was to demonstrate that the restoration envisioned by the prophets had been partially fulfilled in the reforms of Ezra and Nehemiah.

3. During the Maccabean era, the addition of books whose status had been debated, such as Daniel and Esther.

Miller takes a conservative stance, assigning the closing of the Hebrew canon an early date based on the principle that we should trust the ancient writers more than some modern scholars.

Determining an Authoritative Old Testament Text

The precedent for designating certain texts as authoritative can be seen in the ancient Near East. The Egyptians, for example, collected pyramid texts that contained quotations from their gods. Likewise, in Mesopotamia, oracles received by seers, as well as important religious and court documents, were gathered by priests and deposited in temples for preservation and continued instruction.

We have seen already in chapter 2 how the original tablets of the Decalogue and the books of Moses were preserved with the Ark of the Covenant (Deuteronomy 31:9). The Israelite priests guarded the Torah (Deuteronomy 4:2; 12:32) and periodically reread the Law, as Moses commands in Deuteronomy 31:10-12:

> At the end of every seven years, at the time of the year of remission of debts, at the Feast of Booths, when all Israel comes to appear before the LORD your God at the place which He will choose, you shall read this law in front of all Israel in their hearing. Assemble the people, the men and the women and children and the alien who is in your town, so that they may hear and learn and fear the LORD your God, and be careful to observe all the words of this law.

The authority of each author of Scripture was determined by his position as an "anointed of the Lord" (king, priest, prophet)—and, especially in the case of prophets, by the principle of prophetic certitude. While Moses was also a prophet (Deuteronomy 18:18; 34:10a), his unique relationship with God as a conduit of divine revelation (Exodus 33:11; Deuteronomy 5:4; 34:10b) made his writings canonical beyond question. This required that every prophet's message agree with the truths of the Torah, already acknowledged as God's words (Deuteronomy 13:1-5), and also be proven by a prophecy near in time whose fulfillment could be observed (Deuteronomy 18:21-22; see Jeremiah 28:15-17).

It appears that the authority of those books written by prophets, or associates of the prophets (for example, Jeremiah's scribe Baruch), was accepted from the time of their composition, since later prophets cited the works of their predecessors as Scripture. For example, Jeremiah 26:18 cites Micah 3:12 as a prophecy of the impending Babylonian invasion and destruction of Jerusalem. Daniel 9:2 refers to Jeremiah 25:11-12 concerning the prophecy of 70 years' duration for the Babylonian captivity.[4] As for the Writings, the test was their capacity for inspiration.

When Was the Old Testament Canon Decided?

When the canon was recognized as such within Judaism is still a matter of debate. The 39 books that comprise our Old Testament were accepted as Scripture at the time of the writing of the New Testament, since no other texts but these are cited as Scripture. It seems that most sects within Judaism believed (see TB *Berakoth* 34b) that the production of inspired Scripture had ended with the cessation of prophetic activity in Israel—the end of the fifth century BC.

Old Testament scholar David Noel Freedman argues that a canon was established by that time or earlier, creating the "first Bible":

> The major components of the Hebrew Bible in substantially the form in which they have come down to us were organized and compiled, published and promulgated during the Babylonian Exile.[5]

Although he employs source criticism in his analysis, Freedman's historical conclusions with respect to the completion of the canon are plausible. According to his view, the historical books of Joshua, Judges, Samuel, and Kings were fixed in the canon before the Jews' return from Exile, and the entire canon was completed no later than 400 to 350 BC. Even though by this time the canon may have been recognized as completed, it would not be until the production of the Masoretic Text that there would exist an official "authorized" text for all of Judaism.

Other scholars have argued that the canon may have remained open until much later, at least in some sects of Judaism. Based on the way the biblical material was used by the Qumran sect, other scholars argue that the books of the Pentateuch, Prophets, and most of the Writings had been standardized

The Question of
Canon at Qumran

The Qumran sect (ended by Rome's attack in AD 68) contended that the spirit of prophecy was still alive in its midst because they were living in the last days in which the spirit of prophecy would be restored, as had been predicted (cf. TB *Baba Metzia* 59b). Therefore, they believed the sect's "Teacher of Righteousness" was one who could, by prophetic inspiration, interpret the secrets of the former prophets (1QpHab 2:6-10; 7:1-5). Though this is a sectarian view, it is still clear that, while the Qumran sect may have considered their leader an "inspired interpreter" of the prophetic texts, they did not consider his own writings as "Scripture."

This is also the case for the apocryphal and pseudepigraphal texts found in Qumran's "library," which figured prominently in the sect's literature. For example, Ben Sira, or the Book of Ecclesiasticus (which is one of the 15 deuterocanonical books appearing in Roman Catholic Bible and Greek Orthodox Bibles) was found at Qumran and Masada in several different copies. Among them was the first known copy of that book in Hebrew (all other known copies were in Greek). Other apocryphal books, like Enoch and Jubilees, both highly apocalyptic works, were also found in multiple copies; they exerted an authoritative influence on calendrical and eschatological reckoning.

The Qumran sect also included both a one-hundred-fifty-first psalm (though not numbered as such) and 14 other hymns in the biblical Psalms Scroll that were not included in the canonical Hebrew Bible. Works like the Temple Scroll, which its discoverer and translator Yigael Yadin thought was a type of rewritten Torah, also were highly regarded by the sect. Again, however, this does not mean that this or other writings were given the same status as the books they regarded as "Scripture."

by the fourth century BC.[6] The book of Daniel may have been in dispute in some Jewish circles, but at Qumran, Daniel was counted with the Prophets.* Many scholars, however, believe the diversity of texts present at Qumran indicates that at this time (third to first centuries BC) the biblical canon still remained open and was not yet fixed. They claim that, because the scrolls include books differing from those apparently established in Judaism as the official canon of the Hebrew Bible, the construction of the canon was a gradual process, involving many more people than was thought before the discovery of the scrolls. They also believe this implies the canonical process never reached complete unanimity among the various sects of Second Temple Judaism, even as it has not in Christendom until today. Some also see this situation implying that the inspiration and author-ity of Scripture "worked along the path of formation of these texts."[7]

In addition, various scribal features in the Dead Sea Scrolls indicate that the Qumran sect treated biblical and apocryphal texts differently. This implies that they did not regard them with the same degree of sacredness. Therefore, while both had authority for the sect, they probably considered the former inspired but not the latter. The distinguishing Qumran scribal features between sacred and apocryphal books are

1. Interpretive commentaries (eschatological in nature) were restricted to those books considered Scripture, since only these contained divine prophecies.

2. Messianic proof texts (*Testimonia*/4Q175) and other citations in their sectarian literature were drawn only from sacred texts.

3. The sacred texts were copied on more durable material, such as parchment.

4. The sacred Name of God (YHWH) was written in paleo-Hebrew script only in manuscripts of sacred texts.

5. The scrolls reveal a threefold division of the Hebrew Bible that contained only the same sacred books later made a part of the standardized Masoretic Text.

---

*Some of this dispute may have been for reasons other than questions of canonicity, because the book of Daniel was later relocated to the Writings because it caused problems for Judaism as Jews tried to calculate the end of days and find eschatological fulfillment in current events based on its prophetic timetable.[8]

F.F. Bruce, the late Rylands Professor of Biblical Criticism and Exegesis (University of Manchester, England), has explained the conclusion to which the above evidence points:

> It is probable, indeed, that by the beginning of the Christian era the Essenes (including the Qumran community) were in substantial agreement with the Pharisees and the Sadducees about the limits of Hebrew scripture. There may have been some differences of opinion and practice with regard to one or two of the "Writings," but the inter-party disagreements remembered in Jewish tradition have very little to do with the limits of the canon.[9]

As has been previously noted (see chapter 5), the canon of the Hebrew Bible was recognized by the end of the first century AD at latest. This is testified to by the New Testament and the first-century Jewish historian Flavius Josephus. In the late first and second centuries AD the rabbis continued to debate books such as Esther (which does not mention the name of God), Ecclesiastes (which appeared too pessimistic), and the apocryphal Ben Sira. These discussions also show that Ben Sira was decisively rejected (*Yadayim* 2.13), showing that there was already a long-standing opinion about the apocryphal books. Nevertheless, the final point of reference for the Jewish community for the formal canon of the Hebrew Bible is the Masoretic Text of the tenth century AD, as issued in the Bomberg (rabbinic) Bibles edited by Felix Pratensis (1516–1517) and Jacob ben Chayyim (1524–1525).

The Canonical Order of Old Testament Books

Either a twofold or threefold division of the Hebrew Bible was used during the Second Temple period. The earliest evidence for a threefold division appears in the second century BC in the prologue to the apocryphal book of Ecclesiasticus: "Law, the Prophets, and the other books"; and in one of the sectarian texts among the Dead Sea Scrolls, known as 4QMMT: "the Book of Moses and the words of the Prophets and of David" (this last reference standing for the Psalms, which open the third division). The New Testament testifies to a twofold division of "the sacred writings" (2 Timothy 3:15): "the Law and the Prophets" (Matthew 7:12;

Luke 16:6; Acts 13:15; Romans 3:21). Because such divisions are in use as early as the second century BC, it is evident that the canon of the Hebrew Bible was recognized by that time.

Some scholars suggest that a final ordering of the books took place at the end of the Second Temple period (about AD 70). The decision for this, they believe, may have been due to the need to reorganize Judaism after its loss of the Temple and the priesthood, and also in reaction to the rise of Christianity and the emergence of Christian writings being circulated as Scripture. They base their contention on the belief that the Jewish sages who convened the council at Yavneh (Jamnia) in AD 90 met for the purpose of finally deciding the canon.

However, the purpose of this council was *not* to decide the status of any book of the Bible, but rather to discuss how to resolve interpretive problems in the Bible. The problems included Ezekiel's contradiction of Mosaic law in his vision of the reconstituted Temple (Ezekiel 40–48), the problem of philosophical skepticism in Ecclesiastes, the lack of a direct reference to God in the book of Esther, and the issue of eroticism in the Song of Songs. It is clear from the nature of this discussion that the Jewish sages already recognized these writings' canonical status, and this status required them to resolve the interpretive problems.[10]

The Establishment of the Christian Canon

In the case of Christianity, canonization involved recognition of those books that belonged to the Old Testament canon and those that comprised the canon of the New Testament.

As of the fourth century it appears the church was still grappling with questions of canonicity, at least with respect to the Old Testament. This may be evidenced by the fact that it had interspersed the apocryphal books in the Septuagint among the sacred books. The church's lack of contact with the synagogue and the Jewish community apparently prevented it from learning of the rabbinic canon of the Hebrew Bible, and how the Jewish community treated the Apocrypha.

On the other hand, the early Church Fathers had a high regard for the apocryphal books. Even some who questioned their status, like Origen and Jerome, used them in their explanation of Christian doctrine and in their expositions of the New Testament. For this reason,

Books Included by Judaism and Christianity			
The Hebrew Bible	The Septuagint Old Testament	Roman Catholic and Eastern Orthodox Bibles	Protestant Bible
Torah			
Genesis	Genesis	Genesis	Genesis
Exodus	Exodus	Exodus	Exodus
Leviticus	Leviticus	Leviticus	Leviticus
Numbers	Numbers	Numbers	Numbers
Deuteronomy	Deuteronomy	Deuteronomy	Deuteronomy
	Joshua	Joshua	Joshua
Nevi'im	Judges	Judges	Judges
	Ruth	Ruth	Ruth
Joshua	1-4 Kingdoms (1-2	1 Samuel	1 Samuel
Judges	Samuel, 1-2 Kings)	2 Samuel	2 Samuel
Samuel	1-2 Paralipomena (1-2	1 Kings	1 Kings
Kings	Chronicles)	2 Kings	2 Kings
	1 Esdras	1 Chronicles	1 Chronicles
Isaiah	2 Esdras (Ezra-	2 Chronicles	2 Chronicles
Jeremiah	Nehemiah)	Ezra	Ezra
Ezekiel	Esther	Nehemiah	Nehemiah
The Twelve	Judith	Tobit	Esther
	Tobit	Judith	Job
Ketuvim	1-4 Maccabees	Esther (with additions)	Psalms
	Psalms	Job	Proverbs
Psalms	Odes (includes prayer	Psalms	Ecclesiastes
Job	of Manasseh)	Proverbs	Song of Songs
Proverbs	Proverbs	Ecclesiastes	Isaiah
Ruth	Ecclesiastes	Song of Songs	Jeremiah
Song of Songs	Song of Songs	Wisdom of Solomon	Lamentations
Ecclesiastes	Job	Sirach (Ecclesiasticus)	Ezekiel
Lamentations	Wisdom of Solomon	Isaiah	Daniel
Esther	Sirach (Ecclesiasticus)	Jeremiah	Hosea
Daniel	Psalms of Solomon	Lamentations	Joel
Ezra-Nehemiah	Book of the 12	Baruch	Amos
Chronicles	Isaiah	Ezekiel	Obadiah
	Jeremiah	Daniel (including	Jonah
	Baruch	Susanna, Prayer of	Micah
	Lamentations	Azariah, Song of the	Nahum
	Letter of Jeremiah	Three Young Men,	Habakkuk
	Ezekiel	Bel and the Dragon)	Zephaniah
	Susanna	Hosea	Haggai
	Daniel (including	Joel	Zechariah
	Prayer of Azariah,	Amos	Malachi
	Song of the Three	Obadiah	
	Young Men)	Jonah	
	Bel and the Dragon	Micah	
		Nahum	
		Habakkuk	
		Zephaniah	
		Haggai	
		Zechariah	
		Malachi	
		1-4 Maccabees	
		1 Esdras	
		2 Esdras	
		Prayer of Manasseh	
		Psalm 151	

David deSilva suggests that the Old Testament Apocrypha may have been included "more with convenience of reference in mind than as the standards of canonical versus noncanonical books."[11]

Why Was the Apocrypha Included in the Early Church's Old Testament Canon?

By the fourth century AD, the church's relationship to Judaism had become adversarial, and the church exclusively used the Septuagint as their Scripture. Therefore, it may have wanted to recognize a canon in distinction to the Hebrew Bible—with its short list of 39 books—and therefore included the apocryphal books.

It has been popularly thought that the inclusion of the Apocrypha in the Roman Catholic and Eastern Orthodox Bibles was simply the result of their view of the Septuagint and its "Alexandrian canon," which contained the apocryphal books. This is an improper assumption. As we have seen (see chapter 2), the original Septuagint was a translation into Greek of only the Hebrew Torah. It was written in the third century BC, before any of the apocryphal books had come into existence.

Certainly, books were later translated and added to this "Old Greek" version over time. But even when the Hellenistic Jewish commentator Philo (c. 13 BC–AD 45), who not only used the Septuagint but lived in its hometown of Alexandria, wrote his works, he never cited the Apocrypha. The completed Septuagint appears with the apocryphal books in place in the Codices Alexandrinus, Sinaiticus, and Vaticanus; however, these were all composed in the fourth to fifth centuries AD, and were the product of the church. Therefore, while the church's canonical order—interspersing the apocryphal books among the biblical books—was modeled after that of the Septuagint, the Septuagint cannot have been the single factor motivating the early church to include the Apocrypha in its canon.

Determining the Books of the Christian Canon

With respect to the New Testament, the three criteria of apostolicity, orthodoxy, and catholicity were followed as the means of determining which books were Scripture, and therefore canonical.

Apostolicity, the first criterion, was, "Had a book been written by one of the apostles or by someone who had been associated with the apostles?" The test of apostolicity is implied in the way the apostles recognized their fellow apostles' writing as Scripture. This fact is not always recognized, as the opening words in the introduction to a work on the history of the Bible reveal:

> On the brink of execution, the apostle Paul wrote what many believe is his last surviving letter. He addressed it to his close friend Timothy, a leader of a church in what is now Turkey. "All scripture is inspired by God," Paul wrote... (2 Timothy 3:16). The jailed apostle was talking about the Jewish scripture, which Christians today call the Old Testament. Little did he know that one day Christians would consider his private letter part of sacred scripture. Paul was probably no exception in this regard. As far as scholars can tell, none of the biblical writers knew their words would become part of the Holy Bible.[12]

To the contrary, if we consult the New Testament, we can read the testimony of the apostle Peter to the apostolicity of his contemporary Paul:

> Regard the patience of our Lord to be salvation; just as also our beloved brother Paul, according to the wisdom given him, wrote to you, as also in all his letters, speaking in them of these things, in which are some things hard to understand, which the untaught and unstable distort, as they do also the rest of the Scriptures, to their own destruction (2 Peter 3:15-16).

Here, Peter unambiguously recognizes that *all* the letters of Paul are on par with "the rest of the Scriptures." It is from such recognition by an apostle of an apostle that the church deduced this first rule of canonization.

Of first order in this criterion were books authored by one of the apostles who were related to Jesus and repeated His teaching. Next in priority were writers who, though not apostles, were related to them in a vital way, such as Luke. Consequently, by the end of the second century the four Gospels had attained a status equivalent to that of the Old Testament.

Orthodoxy, the second criterion, addressed the matter of books that did not fit the first category: "Did the book agree with the teaching found in the books of the apostles or their associates?" This doctrinal test eliminated the apocryphal Gospels and related works, even though they bore the names of apostles (for example, Thomas, Andrew, Mark, John, Philip, Peter, James, Judas) and those who had been connected with them (for example, Barnabas, Nicodemus, Mary Magdalene).

Catholicity, the third criterion, considered the universal recognition of the book: "Was it accepted early and by a majority of the churches?" Books that were used regularly or had achieved a special place in the worship and life of the churches were carefully considered, though more important criteria could overrule this lesser criterion. Therefore, though the Shepherd of Hermas, Revelation, and Hebrews were all widely used (though there was a regional preference), the Shepherd of Hermas did not gain acceptance because its authorship was uncertain. The books of Revelation and Hebrews did because they were believed to have been authored by apostles (respectively John and Paul).

Other tests: Obvious and irreconcilable chronological and historical inaccuracies, internal contradictions, and theological disagreements with universally recognized canonical books were also reasons for rejecting apocryphal books. Eleven of the fifteen apocryphal books have one or more of these types of inaccuracies or contradictions, and the remaining four are very short or are of a genre that makes it impossible to make this determination. Some religious ideas that separate Roman Catholics, Greek Orthodox, and Protestant Christians, such as prayers for the dead and the doctrine of purgatory, have their source in the Apocrypha. In fact, some scholars have suggested that the chronological errors in these books are intentional and act as signals to the reader that the works are fictional.

First Steps Toward Canonization of the New Testament

That the church by the late second century had taken steps toward determining which books were acceptable is evidenced by the Muratorian

Fragment, or Canon. This document, discovered in 1740 by Ludovico Antonio Muratori in the Ambrosian Library in Milan, is written in Latin and dates to the seventh or eighth century. It supposedly represents a much larger second-century document (usually dated to AD 170*) that was probably composed originally in Greek in the area of Rome. The Muratorian Canon contains the oldest known list of the New Testament books, and therefore it is significant in determining what the early church in the West accepted as canonical in the second century. For example, lines 47 to 59 read,

> ...since the blessed Apostle Paul himself—following the pattern of his predecessor John—writes, giving their names, to not more than seven churches, in this order: To the Corinthians a first; to the Ephesians a second; to the Philippians a third; to the Colossians a fourth; to the Galatians a fifth; to the Thessalonians a sixth; to the Romans a seventh. But although there is one more each to the Corinthians and to the Thessalonians, for the sake of reproof, nevertheless it is obvious that one church is dispersed over the whole globe of the earth. For also John, in his Apocalypse, while writing to seven churches, yet speaks to all.[13]

The list of accepted books in the Muratorian Fragment contains 22 of the 27 canonical books included in our modern New Testament. (Missing were Hebrews, James, and 3 John; and two books not now a part of the canon, the Apocalypse of Peter and the Wisdom of Solomon, were included.) The list also gives an indication of the process and the order of recognition, as well as regional preference. In the Fragment, the Apocalypse (book of Revelation) was included, indicating acceptance earlier in the West than in the East, where the book of Hebrews (excluded here) was accepted earlier.

The Progressive Recognition of the New Testament Canon

From time to time the Church Fathers mention in their writings books they recognized as canonical. For example, Clement of Rome (AD 95) mentioned at least 8 books, Ignatius of Antioch (AD 115) admitted

---

* A second-century date for the original from which the Muratorian Fragment was derived has been challenged by Albert C. Sundberg Jr., who made a case for a fourth-century date and an eastern (rather than western) provenance (place of origin)—in Israel or Syria.[14] If this is so, the earliest witness to the canon is the list in Eusebius, *Ecclesiastical History* 3.25.

some 7 books, Polycarp (AD 108) acknowledged 15 books, Irenaeus (AD 185) included 21 books, and Hippolytus (AD 170–235) accepted 22 books. This reveals a progressive recognition of the canon by the postapostolic fathers.

Shortly after the founding of Constantinople in the early fourth century, the Emperor Constantine initiated an Index of Banned Books. Obviously, the church bishops had to have informed the emperor which books were heretical and which were orthodox in order for such a document to have been created. Therefore, by the time the Council of Nicaea had been held and Constantine had issued his Edict Against Heretics (AD 325), the books condemned as heretical were already clearly differentiated from those books already recognized by the church (both eastern and western) as Scripture.

The first official indication of a definitive list occurred at the Council of Laodicea (AD 363). It declared that only the Old Testament (along with the Apocrypha) and the 27 books of the New Testament were to be read in the churches. This recognition was later affirmed by the Council of Hippo (AD 393). The councils that formed an undisputed decision on the canon took place at Carthage in 397 (60 years after Constantine's death) and again in 419.

What Was Constantine's Role in Canonization?

Fictional books like *The Da Vinci Code* by Dan Brown judged Emperor Constantine as being the instigator of a political conspiracy with the church's bishops. The imagined goal was to oust their political and religious rivals—adherents to alternate "Christianity" (Gnosticism)—by declaring Jesus to be divine and creating a canon at the Council of Nicaea. These acts excluded the Gnostics and their "scriptures" as heretical.

It is, therefore, necessary to clarify exactly what the purpose was for the Council of Nicaea and what role Emperor Constantine played.

After Constantine defeated the rival emperor, Maxentius, in Rome at the Milvian Bridge in AD 311, he converted to Christianity and issued the Edict of Milan (313), which gave freedom of religion, especially to Christians. He issued other edicts, which elevated Christianity to the level of a state religion. Thus he was widely regarded throughout the Christian world as God's champion and gift to the church.

It is questionable, however, that Constantine had a true conversion. He may have simply used the Christian faith and the church to his own advantage. He may also have had a political motive for convening the Council of Nicaea, the first general council of the Christian church (eastern and western), because he feared that disputes within the church (particularly that over Arianism) would cause disorder within the empire.

Whatever his motive, the purpose of Nicaea was not to decide the canon, which was not even discussed by the bishops, but to decide whether Christ was substantively equal to God (the orthodox position) or was in some way subordinate (the Arian concept).

Constantine, first Christian Emperpor of Rome (reigned AD 306–337).

Constantine used the power of his office as emperor to coerce the eastern bishops (who had Arian tendencies) to capitulate in this matter. But neither he nor any of the western bishops invented the divinity of Christ, a truth established repeatedly in the Gospels and throughout the Scriptures, and defended by the postapostolic fathers.

As mentioned, Constantine did order the burning of books that were determined to be heretical by the Council of Nicaea in his Edict Against Heretics (AD 325). The council's determination implies that there was a list of books understood by the church to be canonical long before Constantine and the Council of Nicaea. For this reason, it appears the Orthodox bishops did not see a need to make a formal declaration of a canon until AD 397.

Some scholars lament Constantine's attempt to "stamp out" dissenting views, arguing that such diversity challenged the church to continually define and refine its doctrinal and canonical understanding, and suggesting that after the demise of opposing groups, power-hungry politicians took over positions of church leadership.[15] However, Constantine did not completely eliminate alternative Christianity nor totally suppress their noncanonical Gospels. These heretical movements went underground and continued for another two centuries.

To repeat, the Council of Nicaea did not address the issue of canonicity, nor did Constantine force the creation of the canon for political purposes. The discerning reader will distinguish such fact from the fiction in charges like those in *The Da Vinci Code*.

As alluded to previously, if divine Providence and the superintending hand of the Almighty are removed from our view of history, then, of course, our explanation of the events of history will be limited to the machinations of men who, rightly or wrongly, have sought to shape history according to their own dictates. From this humanistic perspective Bart Ehrman, like Dan Brown, has claimed that the canonical process was a conspiracy to establish an official or orthodox Christianity. His basis for this is because the church of Rome had the money to assure that their version of the Bible was accepted and all competing versions rejected, and because Emperor Constantine, for his own reasons, used his political power to enforce the "orthodoxy" decided at the Council of Nicaea.

However, it is not Constantine's agenda that should be our concern, but that which God expressed in His Word through the apostle Paul:

> There must also be factions [literally, *heresies*] among you, so that those who are approved may become evident among you (1 Corinthians 11:19).

The Council of Nicaea only "made evident" those "who were approved" and clarified their orthodox beliefs in creeds. From Christianity's beginning, heresy provoked the leaders of the church to make decisions concerning the most essential doctrines of the faith.

In the issue of which books would be included in the canon, the decision was made progressively. However, this decision-making was no doubt hastened by the Great Persecution, which came to the church during the pagan emperors Galerius and Diocletian's eight-year war on Christianity

(AD 303–311). When Roman officials began systematically confiscating and burning "Christian Scripture,"[16] the church had to make up its mind which books had sufficient authority to be worth suffering for. By the fourth century (not the sixth, as some critics claim) the majority of churches in both the East and West agreed on the same books, thus "closing" the canon for all intents and purposes.

This recognition was possible only because it was understood that the Holy Spirit attended His church and guided it into "all truth" (John 16:13). It is inconceivable that the God who inspired the authors of Scripture would not give sufficient sense to His church to recognize which books should be a part of that Scripture. While the human process was imperfect, the Head of the church nonetheless brought the leaders of the church to a proper recognition of the books He had inspired.

After all, God has sway over all things, from powerful politicians such as Constantine (Proverbs 21:1) to the decisions of apostles and bishops, who in reality are simply announcing decisions already made in heaven (Matthew 16:19; 18:18; see John 20:22-23). In this world, a fact of God's overcoming divine purpose is that, in spite of wrong seeming to prevail over right, "all things work together for good to those who love God" (Romans 8:28). And if God can make "all things work together for good," He can make sure the right books get into His Bible for the good of His church!

In the end, it is up to us to trust the God of the Bible to be God, and to have given His Word to us in the canon of Scripture. In fact, we have His Word on it. In Jude 3 we read that "the faith" was "once for all delivered to the saints." This statement recognizes that a canon was necessary, since orthodox faith is defined by what is truly Scripture. God gave a fixed number of books to be recognized by the church as Scripture. This being done, there is no reason for the church to be troubled over the unearthing of "lost books" with secret information about a different "Christian" faith. In the 66 books that comprise the canon we have "the faith once for all delivered to the saints."

However, what *are* Christians to make of the discovery of previously unknown books, such as Gospels that contain sayings attributed to Jesus? This is the problem we will tackle in the following two chapters.

Chapter 10

Has the Truth About Jesus in the Original Gospels Been Lost?

The early Christian church was a chaos of contending beliefs. Some groups of Christians claimed there was not one God but two or twelve or thirty…Certain sects maintained that Jesus was human but not divine, while others said he was divine but not human. In *Lost Christianities,* Bart D. Ehrman offers a fascinating look at these early forms of Christianity and shows how they came to be suppressed, reformed, or forgotten…These spectacular discoveries reveal religious diversity that says much about the ways in which history gets written by the winners.

—FROM THE INSIDE COVER OF BART EHRMAN'S BOOK
*LOST CHRISTIANITIES: THE BATTLES FOR SCRIPTURE
AND THE FAITHS WE NEVER KNEW*

I will never forget the feeling I had as my host, a dealer in rare manuscripts, set before me on the table a newly discovered and unpublished text from Egypt.[1] In my hands were some 30 well-preserved papyrus leaves containing lines of text in the Coptic language written with a legible hand. One expert had dated the text to roughly the fourth century AD, and his preliminary translation of the opening lines revealed a creation account. The whole text, it was believed, constituted a lost Gospel.

The reason I remember my feelings that afternoon so well is because, while I was excited to examine such an archaeological treasure, I was also concerned about the effect this discovery, once made known, would have on the Christian community. The ancient Gospel I had handled came not from the ancient Christian church but from one of its most intractable opponents—Gnosticism.

Although long known by scholars from the writings of the Church Fathers, especially those apologists who countered this movement, popular awareness of this group of sects came in 1945. It was then that, near the village of Nag Hammadi, two Egyptian peasants looking for a nitrate ore used as fertilizer stumbled upon a three-foot-tall storage jar filled with 52 papyrus scrolls written in the Coptic (Egyptian Christian) language.[2]

Once these deteriorated fragments had been restored and translated, they revealed the fourth-century AD esoteric teachings of the Gnostic sect—previously preserved only in the written arguments of their opponents in the church. What appeared remarkable was that here—with names attached that also appeared in the New Testament—were "Gospels" and other writings: the Gospel of Thomas, the Gospel of Philip, the Gospel of Mary [Magdalene], the Apocryphon of John, the Acts of Peter, and others.

Papyrus codices (with leather covers) from Nag Hammadi, Upper Egypt, containing Gnostic documents

A Legitimate Contender with Orthodoxy?

Any archaeological recovery of ancient manuscripts is of immense importance to scholars, as it opens up a previously unknown or scantily revealed period of history. In this case, the finding of noncanonical writings that could be associated with the time of early Christianity promised to open a door to understanding the heretical beliefs with which the Church Fathers contended.

However, scholars of the new school did not view the Nag Hammadi texts as heretical, but as lost "Christian Gospels" that provided an alternative perspective on Jesus and formed the basis for a revolution in thinking about history and religion. In their publications, Gnosticism was seen as a legitimate contender with orthodoxy for the truth about the Bible.

And they asked new questions about what the early Christians believed, many of which we will touch on:

- Was there only one God (and which gender was He/She/It)?
- Was Jesus originally considered divine?
- Was Jesus married?
- Did the Gospel of Thomas reveal Jesus more accurately than the Gospel of John?
- Was Judas a hero or a villain?
- Did Jesus actually rise from the dead? Why were some of Jesus' sayings suppressed by the church?

Their answer to such questions and others was that one faction in Christianity prevailed politically over the other. The winner declared its theology "orthodox," branding the loser "heretical" and destroying their version of the Scriptures. (See this chapter's opening quote for a good summary of this view.)

Accordingly, the new school argues that neither orthodox Christianity nor Gnosticism existed in the first two centuries after Jesus, but only a diversity of beliefs about Him. These flourished until one of the heresiologists, Irenaeus of Lyons (c. AD 130–200), along with his followers, enforced an unnatural uniformity based on his brand of belief, causing one form of Christianity (the "proto-orthodox" movement) to emerge as the "true Christianity." The stabilization of this "orthodox" Christianity took place at the Council of Nicaea (see previous chapter), when the money of the hierarchy of the church of Rome and the political power of the Roman emperor Constantine constructed an official canon and creed. The official canon contained only four Gospels and outlawed the rest, while the official creed elevated Jesus to divinity and condemned all other views as heretical.

Several decades passed after their discovery before the Nag Hammadi documents made much impression on modern religious thinking. But once the largely anti-Christian media got its teeth into the idea that these texts of a "lost Christianity" proved that the faith of the church was not the "original" faith, but the product of a centuries-old religious conspiracy and cover-up that "changed the history of the world," the whole new-school interpretation quickly became fodder for Hollywood scriptwriters. It has now shown up in the plots of films such as *The Order, Stigmata,* and *The Da Vinci Code,* the latter based on the novel by Dan Brown, who used the new-school spin to claim his fiction was based on "fact." With the Nag Hammadi documents now becoming public knowledge, people have begun to talk about, and even believe in, the "lost sayings of Jesus."

Could There Be Lost Sayings of Jesus?

Sayings of Jesus that were not recorded in the New Testament are referred to as the *agrapha* ("not written"). Several examples of purported *agrapha* were preserved by some of the Church Fathers of the second century. Further, what is called the *Q Document* is a hypothetical collection of these sayings that were supposedly written down and served as the *source* (German *Quelle*—hence *Q* Document) for those writing the four canonical Gospels. Could there indeed have been such "sayings" that had been lost, but may have been preserved in these apocryphal Gospels?

Because the apostolic age was a time when oral tradition was still considered the main means of preserving teachings, including the words of Jesus, it is plausible that very few copies of the originals were made and circulated. In a time when few people were able to read, books (codices) had not yet been invented, and it was difficult to distribute the bulky scrolls of an illegal religion through the heavily guarded Roman world. Oral communication was far preferable. (As a comparison, the earliest rabbinic writings that we have in the Mishnah come from no earlier than the third century AD, although they contain oral traditions going back to the first century AD.)

Luke writes in the prologue of his Gospel (1:1-4) that "many" in his day had written accounts "of the things accomplished among us" and that these were based on what was "handed down" from "eyewitnesses and servants of the word" (that is, the apostles). Luke's terms "compiled accounts" (verse 1) and "the word handed down" (verse 2) seem to make a distinction in the manner these traditions were received and recorded. If Luke's Gospel was written in AD 60, this means there were 30 years between his writing and the original events witnessed by the apostles.

A Scarcity of Documents

We possess only a small representation of the writings from the apostolic and postapostolic periods (the first to second centuries AD); this is not only true for the lost Gnostic Gospels but also for the canonical Gospels. Frankly, this is the case for all historical documents from the ancient world—only a portion survives, and the closer one comes to the source, the less has survived.

One question that could be asked is this: If, as the new school claims, these authentic sayings of Jesus from the earliest period were lost because they were suppressed or destroyed by the "proto-orthodox" movement (the church), how do we explain the fact that the church's earliest writings were also lost? Who suppressed *them*? Alternatively, the late date of the Gnostic documents could also be evidence that the movement as such simply did not yet exist in the apostolic age.

The greater question is, could there be other sayings of Jesus—sayings that were *not* included in the four canonical Gospels? Since the apostle John wrote in the conclusion of his Gospel that Jesus *did* many other things that were not recorded (John 20:30; 21:25), it is logical that Jesus also *said* many other things that were not included in the Gospel accounts. One such saying—"It is more blessed to give than to receive"—may have been included by Luke in his account of the apostle Paul's teaching in Acts 20:35. (Despite the appearance of a citation formula, some have argued this might not be a saying of Jesus, but merely Paul's summation of Jesus' teaching—"what Jesus said"—on the subject.)

There is a big difference, though, in accepting that Jesus said more—and believing that such sayings can now be identified after 2000 years.

Certainly, the very fact that Jesus said more than what was recorded in the four canonical Gospels, and that this was said only during the last three years of His life, created a desire to "fill in" the gaps or the "missing years" of Jesus' life as well as His words. Some of the noncanonical Gospels may have been written as "inspired fiction" to meet this demand. Others, of course, were forgeries based on the canonical Gospels, invented to support Gnostic beliefs.

If some of Jesus' authentic sayings were preserved in the writings of the Church Fathers or even the Gnostic Gospels, how could anyone ever know for sure? One reason the Gospels were written under inspiration is so we would have the assurance that what was included was indeed Jesus' own words (John 14:26). For this reason, when we compare the Gnostic Gospels with the four canonical Gospels, it is clear that the former contain distorted versions of Jesus' sayings (as well as conflicting with the nature and work of Jesus as recorded in the latter).

Distinguishing the Authentic

However, most people in that day had no New Testament to help them, so how did they distinguish authentic from nonauthentic sayings? One answer is that in the beginning they had the apostles, who as eyewitnesses could verify the sayings. Another answer is that the church memorized the sayings of Jesus and would have recognized any deviation from them. However, as the church grew and as the eyewitnesses died, getting such verification became increasingly difficult. Moreover, the postapostolic era reveals that, despite the safeguards, many people were still deceived as alternative writings such as the Gnostic Gospels began to appear. It was for this reason that the apostolic Fathers (first half of the second century AD), some of whom may have known and been discipled by the apostles and directly maintained their apostolic teaching and traditions, wrote their own letters to the churches.

In turn, from their ranks, in the mid-second century, rose the apologists ("defenders") to make Christianity's case against opposing religions and philosophies. Among this opposition were "alternate" groups that emerged from within Christianity but deviated from the apostles' doctrine. Their battles with heresy forced the apologists to closely examine heretical movements and record their judgments. This process also helped to more carefully clarify the orthodox position until creeds like the Nicaean (promulgated AD 325) would more formally define it.

Therefore, in this early period, the apologists' writings helped protect the church from nonauthentic sayings of Jesus (Gnostic Gospels, among others) by delineating those traditionally recognized as authentic—those in the four Gospels. As a result, even though the Gnostic Gospels claim to be sayings of Jesus, from the perspective of orthodoxy (the four canonical Gospels) they are untrustworthy and add nothing new to our knowledge of Jesus. This is why the *Gospel of Thomas* and the other Gnostic Gospels were not received by the church in the postapostolic period and were later banned at Nicaea. This is also why we should be grateful for having an assessable and testable New Testament (whatever the translation)—as our means for discerning modern, as well as ancient, heresy.

Limited in Size, Sufficient for Faith

Why, then, were not *all* of Jesus' words included in the four canonical Gospels—why were some left out? There are both practical and theological reasons for this. Practically speaking, each Gospel writer constructed his Gospel around a particular scheme. Accordingly, each author had to leave some material out in order to accomplish this task. Since the writers were most likely aware of one another's accounts, they did not feel it necessary to repeat all of the same material or use it in the same way (remember the unique purpose of each) as the others.

Of course, another practical matter was the limited size and length of scrolls, which required a writer to carefully edit his research and draft material. This may offer an explanation for Luke's inclusion of the previously unrecorded saying of Jesus in Acts 20:35, if it in fact is such. Luke was the author of both his Gospel and Acts, and his method of writing reveals he did not prefer to repeat material. Consequently, he may not have used this saying in Luke because it didn't fit his scheme and because he knew he would later cite it in Acts. Likewise, he does not repeat material about Jesus from Acts in Luke (for example, the details of Jesus' ascension in Acts 1:1-11).

Theologically speaking, we believe that the Holy Spirit purposely directed the authors' selection so that what they included was sufficient for faith. John declared this to be the purpose for his own selection of sayings:

> Many other signs therefore Jesus also performed in the presence
> of the disciples, which are not written in this book; but these
> have been written so that you may *believe* that Jesus is the Christ,
> the Son of God; and that believing you may have life in His name
> (John 20:30-31).

Therefore, the problem addressed by the selectivity of the Scripture is the problem of faith. How much must we know in order to have faith? More important, what do we have to believe?

This latter question is at the center of what defines Christianity. Throughout the history of the church one group or another has tried to change or re-interpret the *sine qua non* (the irreducible essential) of the Gospel, stated so succinctly by John: "that Jesus is the Christ, the Son of God." The difficulty of the church as it reached into its world with the Gospel was to maintain this essential truth within cultural contexts of variegated religious influences.

As the multiplicity of religious influences in the Roman world affected new converts to Christianity or spawned movements in competition to it, the church was faced with the problem of Christian heresy. Let us look at the development of this challenge to orthodoxy, especially the Gnostic heresy. This will shed much light on the nature of the debate today over so-called "lost Christianities" and the claim of "missing books" from the original New Testament. The chart on page 167 gives a compact picture of leading Gnostics and Gnostic beliefs.

The Problem of Christian Heresy

It is important to understand that from the beginning of Christianity there was heresy. (Heresy, by definition, cannot exist until the truth has been established.) On a number of occasions the New Testament mentions false religious beliefs: the magic and sorcery of Simon Magus (Acts 8:9-11), Epicurean and Stoic philosophy (Acts 17:18), the worship of Artemis (Acts 19:27-28,34-35), and the polytheism of paganism (Acts 14:12-13; cf. 28:6). The early church battled against many forms of heresy that developed from syncretisms with Judaism, pagan philosophy, mysticism, and foreign religions.

Gnostics and Gnosticism

Key figures	Origin and influence	Beliefs and practices
Cerinthus (late first century)	• had roots in pagan philosophy, especially Platonism	• thought themselves possessors of unique higher insight (*gnosis*)
Basilides (early second century)	• was influenced by Oriental mysticism • had little appeal to the masses	• thought themselves to be of *spirit;* other people of *soul* or *body* • taught that matter is evil
Saturninus (early second century)	• most influential among church leaders • appeared throughout Empire	• held to hierarchy of aeons* • produced either sensuality or asceticism
Marcion (died c.160)	• worship ranged from very simple to very elaborate • forced church to formulate a rule of faith and New Testament canon	• were dualistic • in general, rejected Old Testament and Judaism • used allegorical interpretation; said that the world was created by a demiurge,† Jehovah
Valentinus (died c.160)		
Tatian (110–172)	• caused church to emphasize apostolic succession as repository of truth	• believed Christ's body was an illusion

---

* *Aeons* were "emanations" of God, subdeities that usually came in male–female pairs. The aeons made up the *pleroma*, "region of light."

† A *demiurge* is an aeon that is emanated without its opposite pair (thus being imperfect—not complete), and which therefore should not have come into existence.

Such departures from apostolic doctrine and practice were already being experienced in the first century, and of some of these the New Testament makes special mention:

- forbidding marriage (1 Timothy 4:1-3)

- teaching strange doctrines (Hymenaeus and Alexander in 1 Timothy 1:3-4,6-7,20)

- denying a future bodily resurrection (Hymenaeus and Philetus in 2 Timothy 2:17-18)

- the rejection of apostolic authority (Diotrephes in 3 John 9)

- the denial of Jesus' having "come in the flesh," that is, His appearance in a physical form (1 John 4:1-3)

While these examples of heresy do not warrant the view that Gnosticism made its appearance in this earliest period,[3] it does show that some of the views that would later characterize Gnosticism were already present.

To be sure, these divergent beliefs (heresies) reveal that a diversity of views existed from the beginning. This should not be surprising, in light of Jesus' own examples from the Old Testament of a long history of spiritual apostasy (Matthew 23:34-35), or from the dissent among His own outer circle of disciples (John 6:67), or from the apostasy among the inner circle of the Twelve (Judas in John 6:70-71; 18:2-5).

However, it should be noted that with this diversity is a clear delineation and denouncement of these divergent views and groups as heretical. This precedent preserved a distinctly orthodox Christianity from the beginning.

One such divergent belief, which later became a distinguishing feature of Gnosticism, was the rejection by certain Christians of some or all of the Old Testament. The early Jewish–Christian apostolic church began with the Old Testament as its Bible and continued to embrace it as Holy Scripture even after the New Testament was completed. However, with that completion, and with the rise of increasing conflict between Judaism and Christianity, divergent voices began to view the New Testament as replacing the Old (a view termed supercessionism). They drew this belief from the New Testament's teaching about freedom from the law (contained in the Old Testament); they further concluded that the God of the Jews in the Old Testament was different from Jesus Christ.

Such seeds of spiritual schism sown in the apostolic era sprouted as incipient Gnosticism in the postapostolic era and blossomed in the second century into full-blown Gnosticism. This growth was abetted by such Gnostic leaders as Cerinthus, Basilides and Saturninus, Valentinus, Tatian, and Marcion (see more in chart on page 167). As an example of the heresies characteristic of Gnosticism, let us consider the last of these men.

The Marcionite Heresy

Marcion (c. AD 100–165), the son of a wealthy shipowner, was bishop of a local Christian community in Asia Minor. Around AD 140 he became a prominent member of a church in Rome. There, however, he fell under the influence of the Syrian Gnostic teacher Cerdo. Soon Marcion was teaching the Gnostic concept of two gods.

In his view, one god, the Creator in the Hebrew Bible, was revealed in nature as the demiurge (see chart on page 167) of the cosmos, responsible for evil and misfortune. He was not the highest god; he was just, ruling by the law, but was not merciful. The other god, the unknowable supreme god, was good, but was revealed only in the Gospels. Because he was detached from the creation, Marcion called him "the Alien." Since the highest god did not have a material form, his son, Jesus Christ, did not have a physical body and had not had a human birth. Marcion said Jesus had been revealed in the fifteenth year of the reign of Tiberius as "a man but not a man"—that is, a "phantasm" (a belief similar to Docetism, which taught Jesus was divine but not human).

In the year 144 Marcion attempted to expound his new views to the leaders of the Roman church at a synod and was excommunicated as a heretic. In response, he started a church like the Roman church, with organization, liturgy, and use of scriptures (the first Gnostic to do so). Marcion taught that all of the apostles failed to understand that Jesus Christ was the son of the highest god; only Paul, in some of his letters, had grasped the truth.

Marcion's Bible

Marcion rejected the entire Old Testament as the revelation of the merciless demiurge. He created his own version of the Bible, which contained a "truncated version" of Luke's Gospel (he thought the other Gospels were Judaic forgeries), his own edited version of ten Pauline epistles (excluding the pastoral epistles and Hebrews), and a preface giving his unique theological perspective and allegorical interpretation.

Like other Gnostics, Marcion understood salvation to be physical deliverance from the material world and stressed strict asceticism, not for spiritual sanctification, but as a rejection of worldly things created by the demiurge. Though he embraced many Gnostic teachings, he parted with the Gnosticism of his time by holding that 1) mankind does not participate in the divine essence ("the divine spark"); 2) both the body and soul were created by the demiurge and are imperfect; 3) all, not just a few, people can be "saved" through the mercy of the good supreme deity; 4) this "salvation" is attained through faith in Christ, not through a revealed *gnosis* ("knowledge").

Because of these distinctions scholars debate if it is truly proper to categorize his movement as Gnostic. Also unlike other Gnostics, Marcion traveled as a missionary throughout the Hellenistic–Roman world, establishing his brand of churches. His influence was so extensive that at the height of his movement, it is estimated, Marcionism had influenced some 40 percent of Christians. As a result he was one of the few heretics to be condemned by every Greek and Latin theologian.

By the third century Marcionism had died out and been absorbed into the Manichaean sect. The only positive outcome of the movement was that it, and Gnosticism in general, forced the Church Fathers to formulate a Christian creed (a rule of faith) and formally determine the New Testament canon.

Though Marcion held only some Gnostic beliefs, he paved the way for the spread of full-blown Gnosticism in the late second and third centuries. This Gnosticism held to additional teachings, ones that more fully define the movement, and that need to be considered since they are found in the Gospels of Thomas and Judas, and in other similar works that have also attracted much attention in the last few decades.

What Is Gnosticism?

The term *Gnosticism* is derived from the Greek word *gnosis,* "knowledge." It was first used in English in the 1660s by the Protestant Henry Moore to describe heresy in general. However, the term is appropriate in its more specialized use, since Irenaeus' great treatise *Against Heresies*— subtitled *Exposé and Overthrow of What Is Falsely Called "Knowledge"*— described an early form of this deviant belief, whose chief characteristic was a claim to secret *knowledge.*

While there are a number of theories to explain the rise of Gnosticism, one possible cause was the delay in the return of Christ:

> The early Christians eagerly awaited the imminent return of Christ, who would eliminate the evil and suffering in the world. By the second century, the nonoccurrence of the Parousia ["coming" of Christ] caused a number of Christian teachers to present views of the world and mankind's escape from its oppressions that deviated from the standard Christian beliefs.[4]

If this theory, put forth by Antonía Tripolitis, Professor of Late Antiquity and Director of the Modern Greek Studies Program at Rutgers University, is correct, Gnosticism arose from a disappointed eschatology. It shifted the hope of the physical redemption of the body and of this world to a physical deliverance from this world through the death of the body.

Gnostic self-understanding. Gnostics thought of themselves as "Christians" and claimed to preserve the true revelation of Christ. This self-understanding and the attempt to subvert orthodoxy brought them into conflict with the apologists (heresiologists) of the early church. After the church councils had stabilized the Christian canon and formulated a clear statement (creed) of the Christian faith, the Gnostic movement began to die out. What was perhaps one of the final acts of the cult took place in the late fourth or early fifth century AD, when the Nag Hammadi library was buried in the grave of its last leader.

The biblical text. Gnostics held a nonliteral or allegorical interpretation of the Bible, whose hidden meaning could be understood only by a select few who had special knowledge. Because they held there was a plurality of deities and that the creator god was evil and responsible for the woes of life in an evil material world, Gnostics rejected the Jewish monotheistic concept, of the one God as Creator. Because of this rejection of the Creator God revealed in the Hebrew Bible, most scholars, based in part on the example of Marcion, believe Gnosticism also rejected the Old Testament. Other scholars argue that Gnostics accepted the Old Testament as a "privileged book." However, "like the holy books of other nations, it remained the unsuspecting vehicle of hidden truth to be unlocked by the proper hermeneutical key."[5] As for the New Testament, it served mainly as a source of proof texts to confirm the Gnostic message.

The Gnostic worldview. Gnostic writings vary, drawing upon imagery from the New Testament, pagan myths, and Platonic ideas. Likewise, Gnosticism was quite varied taking many different forms and names in the early church. Even though not all traits are characteristic of every variation, and the further back in time we go the fewer traits we find, there are at least four commonly shared features that comprise and distinguish the Gnostic worldview.

1. *Dualism* is the most generally agreed feature of Gnosticism. The concept of dualism was a prominent teaching of the Greek philosopher Plato, which seems to have had an effect on this sect. Gnostic dualism divides everything into spirit (good) and matter (evil), including God. The false (evil) god, the creator god, is transcendent and unknowable. By contrast, the true (good) god, known as the high god (sometimes called "Father"), from whom the creator god turned, is pure spirit, wise and knowable.

2. *Cosmogony* relates to the origin of the universe. In the Gnostic dualism the creation is a contrast of opposites: spirit versus matter (flesh), knowledge versus ignorance, and light versus darkness. Because an evil god created the world, matter is evil.

Consequently, the world itself is evil and inferior, as are human beings who inhabit it in their material (fleshly) form.

3. *Soteriology* concerns salvation, or in the Gnostic sense, "deliverance." Man's soul or spirit (sometimes called the "divine spark") is good, but it is trapped in both an evil material shell (the body) and in an evil material world. The knowledge about the creation's dualistic nature (including the true god and human condition), once "revealed," is salvation. This knowledge *(gnosis)* brings about a deliverance from ignorance here and, ultimately, a deliverance from the human body and the material cosmos. The revealer (or redeemer) comes from the pure upper spiritual world to a chosen few in order to give them the knowledge that they possess the divine spark within their dark material form; to help them establish a sense of connection with the spiritual; and to help them gain a sense of separation from the material world. Gnostics identified Christ as this revealer/redeemer.

4. *Eschatology* looks to the final goal or end of existence—when the soul or spirit re-ascends to the heavenly realm of its origin and the creation returns to its fullness *(pleroma)*—that is, where good dwells. One can see why Gnosticism wanted nothing to do with the concept of bodily resurrection and rejected the idea that Jesus rose from the dead.

Gnostic Appropriation of Jesus

If this theology seems confusing, imagine trying to apply it to life. Practically, their dualistic theology resulted in a dualistic lifestyle: *asceticism* (a detached self-denial that loathed marriage and procreation) on the one hand, and *antinomianism* (a moral lawlessness that permitted licentious behavior) on the other hand. And like most members of modern "secret societies," Gnostics harbored pride in being those in the know, while feeling arrogance toward those who were unenlightened and therefore inferior.

From this survey of Gnostic teaching, we can understand how Jesus' sayings in the Gospels concerning His having come from above, being the light of the world, declaring that He had overcome the world, and promising His chosen a return to their heavenly home could be reinterpreted in a dualistic way by those already accustomed to Platonic thought and influenced by pagan mythology. N.T. Wright well sums up the character of the Gnostic "Jesus" that was based on these sayings:

> Whatever the "Jesus" of these Gnostic "gospels" has done, the main thing about him is that he has come, not to rescue the world, or to heal or change it, but to give secret teaching about how to escape it.[6]

In order to impart a special knowledge leading to their brand of salvation, Gnostics collected, arranged, and edited "Jesus' sayings," whether actual or apocryphal. Mostly, though, they invented them to fit their beliefs. In contrast to the canonical Gospels, whose stated purpose is to give an account of the life of Christ (Matthew 1:1,18; Mark 1:1; Luke 1:1-4; John 20:30; 21:24-25), the Gnostic Gospels are non-narrative (tell no story).

Their form—a lack of narrative sequence with no specific context— deliberately made the sayings puzzling to readers, but allowed them to be open to any unorthodox interpretation, especially an enlightened Gnostic interpretation. Consider an example from the *Gospel of Thomas:* "Jesus said, 'He who drinks from my mouth will be as I am, and I shall be that person, and the hidden things will be revealed to him'" (logian 108). Who knows what this means? But a Gnostic could tell you!

Gnostic "Wisdom"

The Gnostic Gospels also contain cryptic wisdom sayings (proverbial or parabolic in nature) that require an enlightened interpreter to reveal their hidden meanings. For example, "Lucky is the lion that the human will eat, so that the lion becomes human. And foul is the human that the lion will eat, and the lion still will become human" (*Thomas,* logion 7). Such ideas remind us that paganism was one of the sources from which Gnosticism borrowed its ideas. According to Ben Witherington III, what sayings such as this one "probably reflect is the pagan notion that the life force can be transferred from a lesser being to a greater one (even a god) by the greater being sacrificing or consuming or even strangling (and so squeezing the life breath out of) the lesser being."[7]

The "Gospels" that Present the Gnostic Jesus

The Gnostic Gospels also overplay their hand in promoting their claim to authority. The canonical Gospels as we know them appear as anonymous works, except for Luke, although there was probably an ending in the originals that identified the apostolic authors. For this reason, New Testament scholar Martin Hengel insists that the Gospels never circulated anonymously. Even so, there may be another reason for the anonymity, such as the characteristic Christian virtue of "humility of mind." Because these teachings were things the Lord Jesus had promised to reveal through the Holy Spirit, it may have been thought irreverent to claim authorship. We see this, for example, in the incidental way the apostle John identifies himself—merely as "the disciple whom Jesus loved" (John 21:20,24). Even so, this is an internal witness of authorship (at least in the case of John).

By contrast, the Gnostic Gospels take pains to announce their apostolic identity—their only means of acceptance. In addition, they often make claims to be the guarantee of the true knowledge that leads to salvation (a real selling point!)

In sum therefore, despite the use—or misuse—of Christian texts, Gnosticism cannot be construed as an "alternative Christianity," as the new school would have us believe. It clearly has to be labeled a heretical Christian cult, as Alastair H.B. Logan concludes in his textbook on the subject.* After surveying various theories on the nature of the Nag Hammadi community, he concludes,

> If one is thus led to rule out the monastic hypothesis in its various forms, as well as that of an individual and the heresiological one, then that of the codices as comprising the library of a Christian ascetic Gnostic cult is the only remaining plausible candidate... the Nag Hammadi library...is the library of a Gnostic cult for whom everything was grist to their mill.[8]

---

*Logan is Senior Lecturer in Theology at the University of Exeter.

There is an old saying, "If it's true, it's not new." This should especially apply to spurious teachings about Jesus. Is it possible that the church that He founded (Matthew 16:18; see Ephesians 2:29; 5:23) never knew the real Jesus until the discoveries of Gnostic texts at Nag Hammadi? Is it possible that the Church Fathers and their successors for the past twenty centuries got it all wrong?

When we are told we now have new teachings of Jesus never before known—teachings that radically change our concept of Him and of Christianity—we must be inclined to say, "If it's new, it probably isn't true." It is not that the Jesus of history cannot be found in the Gnostic Gospels,[9] it is that whatever historical information may be present is couched within a heretical context…for the purpose of altering our view about the Jesus of history.

As we look more closely at the Gnostic Gospels in the next chapter, the contrasts between orthodox Christianity and the Gnostic heresy will become still clearer.

Chapter 11

What the New Gospels Say About the Christian Faith

Included in [the Nag Hammadi documents] are several gospels of Jesus' life that never made it into the modern Christian Bible as well as a treasury of lost, esoteric wisdom that portrays a side of Christianity suppressed by the institutionalized church.

—FROM THE JACKET OF MARVIN MEYER'S BOOK
THE GNOSTIC DISCOVERIES

My first real acquaintance with Gnostic thought came during my graduate studies at the Hebrew University in Jerusalem. In a course titled "Judaism and Gnosticism," co-taught by Professor Michael Stone of the Hebrew University and Father George MacRae of Harvard, our coursework consisted of reading scores of apocryphal and pseudepigraphal texts and then discussing them at Professor Stone's home in Jerusalem.

This all took place back in 1980, but I have never had as many strange religious ideas in my head since! One of those texts we studied, the *Gospel of Thomas*, has since been nominated by some in the new school to be a fifth Gospel in the New Testament, or even to replace the Gospel of John! It has recently been joined by the newly discovered *Gospel of Judas*—said to be another missing piece in recovering the Jesus we never knew. In order to understand these highly publicized "Gospels," let us examine them more closely.

The Gospel of Thomas

The *Gospel of Thomas*, the most famous of the Gnostic Gospels because of its early translation and popular publication as "a fifth Gospel," consists of 114 *logia* ("sayings") of Jesus. It is also notorious for being one of the "heretical books" the Church Fathers mentioned by name.

The new school believes these sayings once existed as part of the hypothetical written document known as Q, which contained all of the oral Jesus tradition and was circulated in the early church. However, after an individual assessment of each saying in *Thomas*, scholar Hans-Josef Klauck concluded that some 50 percent of the sayings have no contact with anything recorded in the New Testament.[1] Could that much material have been overlooked by the canonical Gospel writers? If, though, the writing of *Thomas* postdates the apostolic era, then this 50 percent was not used by the apostles (or even the apostolic Fathers) because it did not yet exist.

Gospel of Thomas (Nag Hammadi Codex II), fourth century AD
(Coptic Museum, Cairo, Egypt)

Thomas's Sources

Klyne Snodgrass has shown that *Thomas* borrows from Luke and the synoptic tradition.[2] Nicholas Perrin has demonstrated that *Thomas* has affinities with Tatian's *Diatessaron* (Greek, "harmony of the four"), the earliest Syriac version of the four Gospels,[3] dated c. AD 175. Consequently, most scholars would not see *Thomas's* composition before AD 175 to 180.[4] This evidence indicates that even the roots of *Thomas* come later than the composition of the four Gospels, and therefore it did not arise in a parallel fashion from the same source—the hypothetical Q document.

However, it is also argued that if some portions of the material appear to come from sources *outside* the synoptic Gospels, they could contain some authentic "unknown" sayings of Jesus. There is no way to affirm or deny this, for the simple reason that the church has recognized only canonical Scripture, with the qualifications necessary to attain this recognition as the determining factors (see more in chapter 9). Further, while some of the sayings are taken from the authentic synoptic Gospels, they are recast in the Gnostic mold. Anyone acquainted with the sayings of Jesus in the canonical Gospels will have little trouble identifying the forged pseudo-sayings in *Thomas,* for example: "Jesus said, 'Where there are three gods, they are divine. Where there are two or one, I am with that one' " (logion 30). What reader of the synoptic Gospels would believe that Jesus the Jew, who spoke of only one God,* could ever utter such a thing?

Sometimes *Thomas's* sayings clearly betray themselves:

> The disciples said to Jesus: We know you will go away from us. Who is it who shall be great over us? Jesus said to them: Wherever you have come, you will go to James the Just for whose sake heaven and earth came into being (logion 12).

Jesus could never have said this because during His lifetime James was an unbeliever (John 7:3-5). Only after Jesus' resurrection did James believe,

---

* See Matthew 4:10; 23:22; 27:46; Mark 2:7; 10:6,18; 11:22; 12:30; Luke 10:27; 20:25.

and only later did he become leader of the Jerusalem church. Moreover, the designation "James the Just" was never used by the early Christian community but rather by outsiders, such as the Jewish historian Flavius Josephus, and in later traditions (for example, by the fourth-century church historian Eusebius).

The author of the *Gospel of Thomas*, like other apocryphal writers, took a pseudonym of an apostle in order to gain recognition as an authentic and authoritative, rather than apocryphal, Gospel. However, as noted previously, the Gnostic author exposes his pseudonymity by deliberately making this point, and by declaring the secret nature of his private revelation from Jesus:

> These are the secret words which the living Jesus spoke and Didymus Judas Thomas wrote. And He [Jesus] said: "Whoever finds the explanation of these words will not taste death" (Prologue to *Thomas,* logion 1).

To better grasp the differences between this "Gospel" and the canonical Gospels, let us consider some of the teachings in the book.

Teachings in the Gospel of Thomas

We would expect to start with *Thomas*'s teaching about God, but there is very little discussion about God in the book. In fact, the word *God* rarely appears in the English translation, although the term *Father* is used indirectly some 15 times.

It should be recalled that this "Father" in Gnostic thinking is the good high god that is unknowable and detached from the world he didn't make. No real information is given about this "Father," other than that he is "living" (also used of Jesus) and has a heavenly "Kingdom." One saying reveals that the image of the "Father" is, or has, "light," but is uncertain of much more than this:

> The images are manifest to man, but the light which is within them is hidden in the image of the light of the Father. He will manifest himself, but his image is concealed by his light (logion 83).

However, another saying, which does not mention God, nevertheless explains that Jesus is "the light," but then goes on to describe him in pantheistic language:

> Jesus said, "I am the light that is over all things. I am all; from me all came forth, and to me all attained. Split a piece of wood; I am there. Lift up a stone, and you will find me there" (logion 77).

While it would appear commendable that *Thomas* expresses a high Christology, identifying Jesus as the creator, such language is inappropriate for the Gnostic Jesus, whose role is only to reveal the mysteries so the individual can become enlightened and attain self-deliverance from the material world. In fact, it sounds like Jesus and the material world are one, yet the material world in Gnostic thought is evil, as is the god who created it. Nonetheless, Jesus claims in this saying that "from me all came forth." Is Jesus then being identified with the evil god of creation, or is *Thomas* here something less than Gnostic? When we read logion 61, however, we find that the seemingly high Christology has been significantly lowered: "Jesus said, 'I am he who exists from the undivided. I was given *some* of the things of my Father.'" (James M. Robinson translation).

If it is difficult to understand *Thomas*'s concept of God, perhaps his concept of man will be clearer. It is, but it is no more encouraging. Consider logion 87: "Jesus said, 'Wretched is the body that is dependent upon a body, and wretched is the soul that is dependent on these two.'" In other words, the body is evil and worthless to the soul. However, logion 112 declares that the soul is also worthless to the body: "Jesus said, 'Woe to the flesh that depends on the soul; woe to the soul that depends on the flesh.'"

Elsewhere *Thomas* states that the [human] "spirit," which in Gnostic thought belongs to the upper realm, is imprisoned in the human body:

> If the flesh came into being because of the spirit, it is a wonder. But if the spirit came into being because of the body, it is a wonder of wonders. Indeed, I am amazed at how this great wealth has made its home in this poverty (logion 29).

This understanding is clearly in line with Gnostic thought that the body is evil and escape from it is the apex of the one who has been enlightened.

Salvation According to Thomas

Having seen *Thomas's* concept that man's spirit is captive to his flesh, we next need to consider the manner of salvation it offers. In the very first "saying" of Jesus in the *Gospel of Thomas* we have seen that salvation can be attained only if one can figure out the hidden meanings in Jesus' sayings. But this applies to only a select few: "Jesus said, 'I disclose my mysteries to those who are worthy of my mysteries' " (logion 62). How does one become worthy? By continuing to understand the hidden meaning until he succeeds:

> Jesus said, "Let him who seeks, not cease seeking until he finds, and when he finds, he will be troubled, and when he has been troubled, he will marvel and he will reign over all" (logion 2).

Now, if one has to be worthy to understand the mysteries, how can he understand the mysteries and become worthy? Can the path to salvation be this self-contradictory? The answer apparently is yes. Consider the very next saying: "The Kingdom is within you and it is without you. If you will know yourselves, then you will be known and you will know you are the sons of the Living Father" (logion 3). This sounds much like the self-help psychotherapy coming out of some pulpits today. Essentially, in Gnostic expression, it is a self-salvation of self. Logion 70a makes this point precisely: "Jesus said, 'If you bring forth that within you, that which you have will save you.' "

However, even though this is an individualistic salvation, it is not for *every* individual. In fact, one entire sex of the human race is excluded:

> Simon Peter said to them: "Let Mary go out from among us, because women are not worthy of the Life. Jesus said: See, I shall lead her, so that I will make her male, in order that she too may become a living spirit, resembling you males. For every woman who makes herself male will enter the Kingdom of Heaven" (logion 114).

This is because in Gnostic thought only the male mind is capable of "knowing" and therefore of attaining salvation, which is based on knowledge. Apparently, women also are not "living spirits"!

If this concept of elite, worthy-male self-salvation appears discouraging, unfortunately things do not get better when *Thomas* describes the future. When the disciples ask Jesus "how our end will be," his reply is as enigmatic as ever: "For where the beginning is, there shall be the end. Blessed is he who shall stand at the beginning and he shall know the end and he shall not taste death" (logion 18b). In like manner, when they ask, "When will the rest for the dead come about, and when will the new world come?" the reply of Jesus is, "What you expect has come, but you don't know it" (logion 51). This reveals that *Thomas*, in keeping with other Gnostic Gospels, has no eschatological focus in this world and no expectation of a coming kingdom as found in the canonical synoptic Gospels.*

In conclusion, *Thomas's* teaching is individualistic and moralistic—that is, each person innately has what they need for salvation, and in pursuing this to final enlightenment they may attain what they seek. *Thomas* also is pluralistic and somewhat pantheistic, finding God (or Jesus) in everything, except external revelation, since the spirit in man is essentially divine.

As a "Gospel," however, *Thomas* really tells us very little about what Jesus thought of Himself or what others thought of Him. While there are a few contradictory logia hinting at an exalted view of Jesus, or implying His suffering, for the most part all we have is an assortment of cryptic wisdom sayings requiring secret knowledge for their interpretation. Though they do say Jesus is a wisdom teacher, the exclusion of any saying directly related to Jesus' death or resurrection (such as the passion narratives of the canonical Gospels) reveals a Jesus much diminished from the picture history draws of Him.

The Gospel of Judas

The *Gospel of Judas* made its public debut on April 9, 2006. On that date the National Geographic Society aired a television special simultaneously with the release of a book on the sensational discovery of a new Gnostic Gospel. At the time I was in Athens, Greece, and had to content myself with the local newspaper, which headlined the find as a "lost Gospel" that

---

* See Matthew 6:10; 16:28; 19:28; 25:31,34; Mark 11:10; 15:43; Luke 1:33; 13:29; 14:15; 19:11; 22:16; 23:43.

told a very different story concerning the role of Judas than that recorded in the New Testament. I wondered what the local priests were going to tell their parishioners in this country where the Greek Orthodox Church strictly dominates religious thought. A week later I was in Turkey, where the newspapers in this Islamic country were more than pleased to imply that the discovery of the *Gospel of Judas* refuted Christianity! Back home I was finally able to settle down and understand the details of this newly found document.

Like the unpublished Gnostic document I had handled at the manuscript dealer's home, the *Gospel of Judas* had come to light in the antiquities market in Geneva, Switzerland. According to those investigating its provenance, it was part of a collection of texts (codices) that had apparently been discovered in a cave in Egypt around 1978. Thereafter, it had made its way around the Egyptian antiquities market, then to Geneva (where it was scientifically studied and authenticated by experts) and the U.S., and finally back to Switzerland where the Maecenas Foundation was finally willing to pay the high asking price.

As with the Nag Hammadi Library, the text was written in Coptic and was dated to the fourth century AD. With help from the National Geographic Society, about 85 percent of the badly eroded text of the *Gospel of Judas* was carbon dated to the late third century and partially reconstructed.[5] Even so, it was later discovered that some 42 pages of the complete codex are missing.

An Opposite "Revelation"

Unlike the *Gospel of Thomas*, this Gospel includes narration. However, in keeping with *Thomas* the opening lines of *Judas* betray its exclusively Gnostic character: "The secret account of the revelation that Jesus spoke in conversation with Judas Iscariot." The reason Judas is singled out is later explained by Jesus: "I know who you are and from where you have come. You are from the immortal realm of Barbelo. And I am not worthy to utter the name of the one who has sent you."[6] For this reason Judas is elevated as the premiere disciple; Jesus even demeans the other disciples' prayers and acts of worship as a waste of time.

Jesus teaches Judas privately and instructs him concerning the sacrifice that really matters: "You will exceed them all. For you will sacrifice the man who clothes me."[7] In other words, in making sure Jesus was killed, Judas would become the greatest disciple. This is the gist of the text. No trial, crucifixion, or resurrection is included, probably because the purpose for which the Gospel was written was completed with the account of Judas's handing Jesus over to the Jewish authorities. Of course, we would not expect resurrection in this account, since it would work against the Gnostic purpose of salvation: release from the physical body.

The Real Story

The *Gospel of Judas* is a good example of how false theology rewrites history. According to the historical accounts in the canonical Gospels, Judas is the "son of perdition" (John 17:12) into whom Satan entered (Luke 22:3). Jesus' crucifixion was a wicked act (Acts 1:18a; 2:23), and because Judas betrayed Him "it would have been good for that man if he had not been born" (Matthew 26:24). Finally, in remorse over his act of condemning Jesus, Judas hanged himself (Matthew 27:3-5).

Luke in particular wants to make sure his audience understands what Judas did and that he got what he deserved. He adds details of Judas's suicide—an act according to the Old Testament that is connected with shame and failure (see 2 Samuel 17:23). Jews also preferred deaths that did not deface the body (see Leviticus 19:28), which was looked upon as a disgrace (see 1 Samuel 31:9-13; 2 Samuel 2:4-6), so Luke describes Judas's body as falling after his hanging and being horribly disemboweled (Acts 1:18). Finally, Peter states that Judas "turned aside to go to his own place," a euphemism for his receiving the punishment of the unjust in the afterlife (Acts 1:25).

The *Gospel of Judas* is just the opposite of the canonical Gospel accounts, because the Gnostic means of "salvation" is the opposite of that in orthodox Christianity. In Gnostic thought the body is evil, and the spirit is imprisoned within it. For the Gnostic Jesus, the greatest thing is the spirit's deliverance from the body. Since Judas is the agent of this he attains the rank of the greatest disciple. By the reader understanding this secret revelation he can grasp the esoteric knowledge that will lead him to "salvation." Gnosticism's method is to reinterpret the obvious to make it obscure; or in this case, to "reveal" that something that has been thought to be obvious—that Judas was evil—is in fact the opposite. The justification for this lies in the Gnostic teaching that the god of this world—the creator god—is evil, and therefore anyone he hates must really be good.

How has this Gnostic historical revision of the betrayer and the betrayed been packaged and presented to the public? Just as it appears. There has been no attempt to dilute or conceal its clearly Gnostic message, which is dramatically opposite of the Christian message. In fact, this distinction is celebrated—as though finding the *Gospel of Judas* has finally unveiled the real story. Listen to Bart Ehrman, who although a professing agnostic, concludes his book on the *Gospel of Judas* in an almost evangelistic appeal for this "alternative truth":

> The Gospel of Judas presents a different view, insisting that Judas was the only one of the disciples who understood his Lord. Jesus came not from the creator god but from the "realm of Barbelo." So, too, did some of us. Some of us are trapped here in the prisons of our bodies, but once we learn the truth that Jesus delivered to his one faithful disciple, Judas, we will be able to escape to return to our heavenly home. Judas is the one who leads the way. He is the "thirteenth," because he stands outside the number of Jesus' twelve disciples, who never did grasp his teachings and never did realize that their devotion to the creator god is misplaced. Only Judas had a glimpse of the truth. And so to him alone did Jesus reveal all that needs to be known.
>
> In return, Judas performed for him the greatest service imaginable. His betrayal was not the act of a traitor to the cause. It was a kind deed performed for the sake of his Lord. He turned Jesus over to the authorities so that Jesus could be killed and escape the confines of his body. In so doing, Judas is the greatest of all the apostles. In the memorable words of Jesus, "You will exceed them all. For you will sacrifice the man who clothes me."[8]

In a word, Judas is seen as Jesus' friend and closest ally, a man who does the greatest good by helping Jesus rid himself of the defilements of the fleshly life and attain (through death) the bliss of the disembodied state. This is in stark contrast to the historical accounts of the canonical Gospels, which depict Judas as follows:

- He is a preordained traitor (Matthew 26:24 with Psalm 41:9), confirming Jesus' place—as the suffering Messiah—at the end of the line of Israel's persecuted prophets (Matthew 23:30-37; Luke 11:47; 13:34; see Matthew 5:12; Luke 6:26).

- His act of betrayal is depicted as satanic activity (Matthew 26:24; John 13:26-27,30).

- The details of his death are given to verify his divine condemnation (Matthew 27:3-5; see Acts 1:16-18, 25).

A Prime Example of Gnostic Thought

Back in the second century AD the apologist Irenaeus wrote against this Gnostic reversal of history. He addressed a group he called "Cainites" because they rewrote biblical history, making heroes out of villains such as Cain, Esau, Korah, and the men of Sodom. Here we find that the *Gospel of Judas* is not at all new, for Irenaeus mentioned it in *Against Heresies* 1.31.1, judging it to be the "invented history" of heretics:

> They declare that Judas the traitor was thoroughly acquainted with these things, and that he alone, knowing the truth as no others did, accomplished the mystery of the betrayal; by him all things, both earthly and heavenly, were thus thrown into confusion. They produce a fictitious history of this kind, which they style the Gospel of Judas.

The *Gospel of Judas* has reappeared in the twenty-first century with media fanfare, but like its first appearance some 1800 years ago, it will not fool the church into thinking the canonical Gospels got it wrong and nominating Judas for sainthood! Rather, as N.T. Wright has pointed out, the very public promotion of the *Gospel of Judas* may well work against the new school, not for it:

> The "Gospel of Judas" might indeed represent the point at which the ordinary reader, long used to being fed a diet of conspiracy theories, "secret gospels," "lost sources," and a host of similar

things, would at last wake up, rub her eyes, and declare that if *that's* what it's all about—meaning by "that" the kind of thing we find in "Judas"—then it's obviously all a mistake, and maybe there is something in classic Christianity after all.[9]

Alternative Christianity?

The *Gospel of Thomas* and the *Gospel of Judas* are said by the new school to be examples of "lost Christianities" or "vanished Christianities"—that is, early forms of Christianity that did not survive the orthodox chopping block. Supposedly, these "Christianities," now restored to us through archaeological discovery or the antiquities market, not only show the diversity that existed in early Christianity, but record alternative views about Jesus and the church that were just as legitimate as those that survived in the New Testament. For example, Gnostic expert Elaine Pagels writes,

> Many Christians today who read the Gospel of Thomas assume at first that it is simply wrong; and deservedly called heretical. Yet what Christians have disparagingly called Gnostic and heretical sometimes turns out to be forms of Christian teaching that are merely unfamiliar to us—unfamiliar precisely because of the active and successful opposition of Christians such as John.[10]

Orthodoxy and Heresy in the Early Church			
Writing (or Church Father)	Date written	Location	Heretical movement
Apostolic period (AD 30 to 100)			
Matthew	c. 60s	Syria	
Mark	c. 50s	Rome	
Luke	c. 60	Rome	
John	c. 80s	Ephesus	incipient Gnosticism

Period of the apostolic Fathers and heretical movements (AD 100 to 150)			
Clement	75-110	Rome	Docetism
Marcion	before 150	Rome	Marcionism
Gospel of Thomas	before 150	Egypt	Gnosticism
Justin Martyr	100-165	Asia Minor, Rome	
Period of the apologists and more heretical movements (AD 150 to 400)			
Tatian*	c. 130–170	Syria	Gnosticism
Gospel of Judas	before 180	Egypt	Gnosticism
Irenaeus' Against Heresies	175	Lyons, Gaul (now France)	Gnosticism
Tertullian's Apology	d. 220	Carthage	Ebionism
Origen, Against Celsus	d. 254	Alexandria, Caesarea	Montanism
Eusebius	d. 340	Caesarea	Arianism
Period of the orthodox church councils and creeds (AD 400 to 800)			
Council of Nicaea	325	Nicaea	Arianism
Council of Constantinople	381	Constantinople	Apollinarianism
Jerome, Vulgate	d. 420	Bethlehem	
Council of Ephesus	431	Ephesus	Nestorianism
Council of Chalcedon	451	Chalcedon	Eutychianism
Council of Constantinople	553	Constantinople	Monophysitism
Council of Constantinople	680–681	Constantinople	Monotheletism
Council of Nicaea	787	Constantinople	Iconoclasm

*After about the year 172, Tatian apostatized from Christianity and became a Gnostic of the Encratite sect.

Similarly, Bart Ehrman writes concerning the ultimate significance of the *Gospel of Judas* that "the Gospel provides us yet another ancient Christian writing that does not belong to the orthodox camp. It instead presents a form of Gnostic religion that came to be suppressed by the victorious party in Christianity in the third or fourth century."[11]

So extensive is the literature on this subject that modern bookstores now have a section called "Alternative Christianity." Though the *Gospel of Thomas* and *Gospel of Judas* differ substantially from the canonical Gospels, could they not simply represent one of these "alternative Christianities" that the new school tells us grew up alongside what would come to identify itself as orthodox Christianity?

To be sure, the Gnostics called themselves "Christian," but this does not make them Christians any more than modern Mormons, who also refer to themselves as "Christian." In contrast the term *Christian* first occurs in Acts 11:26 as a derisive name used by the Antiocheans for the followers of Jesus.* In 1 Peter 4:16, it is found as kind of a legal charge, like "thief" or "murderer"; it also appears in this sense in Roman accounts, to describe the victims of Nero's persecution. The point here is, by the second century, when the church adopted it for its members, the term already had a history of application to the particular movement known previously as "the Way" (Acts 19:9,23; 24:14,22), which had emerged from Judaism.

The significance of this is, when we consider the historical origin of the church from the apostles as recorded in the New Testament, it is a movement still defined in terms of Judaism and still looking forward to the fulfillment of the eschatological promises made to national Israel.† This shared hope initially linked the early church to the Jewish community, with the synagogue being not only the regular place of Jewish-Christian worship,†† but recommended by the apostles to Gentile believers in order that they might gain a proper background in the Scriptures (Acts 15:21). For this reason, frequent positive references are made to the Law, Psalms, and Prophets in the canonical Gospels as well as other orthodox writings.

---

* The term is formed on the analogy of adherents to a political party, such as the *Caesarians,* the *Herodians,* or the *Pompeianians.*

† For example, Acts 1:6-7; 3:19-21; 26:7; Romans 11:25-28.

†† See Acts 13:14-15,43; 14:1; 17:1,10,17; 18:4,7-8,17-26; 19:8.

By contrast, however, this linkage to the Jewish community and any similar appeal to the Old Testament is strikingly absent in the Gnostic texts. If they emerged from the same original source, there should have been at least a trace of this. However, the Gnostic texts promulgated secret knowledge that needed no tradition, written or oral, for its support. For this reason, among many others, it is obvious that the Gnostic writings have a significantly different origin and come from a much later period (mid to late second century AD). Gnostics may have called themselves "Christian," and the new school may wish to see them as an "alternative Christianity," but they have no historical claim to that name because they do not share true Christian origins. Craig A. Evans makes this point in the conclusion to his book *Fabricating Jesus:*

> These hypothetical Christianities did not exist in the middle of the first century. But lack of evidence and anachronism need not prevent the creation of novel scenarios. All one needs is imagination and uninformed readership.[12]

Are These New Gospels Really "Gospels"?

The Gnostic documents have been popularly labeled "Gospels" because they were written by figures whose names appear to identify them as disciples of Jesus. This was done deliberately to give the impression they held the same authority as the canonical Gospels. Below, one of the leading experts on these documents, James M. Robinson, explains that the literary genre of the *Gospel of Thomas* (he also addresses in context the *Gospel of Philip,* the *Gospel of the Egyptians,* and the *Gospel of Truth*) is distinct from that of the canonical Gospels:

> It is clear that the *Gospel of Thomas* was hardly designated by its original author or compiler as a *Gospel*. Rather he or she would have called it a collection of *sayings*. But then, in the effort to get it accredited by the church as being on a par with the *Gospels* gaining canonicity in the emerging New Testament, this collection of *sayings* was secondarily named a *Gospel*.[13]

When we further compare the two distinct genres of the collections of sayings and the canonical Gospels, we find that the Gospels are narrative, purposefully telling a story (the career of Christ). This choice of genre was ideal for proving historically 1) that Jesus is the fulfillment of Israel's expected Messiah and 2) that through His death and resurrection He has accomplished redemption, and therefore has become the object of the believer's faith as "the mediator between God and man." This fits the meaning of the term *gospel:* "good news."

By contrast, the Gnostic writings that are called "Gospels" represent collections of sayings attributed to Jesus (in relation to His disciples). Their purpose, aside from private meditation, appears to have been to create an authoritative basis for Gnostic teaching—specifically, the attainment of a state of disembodied perfection through the practice of an enlightened spirituality.

Orthodoxy vs. Heterodoxy

The difference between apostolic teaching (orthodoxy) and Gnostic teaching (heterodoxy) can be understood by the meaning of these opposing terms:

Orthodoxy: the quality or state of "conforming to established doctrine especially in religion…from Late Greek *orthodoxos,* from Greek *orth-,* straight, right, true + *doxa,* opinion"

Heterodoxy: the quality or state of being "contrary to or different from an acknowledged standard, a traditional form, or an established religion…from Greek *heterodoxos,* from *heter-,* other than usual, different + *doxa,* opinion"

In our brief overview of this question of newly discovered Gospels, we have made the case that these Gnostic Gospels were hidden away (not lost) because they had been judged to be heretical by the church from the time of their initial appearance. The evidence of church history reveals that Gnostic teaching was always strongly opposed, but there was no official means of restraining its influence until the rise of Constantine. This means that there was not a comfortable diversity in the early church, where "alternative Christianities" flourished side by side. Rather, there was a pure stream of truth and tradition—coming from Christ and His apostles and preserved through their successors—that experienced conflict with heretical views and groups that arose. This is what history has taught us, and nothing discovered at Nag Hammadi has changed it.

For this reason, we can affirm that orthodoxy was not merely one view amid competing legitimate Christianities—a view that forced its way to hegemony in the third and fourth centuries. Rather from the beginning, orthodoxy was the only legitimate view, taught by Jesus and His apostles and handed down in a defined form. Their successors' recognition of what constituted orthodoxy was applied to the "sayings of Jesus" being circulated in their day, as well as to those teachings and writings of opposing groups. In the final analysis, it was not an apologist like Irenaeus who produced orthodoxy, but orthodoxy that produced Irenaeus. Moreover, it was not because one group won that it became orthodox; it won because it was orthodox and all others were heterodox.

Chapter 12

Do We Have Now What They Had Then?

[The Hebrew text of the Bible] is a carefully annotated product of a centuries-long tradition throughout which the sacred words were meticulously guarded, copied, and checked by Jewish experts.

—JAMES VANDERKAM,
THE DEAD SEA SCROLLS TODAY

The New Testament was copied in such a way that we can recover most of the original wording. The suggestion that the scribes went wild on the text, that there were no controls, and that scholars cannot determine the wording of the original because of such chaos is nonsense.

—KOMOSZEWSKI, SAWYER, AND WALLACE,
REINVENTING JESUS

The question "Do we have now what they had then?" is not simply an academic matter. It is not an armchair debate concerning the value of one modern version of the Bible over another. Rather, this question's answer affects the essential integrity of both Judaism and Christianity in their claim to possess an authoritative text from God.

Whose Text Is Authoritative?

Therefore, in this chapter we will consider some additional points about the trustworthiness of the Bible's transmission down to us and draw them together with some of the conclusions made in earlier sections of this book—especially chapters 6 and 7—in order to reach a reliable answer.

Islam, the foremost opponent of both Judaism and Christianity today, argues that it alone has an authoritative text—the last word from "God"— and that both the Old Testament of the Jews and the New Testament of the Christians were corrupted and changed at some time in the past:

> The Jews repeatedly lost their revealed books…they distorted and perverted Allah's word and changed its meaning…The Old Testament in the Bible cannot, for these reasons, be regarded as the book revealed by Allah to Musa [Moses]….
>
> "Those who call themselves Christians…forgot a good part of the message that was sent to them" (Sura 5:15)…. They exceeded the limits of religion and perverted it and introduced the doctrine of "trinity" and that of redemption through the so-called crucifixion of 'Isa [Jesus]….
>
> By the time of Muhammad all of the books revealed up to that time had either been totally lost, or their original contents and the true message had been grossly perverted and distorted. The time had come for Allah to send a fresh, final and complete revelation—which is the Qur'an.[1]

The Qur'an, according to Islam, is the latest and greatest revelation of Allah to mankind, and according to it the Bible (or biblical figures) must support the Qur'an. Since the Bible and the Qur'an differ on major points, however, then the Bible must have been corrupted at some point in the past.* The Muslim viewpoint is not simply an abstract theological notion, but has very real-world applications, especially with regard to the Middle East conflict and its global offshoots.

---

* One primary accusation is based on an out-of-context reading of Jeremiah 8:8: "How can you say, 'We are wise, and the law of the LORD is with us'? But, behold, the lying pen of the scribes has made it into a lie." Based on this, the Islamic Web site "Answering Christianity" declares, "We clearly see that the Jews had so much corrupted the Bible with their man-made cultural laws, that they had turned the Bible into a lie!" (page 1).

   Now, of course, these texts refer to Israelite henotheism (the worship of one god without denying the existence of other gods), syncretism, and pagan apostasy. All of these practices involved false prophets and false scribes. When the proper context is supplied—from the following verse, Jeremiah 8:9—we find it stated that these "wise men…have rejected the word of the LORD." There is no declaration here that the Bible was changed or corrupted—only that some people acted corruptly and stood condemned by the pure and unchanging word of God.

Other well-known religions, Mormonism being one,[2] have made the same accusation against the Bible—that it is corrupt, and their authoritative texts take precedence over the Christian Scriptures. We have seen in earlier chapters how many hundreds of Hebrew manuscripts of the Old Testament and tens of thousands of Greek manuscripts and versions of the New Testament are in existence. The variants in these serve as witnesses to the Original Bible, which can be restored through textual criticism (see the next chapter). However, the accusation of corruption and alteration in these manuscripts has not yet been answered. How do we know that what was written by those who had initial contact with God really remains in our text? How do we know that those countless scribes who copied the text for thousands of years did not, in fact, lose the original words or distort them, as Muslims maintain? Is it possible for us to say that we still have now what they had then?

Scribal Preservation and the Old Testament

The Old Testament (as well as the New Testament) was preserved through the work of professional scribes whose duty was to ensure the accuracy of the text as it was copied. In the ancient Near East the scribal preservation of royal and religious documents was of vital importance. Therefore, scribes of varying qualifications were assigned to all governmental and temple offices. As in the lands that surrounded Israel, Israelite scribes were members of tribal or family guilds (see 1 Chronicles 2:5). In the time of Moses, certificates of divorce were written by scribes (Deuteronomy 24:1,3; see Matthew 19:7). According to a fifteenth century BC cuneiform text, scribal schools were already present in Canaan when the Israelites arrived.

However, because the Hebrew Bible is written in the postexilic Hebrew language (some 900 years after Moses' time), higher critical scholars have argued that this period must also be the time of its original composition. They assume it was the work of scribes of this period who needed religious fiction concerning the origins of the Jewish people to inspire the postexilic community. But simply because a text was copied in a more modern form of the language (in regard to script and grammar), this does not mean it did not previously exist in an archaic form. This is evidenced by the use of the paleo-Hebrew script in the Samaritan Pentateuch and for some of the biblical books of the Dead Sea Scrolls (for example, paleo-Exodus and paleo-Leviticus), as well as in a biblical inscription of Numbers 6:22-27, dating to the mid-seventh century BC, found on silver amulets from Ketef Hinnom.*

Recently, nonconservative Cambridge scholar John Emerton has argued for the existence of a highly trained scribal contingent in Jerusalem in the tenth century BC—the time of David and Solomon—on the basis of the fourteenth-century BC Amarna letters (written by Canaanite authorities in Jerusalem to rulers in Egypt):

> They were written by people who could write Akkadian cuneiform as well as knowing the local language. They were evidently scribes, and they must have received a thorough training....It is difficult to see why there could have been capable scribes in Jerusalem in the Amarna age, but not in the tenth century.[3]

If a developed scribal school was already in existence at the beginning of Israel's monarchy, then how far back could scribal activity go?

How Accurate Were the Scribes?

The Hebrew Bible, of course, sees this activity first taking place with Moses in the fifteenth century BC and then throughout the compositional history of the text.[4] But how accurate were the scribes? Isn't it possible they could have so changed the original wording of the text that it is impossible to know what the original authors wrote? Let us set about to obtain an answer.

We know that those Masoretic scribes (such as Aaron ben Asher) who in the tenth century AD analyzed hundreds of Hebrew manuscripts to produce authoritative codices, employed scribal methods to maintain a fixed text. They counted the words and consonants of each book, the middle word and middle consonants, taking special note of everything in the text that had been the result of errors in transmission (even though they accepted the text they had as inspired, with no variants as such). If we consult the rabbinic sources,[5] we find descriptions of the rules for scribal practice during the Talmudic period for preparing new scrolls for use in the synagogue:[6]

---

* See page 71 for Pentateuch photo; page 92 for amulet photo.

Rules for the Scribe

1. Every scroll must contain a certain number of columns, equal throughout the entire codex.
2. The length of each column must not extend over less than 48 or more than 60 lines; and the breadth must consist of 30 letters.
3. The entire copy must first be lined; and if three words are written without a line, it is worthless.
4. An authentic copy must be the exemplar (master copy), from which the transcriber ought not deviate in the least.
5. No word or letter, not even a *yod* (the smallest Hebrew letter), must be written from memory, the scribe not having looked at the codex before him.
6. Between every consonant the space of a hair or thread must intervene; between every *parashah* (section), the breadth of nine consonants; between every book three lines.
7. The fifth book of Moses (Deuteronomy) must terminate exactly with a line; but the rest need not do so.
8. The scribe when transcribing must sit in full Jewish dress.
9. The scribe must wash his entire body (ritual purification necessary before handling sacred texts).
10. The scribe must not begin to write the name of God (YHWH) with a pen newly dipped in ink.
11. Should a king address a scribe while he is writing the name of God, he must take no notice of him.

These accounts reflect later rabbinic scribal practice, but granting that scribes inherited their positions within their families and were part of guilds that maintained strict traditions, it is not unwarranted to extend these rules to the Jewish scribes of ancient Israel. Evidence for this may be had from the biblical texts among the Dead Sea Scrolls produced at Qumran more than 1000 years before the above rules for scribal practice. Emanuel Tov has shown that scribes at Qumran clearly followed a set of rules which agree (as well as disagree in some respects) with the rules prescribed in the rabbinic literature.[7]

The Masoretes sought to preserve the original understanding of the text, which had been written without vowels. The correct vocalization of this text had previously been transmitted orally, and by memory, from generation to generation. After six centuries in the Diaspora, a fear arose that the memory of the original Judean dialect was fading. Therefore, the Masoretes inserted markers in the text to indicate the original understanding of the vowels.

But how well was this understanding preserved by the oral tradition? In brief, the scribes' memory of the text was so accurate that they preserved all of the rare and difficult forms of words as well as the common and well-known ones. Therefore, these men were not inventing vowels or making up words, but were creating a system of signs and marks to preserve what had been given to them.[9]

The scribes of the Dead Sea sect who copied the scrolls faced a similar problem. They included consonants within the text that served as vowels. Here also, the comparison between the Isaiah scroll and the Masoretic Text (see sidebar) reveals how accurate the transmission of the text by oral tradition had been. Overall, therefore, with respect to the witness of the Jewish scribal practice, R. Laird Harris has concluded,

> We can now be sure that copyists worked with great care and accuracy on the Old Testament…indeed, it would be rash skepticism that would now deny that we have our Old Testament in a form very close to that used by Ezra when he taught the word of the Lord to those who had returned from the Babylonian Captivity [538 BC].[10]

The Accuracy of the Scribes

The textual accuracy of the Masoretes—as well as of the Qumran scribes—can be seen by a comparison of text of the Dead Sea Isaiah Scroll (1QIsa^a) with the Masoretic Text. It shows that the two texts are almost identical—only three words are spelled differently.[9] For a book that runs 66 chapters (about 100 pages in our English Bibles), this reveals a remarkable degree of care taken in the textual transmission between the time of the Dead Sea Scrolls and the Masoretic Text.

And if such a state of textual preservation could be maintained for a millennium forward in time, why could it not have been maintained for a millennium backward in time—the very time of the composition of most of the Hebrew Bible?

The result of this for both Jewish and Christian scholarship is stated by Halvor Ronning, Director of the Home for Bible Translators, Jerusalem:

> This incredible faithfulness of the Jewish scribes in honoring that written text and preserving it for us has led in the scholarly world to an increased respect for that Hebrew text. This was especially the case in the Christian world, where there had been an almost exclusive interest in the Septuagint text of the Bible.[11]

The Masoretes were reluctant to change anything in the consonantal text before them, as we saw in chapter 4. They devised numerous kinds of scribal notations to indicate that something was not right with the text, but they would not alter it even if they knew with certainty it was incorrect. The system of notation known as *Kethiv-Qere* ("what is written"—"what is read") enabled the scribes to place in the margin of the text what they thought to be the correct (or original) reading while avoiding any change to the text itself. The tradition of preserving the sacred text was an inherited one that surely went back to antiquity. It again shows the high degree of care exercised in transmitting the text and assures us that, in the case of the Hebrew Bible, there was no tampering with or distortion made to the received text.

Scribal Preservation and the New Testament

The scribes who initially copied the New Testament were connected with the early Christian community and were employed for the purpose of making copies for distribution to various churches. Although we are lacking examples from the earliest period, the apostolic Fathers of this period cited from the texts they had on hand and—whether they were citing from memory or had an actual manuscript before them (see chapter 7)—it is clear that the pristine text they referenced has remained largely unchanged up to our day. Even a skeptic like Bart Ehrman has had to admit that "most scribes, no doubt, tried to do a faithful job in making sure that the text they reproduced was the same text they inherited."[12]

Nonetheless, at the same time, this scholar has also commented, "The more I studied the manuscript tradition of the New Testament, the more I realized just how radically the text had been altered over the years at the hands of the scribes."[13]

What Has Changed?

Now, it is true that scribes have made changes to the text, but these can easily be identified and in fact are quite insignificant. Far too often, though, as in the statement by Ehrman, the insignificance of the changes has not been explained. And therefore the typical reader has been left to imagine the worst—especially when, as we noted in chapter 7, it is revealed that as many as 400,000 variants exist for the Greek New Testament!

As we have said, change—in the sense that an alteration in the meaning of a text—has not taken place. Rather, most changes are extremely minor and insignificant. (See the discussion of types of textual variants found in the New Testament manuscripts on pages 116–117). But it is "those variants that are both meaningful and viable"—which most New Testament scholars would say "constitute much less than 1 percent of the total[14]—that the skeptical scholars such as Ehrman play upon when they trumpet the "orthodox corruption of scripture" or the "misquoting of Jesus."

Deliberate Corruptions or Necessary Repairs?

Intentional variants, known as *conjectural emendations,* exist in every copy of every kind of ancient literature, primarily because information is missing. In such cases the scholar, using the best comparative linguistic and historical information available, makes a scientific decision to supply a word or words in order to complete the text and preserve its meaning. For example, because of the poor condition of some of the Dead Sea Scrolls it was necessary for those reconstructing the text to make many conjectural emendations. However, this was necessary only in the case of *sectarian* documents, since the *biblical* scrolls had the Masoretic Text as a referent.

In secular literature, for some striking examples, we are missing *107* of the 142 volumes of Livy's *History of Rome* and *10* of the 14 volumes of Tacitus' *Histories,* and in even the very best-preserved copies significant *lacunae* ("gaps" in the text) exist.[15] Yet, these references are still the standard authorities for classical historians, and no one complains that they are unreliable because so much is lacking or because so much of the text has been reconstructed by both ancient and modern editors.

In amazing contrast, as we have already seen, the New Testament is lacking nothing and has tens of thousands of manuscripts and versions— (far more than any other literature)—including the earliest and best manuscripts (earlier and of higher quality than any other literature). Further, such conjectural emendations as do exist are easy to identify because they have no manuscript support. Since they are unique, they are found only in isolated manuscripts and are therefore understood by textual critics as not authentic.

Notorious Emendations to the New Testament

There are some well-known examples of emendations that have been easily distinguished. In 1516 Erasmus, the Roman Catholic Humanist, was hurried into publishing the first printed edition of the Greek New Testament to beat out competitors. In his haste he made hundreds of typographical errors and had to "create" his own text at places, most notably for the last six verses of the book of Revelation. Since he had only a Latin manuscript of this passage, he made up his own Greek translation from the Latin. His conjectural emendations introduced 17 new variants that do not exist in any other Greek manuscript of Revelation.

Another example, which also involves Erasmus, is 1 John 5:7-8 in the third edition of his Greek New Testament. It reads "there are three witnesses in heaven, the Father, the Word, and the Holy Spirit." This supported the Roman Catholic Church's teaching of the Trinity with a Trinitarian-formula "proof text," although, as Erasmus had earlier protested to the Church authorities, no manuscript available to him in any language had such a reading. He inserted it only because his hand was forced—a scribe at Oxford in 1520 had produced a manuscript with this reading (codex 61, now in Dublin) at the Church's request.

Today only a few variants support this reading, but none of them is earlier than the sixteenth century! All current critical Greek editions and the translations based on them, except the King James Version, have excised these words as unauthentic. And this has been done, not from an insidious motive to "corrupt" the Bible, but rather to preserve the purity and accuracy of the text from human emendations.

And the fact is, there has been no real need for conjectural emendations in the New Testament because the state of the text is so complete. According to Daniel Wallace,

> Of the 138,000 words of the original text, only one or two might have no manuscript support. And in the places where conjecture may be necessary, this does not mean that we have no idea what the original text said. Instead, precisely because almost all the possible variants are already to be found in the manuscripts, scholars have a rather limited number of options with which to contend.[16]

For this reason, two of the leading textual critics in the world, Kurt and Barbara Aland, declared,

> Every reading ever occurring in the New Testament textual tradition is stubbornly preserved, even if the result is nonsense.... Any reading ever occurring in the New Testament textual tradition, from the original reading onward, has been preserved in the tradition and needs only to be identified.[17]

In sum, it may be confidently stated that the variants in the manuscripts of the New Testament do not support the claim that the original text has been changed in transmission; rather, they have aided textual critics in keeping the text of the New Testament as trustworthy as possible by *restoring* it to the original.

Was the Sequence of the Old Testament Books Corrupted?

Let us go back again to the story in chapter 2 of the three women who bought three different Bibles, one a Jewish translation of the Hebrew Bible, another the Douay Bible, the official translation of the Catholic Church, and the last a Protestant translation. Besides the difference in the number of books included in each, we can also see a difference in the canonical arrangement, or order, of the books in these Bibles. The chart on the next page illustrates this variation.

As is obvious, the Hebrew (Jewish) Bible with its order of books came first. When the Septuagint translation was made into Greek, starting about 250 BC, a number of changes came about in the order of the books, the most notable being the placement of prophetic books at the end. In

Jewish and Christian Divisions of the Bible

Jewish Bible					Christian Bible			
Twofold — 24 Old Testament books (Jesus' Day)		Threefold — 24 Old Testament books (After Jesus' Day)			Fourfold — 39 Old Testament books			
Law (5)	Prophets (19)	Law (5)	Prophets (8)	Writings (11)	Law (5)	History (12)	Writings (5)	Prophets (17)
Genesis	Joshua	Genesis	Joshua	Psalms	Genesis	Joshua	Job	Isaiah
Exodus	Judges, Ruth	Exodus	Judges	Job	Exodus	Judges	Psalms	Jeremiah
Leviticus	1, 2 Samuel	Leviticus	1, 2 Samuel	Proverbs	Leviticus	Ruth	Proverbs	Lamentations
Numbers	1, 2 Kings	Numbers	1, 2 Kings	Ruth	Numbers	1 Samuel	Ecclesiastes	Ezekiel
Deuteronomy	Job	Deuteronomy	Isaiah	Song of Songs	Deuteronomy	2 Samuel	Song of Songs	Daniel
	Isaiah		Jeremiah	Ecclesiastes		1 Kings		Hosea
	Jeremiah		Ezekiel	Lamentations		2 Kings		Joel
	Ezekiel		Book of the 12	Esther		1 Chronicles		Amos
	Book of the 12			Daniel		2 Chronicles		Obadiah
	Psalms			Ezra-Nehemiah		Ezra		Jonah
	Proverbs			Chronicles		Nehemiah		Micah
	Song of Songs					Esther		Nahum
	Ecclesiastes							Habakkuk
	Lamentations							Zephaniah
	Esther							Haggai
	Daniel							Zechariah
	Ezra							Malachi
	Nehemiah							
	Chronicles							

the Hebrew Bible, what Christians would call books of poetry and history are final in the sequencing. (See the chart on page 149 for a listing of the order of books in both the Hebrew Bible and the Septuagint).

The textual preference for the Septuagint (the Bible of the early church) determined the order loosely followed in the church's canonical arrangement. The continuation of the Septuagint's deviation from the order established in the Hebrew Bible was the result in part of theological differences between Judaism and Christianity.

Jewish apologists argued in part against Jesus being the fulfillment of messianic prophecy from the canonical order of the Hebrew Bible. Because the Hebrew Bible ended with the Writings, rather than the Prophets, and with the books of Chronicles, rather than Malachi, Jews could argue that the return to and restoration of Israel, not the coming of the Messiah (as Christians saw in the Gospels) was the focal point and the expected means of fulfillment in the prophets.

However, if the Prophets ended the Old Testament canon—especially Malachi, whose final words predict the coming of Elijah before the Day of the Lord to restore the hearts of the children of Israel (Malachi 3:5-6)— that would provide the ideal lead-in to the opening words of the Gospel of Matthew, which shows the fulfillment of messianic expectation in "Jesus, the son of David, the son of Abraham" (Matthew 1:1).

But is this difference in sequencing a *corruption?* The answer is no. The issue of *the order of the books* of the Bible is not the same as the issue of determining *which books are part of that order.* The latter issue is crucial, involving the recognition of inspired, authoritative Scripture. Sequencing the books, however, involved a textual preference for the Septuagint and the theological perspective of the postapostolic Fathers, who had been influenced by an adversarial relationship with Judaism.*

In a word, it is the canonical books themselves that are regarded as inspired, not the order in which they are arranged. The sort of skepticism that thinks a difference in the arrangement of books between the Hebrew and Christian Bibles is evidence of corruption or change that has obscured or obviated the text of the Original Bible is simply unwarranted.

---

* While I do not advocate that Christian Bibles return to the original Hebrew order, since such arrangement was not "inspired," Christians would do well to understand the historic and theological reasons for these differences.

Inspiration vs. Preservation

The presence of so many textual variations in the original language texts behind our English translations, as we have seen, raises one sort of issue for the new-school critics and those who follow them. The variations raise a different question for many Christians. This concern is often voiced in ways that reveal a crucial misunderstanding: "If we don't have the original inspired text, then we don't have a Bible!"

To properly answer this concern we must distinguish between *inspiration* and *preservation*. *Inspiration* involves the original autographs of the Bible as given by God through men, while *preservation* involves copies that have been passed down through human agency alone. Those who confuse these two must logically contend that nothing in the copies that have come down to us can have been altered in any way from the autograph. In other words, their translation must be "inspired."

For this reason such people chose a translation based on a text type they believe is the most stable or has the best chance of having preserved the original. This has often been considered to be the Byzantine text type. It is said to have been used to produce the *Majority Text*, which is supposed to have been the basis of the King James version.[18]

Now, even if the Byzantine text type could be said to have been stable (although its earlier and latter forms differ), it is against fact, and against Scripture, to claim that any copy of the Bible is inerrant. What is to be done with the Masoretic Text, the only text behind the translation of the Old Testament of the King James version? The scribes that compiled it, as we have seen, left marginal notes of things they *knew* to be errors in the text.

However, nothing in biblical statements such as "All Scripture is inspired by God" (2 Timothy 3:16), or "Until heaven and earth pass away, not the smallest letter or stroke shall pass from the Law, until all is accomplished" (Matthew 5:18), or "Heaven and earth will pass away, but My words will not pass away" (Mark 13:31) requires that every inspired word must be likewise preserved *outside* of the autographs. Nevertheless, we may say—and say with greater confidence than ever, based on the manuscript evidence—that our present text is accurate and reliable, and that nothing affecting the doctrine of the original has been compromised or changed in any way in the manuscript copies.[19]

In the case of the Hebrew Bible, as we have seen, the Dead Sea Scrolls have revealed that the Masoretic text behind our English translations was carefully preserved. Furthermore, the very preservation and recovery of these biblical scrolls has added to the colorful history of preservation of other copies of the Scriptures, all of which testifies to the providential element in their safekeeping.

In regard to the New Testament, for over four-fifths of it, the Greek text is considered 100 percent certain, regardless of which text type might be favored by any critic. Moreover, regarding the entire Bible, through the science of textual criticism at least 95 percent of the original text of the Old Testament has been recovered, and 99 percent of the New Testament. Any historian would be thrilled beyond measure to have such a transcription rate for any ancient document.

Therefore, whether we are replying to the world of Islam or some other religion, to the secular world, or to the world of skeptical scholars within the biblical tradition, we may say with assurance that the word of God has not changed. Rather, it has been brought closer to the original than in previous times. Truly, what we have now is what they had then!

PART FOUR

Searching for
THE RESTORATION OF
THE
Original
Bible

Chapter 13

Can the Original Bible Be Recovered?

Faithful scribes through the centuries have labored to preserve and transmit the written Word as originally given by the inspiration of God. Building upon this tradition, the textual critic seeks not to produce a merely "good" text, nor even an "adequate" text, but instead to establish as nearly as possible the precise form of the written Word as originally revealed.

—FROM THE INDTRODUCTION TO
*The Original Greek New Testament According
to the Byzantine/Majority Textform*

In the midst of researching this chapter I attended a scholar's convention in Washington, DC, the very city in which an important early New Testament manuscript known as *Codex Washingtonensis* (Codex W) is housed—at the Freer Gallery of Art, part of the Smithsonian Institution. One of the attractions of this meeting, other than listening to academic papers being read, was the vast display of books by academic religious publishers in the convention showroom. However, upon entering this area, to my surprise, I caught sight of a large banner over a display area, which announced "The Discovery of the Original Bible."

As it turned out, the alleged discovery was of the original Four Gospels, yet this—if it were true—would be the most important discovery in the history of Christianity! Surprisingly, the manuscript that was being heralded as the original was none other than Codex W! Dr. Lee Woodard, one of the display's presenters and the author of a self-published book on the discovery,[1] explains the basis for the group's belief:

An accidental discovery has revealed an ancient Greek manuscript to be the actual First Century version of the four gospels Matthew, Mark, Luke, and John....They are signed by (or on behalf of) all four of the famous writers of the gospels, marked with their own seals, dated with the year of completion (in the Roman dating system), and even recorded with the place of their final editing and collation, which was Aun, Egypt, known in the Old Testament as On and today as Heliopolis.[2]

Four Gospels from Codex Washingtonensis (fourth-fifth century AD), Freer Gallery of Art, Washington, DC

This group's case, based on the alleged "discovery" of encoded "Aramaic Hebrew" letters and on the counting of marks embellishing the tails of birds at the end of the manuscripts, has not convinced any New Testament scholars. The reason is that Codex W, according to paleographers (experts who date manuscripts based on the shapes of their letters), can date no earlier than the late fourth or early fifth century AD (300 to 400 years *after* the original).[3] The decorations at the end of the Gospels are known from other manuscripts of this period and served merely to formally mark off the end of a text or to signal the end of the codex.[4]

Moreover, scholars confirm Codex W consists of "a compilation of unrelated copies of the Gospels by a single scribe in a single codex,"[5] not individual originals. In addition, this codex is enclosed in painted wooden covers depicting the four evangelists in the Egyptian-Coptic style. Though Woodard contends these portraits were painted during the lifetime of the apostles and are also encoded with Aramaic characters, they can be confidently dated to the seventh century AD.[6]

There have always been "historical rumors" connected with the discovery of the originals, such as one in AD 489 that the autograph of the Gospel of Matthew had been discovered in the grave of Barnabas in Cyprus;[7] or that the original Gospel of Mark had been found in Venice (which turned out to be a seventh-century AD fragment of the Vulgate),[8] or that the original epistle of Peter had been located.[9] Even if such claims up till now, including that of Codex W, are only wishful thinking, in light of the large number of early manuscripts that have been discovered (see chapters 4 and 5), is it possible that someday an original manuscript of the Bible might be brought to light?

Possible Places for Recovering the Original Bible

As an archaeologist who has been surprised many times by "impossible" finds, I have to admit that recovering the original manuscript of some part or book of the Bible is *possible*, although I do not think it is probable. In the case of the Mosaic Torah, if the Ark of the Covenant was hidden (and not taken as loot or destroyed with the First Temple) and the priests also hid this original document with it, then—if it is possible to find the Ark—it might be possible to find the Mosaic Torah, as well as the original tablets of the Ten Commandments.

It is also possible that original biblical scrolls were deposited in the Temple archives and were removed before the destruction of the First, and later the Second, Temple and then hidden somewhere. The Dead Sea Scrolls astonished the world when they were discovered hidden in jars in the Judean desert—many in a very fine state of preservation after 2000 years. And since some of them were hidden at the time of the Second Temple's destruction, it is possible that somewhere in the vicinity of Jerusalem, or out in the Judean desert, the Temple archives might yet be found.

Temple Mount (Jerusalem, Israel), possible site of hidden manuscripts

However, if the testimony of Flavius Josephus in his autobiography is to be believed, the Roman general Titus, who sacked the Temple, gave the sacred Temple scrolls to him. There may be some truth to this since Josephus, even though from a priestly family, knew a great deal more about details of the Hebrew Bible than simply a learned Jew could know. Not only was he able to give a full account of biblical history, but he also described the contents of the scrolls and their threefold division. If Josephus had these scrolls, then the trail ends with him.

The New Testament autographs went to various churches and possibly remained with them or were deposited in a central location. It has been suggested that this central location might be Pella, one of the cities of the Decapolis on the other side of the Jordan River (today in the modern country of Jordan across from the Israeli city of Bet She'an). Scroll scholar William H. Brownlee once considered this a prime site for ancient manuscript discovery:

> The recovery of the Dead Sea Scrolls indicates that such discoveries may no longer be considered impossible. The vicinity of Pella,

for example, to which Jewish Christians retired from Jerusalem during the First Jewish Revolt against Rome (AD 68–70), needs to be searched for the possible survival of Hebrew and Aramaic Christian literature.[10]

A large portion of the Jewish-Christian community fled to Pella before the Roman destruction of Jerusalem in AD 70. Perhaps some of the autographs still lie hidden in an archive in the remains of one of the early Byzantine churches at this site. However, a central location for depositing documents shared by all of the churches would probably have been a place significant to the growing church, rather than a place to which just part of the church had fled. (This may also rule out burial crypts or monasteries in Egypt and *genizaot* in synagogues.)

Remains of a Byzantine church, Pella (in Jordan), possible site of hidden manuscripts

If it is possible that some of the originals still existed by the fourth century AD, then they might have been sent to a central location like Constantinople. However, we know that Emperor Constantine ordered Eusebius, bishop of Caesarea, to have 50 copies of the Bible made for new churches in the city. If any autographs had been available, Eusebius would have had them used in the production of these copies and, knowing the personal pride he displayed in his writings concerning the project, certainly would have bragged about it!

Finally, it is also possible that the theory of deposition in a central location is wrong, and the individual recipient churches of autographs had copies made for distribution to other churches and retained their originals. Thus it is possible they could have been stored away in a hidden archive room connected with one of these churches.

As you can see, there are a lot of possibilities, but again, not much is probable. In conclusion, Daniel B. Wallace says of the New Testament autographs,

> The originals are gone....Tertullian and others mentioned that the original manuscripts had disappeared or had worn out by the end of the second century....No other ancient Greek or Latin literature has been preserved in the original documents. Why would we expect the New Testament autographa to be any different?[11]

However, having said this, we want to explore the question whether the original text can be recovered by a different means. Let us first consider why we need to recover the original text.

Why We Need to Recover the Original Text

The average person in the English-speaking world may sometimes forget that the Bible was not written on a word processor, and that no "master text" of the Bible exists from which the various modern translations have been made. The "Bible" we possess has come to us in thousands of manuscripts, all of which contain differences of greater or lesser degree.

While we have shown that the scribes were professionals at transcribing manuscripts and had an extremely high degree of accuracy, they were still human and made mistakes. Like us, they sometimes had poor memory, misheard texts that were read aloud, had errors of sight, or suffered from impaired judgment. To these unintentional mistakes we may add intentional changes that were made to correct earlier scribal mistakes, smooth out a text, harmonize difficulties, or make theological adjustments.

The biblical texts of the Dead Sea Scrolls also offer evidence of reworking by copyists, reflecting exegetical techniques such as harmonization, *halakhic midrash* and *targum* (legal interpretation, paraphrase), and *pesher* (commentary). These scribal habits introduced variants into the Qumran manuscript copies.

Copying practices may be determined by evaluating the variants that exist among copies. These variants are classified into one of three categories: *stylistic, substantive,* and *error.* The chart below lists some of the tendencies of scribes (both ancient and modern) in producing variants. These apply to both the Hebrew Old Testament and Greek New Testament (though some apply more to one or the other).

Scribal Tendencies that Produced Textual Variants

Unintentional changes
(scribal accidents or mistakes)

1. *Confusion of similar letters.* Although the scribes were experts with letters, confusion between similar appearing letters, especially in worn documents with faded script, could result.

2. *Confusion of words that sound alike.* In cases where a document was being read aloud to the scribe as he copied, similar sounding words could result in errors of judgment in writing.

3. *Omission because of similar endings (homoeoteleuton).* The scribe's eye may have skipped a word or a line in a sentence where the ending of another word or line in a sentence appeared similar. In this case the material in between would be missed.

4. *Omission because of a similar beginning (homoeoarchton).* The scribe's eye may have skipped from the beginning of one word or line to the next similar word or line, excluding the material in between. This is not as common an error as the previous one.

5. *Haplography, or single writing.* The scribe wrote two letters or words that appear together as a single letter or word. This also applies to the accidental omission of letters or words.

6. *Dittography, or double-writing.* The scribe accidentally repeated what he had just written.

7. *Incorrect word division.* This problem is due to line spacing, but is more common in Greek manuscripts than in Hebrew.

8. *Incorrect vocalization.* This occurred in Hebrew manuscripts where the scribe was adding vowel markings to his copy from an unpointed manuscript. The scribe either missed placing a vowel marking beneath a consonant or mispointed it.

9. *Transposition of words or letters (metathesis).* The scribe reversed letters, which affected the meaning of the word.

10. *Substitution of synonyms.* The scribe substituted a similar, or more familiar word, for the word in his text. This may have occurred because he was working from memory.

11. *Assimilation of the wording in one passage to the slightly different wording in the context or in a parallel passage.* The scribe seems to have substituted a word frequently used in a similar context.

12. *Mistaken inclusion of marginal comments into the text.* The scribe accidentally included a word from a scribal notation (sometimes a single letter) that was then interpreted by the next scribe as a different word.

13. *Scriptio continua.* This occurs in copies of the earliest uncial Greek manuscripts of the New Testament, which were written in continuous script. Because there were no breaks between words, a scribe who attempted to divide words in copying might misdivide a word and thereby create a variant.

Intentional changes
(scribal corrections, clarifications)

---

1. *Changes in spelling or grammar.* The scribe made slight changes in order to smooth out readings, make verbs agree grammatically with their subjects, or improve or clarify a reading.

2. *Harmonizations.* The scribes tried to make a line harmonize with other things indicated in the context by adding words.

3. *Conflation of variant readings.** The scribe included both variants without realizing the original contained only one.

4. *Filling out names and epithets.* The scribe liked to give the fuller spellings of names, which resulted in conflated readings.

---

* To conflate is "**1a:** to bring together: fuse **b:** confuse. 2: to combine (as two readings of a text) into a composite whole."

5. *Supplying subjects and objects.* When the text being used by the scribe lacked a clear reference to the subject or the object, the scribe added them for the reader.

6. *Expansion from parallel passages.* These were additions to the text taken from familiar parallel sections by the scribe.

7. *Removal of difficult expressions.* References or expressions to history, geography, or theology that the scribe felt were incorrect or offensive. For example, in Job 1:5,11 and 2:5,9 we find the words "blessed God/bless God" in the Hebrew where obviously the text originally read "cursed God/curse God." Since saying this in reading would be to blaspheme God, the rabbis substituted the euphemism "bless God."

8. *Replacement of rare words with more common ones.* Scribes might have had a tendency to use a more familiar term in the copy.

These examples of scribal variants help us understand why we have texts that differ, and they reveal the very human way the word of God has been transmitted to us. The translations that we use result from a compilation and analysis of all these divergent manuscripts. Now, since our present text is far removed from the originals and our many source manuscripts contain a large number of variants, is recovery of the original text even possible?

Is it Possible to Recover the Original Text?

To some scholars the large amount of manuscript and other textual data we possess is an argument against recovering the original text. To these scholars it is not the *amount* of data we have, but the *quality* of it, that matters. They argue that the huge number of variants in all of these texts is evidence of a corruption so great that no one can have any confidence in the present state of the text. This corruption, they believe, is the result of so many people manipulating the text (some unconsciously, many more deliberately) that what it now says cannot possibly reflect what was originally written.

As an illustration of how this happened, these scholarly skeptics remind us of the old "telephone game," where the first person in a circle of people speaks a phrase or sentence to the next person, who repeats it to the next person until it goes full circle. The point of the game is to demonstrate that by the time the original message gets back to the original speaker, it has been completely changed.

The comparison of the telephone game may sound quite plausible, but the situation with the textual data is not at all the same. In the telephone game, no one has any source to compare to other than the words they receive from the person who spoke to them. However, if everyone could hear a recitation of everyone else's words, it would not be too difficult to reconstruct the original message to a reasonable degree. And that is exactly what we have in the textual data.

However, there is another issue at stake. In the telephone game, some players try to faithfully reproduce what they hear, and some intentionally try to alter words (even though they are told not to) just to guarantee a laugh at the end. Are we really to believe that the Jewish and Christian scribes capriciously altered the text however they pleased? In the case of the transmission of sacred Scripture, as we have seen, this could not have been the case.

True, some scribes may have corrected the text because a word was obscure (a *conjectural emendation*—see pages 202–204) or, less often, to strengthen a theological point. However, such changes rarely affect the sense of the text and can usually be identified for what they are.

These examples, though, pale by comparison with the overwhelming evidence in our manuscripts of faithful transcription. Therefore, unlike the telephone game, where the message becomes further removed from the original the longer the game is played, as time goes on, the increasing abundance of manuscripts is making it possible for the textual critic to get ever closer to the original.

The Advent of Textual Criticism

For nearly 2500 years the text of the Hebrew Bible was transmitted through manuscript copies that contained variants, and through various versions translated from these, without a comparison being made between them in order to create a standardized form of the text.[12]

However, with the revival of classical learning in the Renaissance period and the massive spread of the printing press, there arose a desire to recover texts from the ancient world and present them in their pristine form. This availability invited an evaluation between different texts, and it soon produced the role of the scholarly editor and the science of textual criticism, as John Van Seters observes:

> The recovery of multiple divergent manuscripts of the same literary work gave rise to the development of textual criticism, which became the primary activity of the scholarly editor in his concern to produce the definitive edition of the text.[13]

This age of the scholarly editor saw the dawn of authorized editions such as that of the Masoretic Text—the second edition of the Bomberg Rabbinic Bible, edited by Jacob ben Chayyim—and the *Textus Receptus,* produced by the great humanist scholar Desiderius Erasmus. Each of these standardized texts was the result of the careful study of the textual witnesses.

This process of diligent appraisal and comparison of text types in order to produce a text that represents the original as much as possible is known as *textual criticism.* It should be remembered that *criticism* (from the Greek *krinen,* "to judge") is a positive activity when its object is to recover and restore the accuracy of the original text. It has sometimes been called *lower criticism* to distinguish it from *higher criticism,* which examines (often negatively) questions of composition, authorship, and historicity (though these terms are not often used by modern scholars).

Every person who has ever read a newspaper has engaged in a form of textual criticism. In a newspaper there are often misspellings, errors of omission, and displaced letters, words, or even lines of type. The reader must quickly decide what has occurred and reconstruct the original version in his or her mind to gain the proper sense, in order to proceed with reading. As David Parker reminds us, "Textual criticism is not an arcane science. It belongs to all human communication."[14]

Textual criticism of the Bible as a practice began when scholars started to compare the manuscripts and versions available to them. An early example is Origen's *Hexapla,* an edition of the Old Testament produced about AD 240, which arranged the Hebrew text, different Septuagintal Greek texts, and Greek translations by others in six parallel columns for comparison. However, the development of textual criticism as a science resulted from the discovery of ancient sources, the use of the printing press as mentioned,

Textual Criticism Timeline

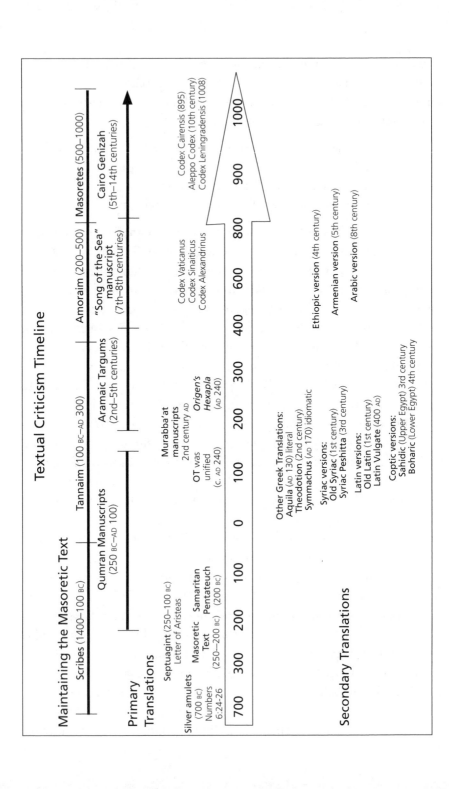

Maintaining the Masoretic Text

Scribes (1400–100 BC) | Qumran Manuscripts (250 BC–AD 100) | Tannaim (100 BC–AD 300) | Aramaic Targums (2nd–5th centuries) | Amoraim (200–500) | Masoretes (500–1000)

"Song of the Sea" manuscript (7th–8th centuries)

Cairo Genizah (5th–14th centuries)

Codex Cairensis (895)
Aleppo Codex (10th century)
Codex Leningradensis (1008)

Codex Vaticanus
Codex Sinaiticus
Codex Alexandrinus

Primary Translations

Septuagint (250–100 BC)
Letter of Aristeas

Silver amulets (700 BC)
Numbers 6:24-26

Masoretic Text (250–200 BC)

Samaritan Pentateuch (200 BC)

Murabba'at manuscripts 2nd century AD

OT was unified (c. AD 240)

Origen's Hexapla (AD 240)

Secondary Translations

Other Greek Translations:
Aquila (AD 130) literal
Theodotion (2nd century)
Symmachus (AD 170) idiomatic

Syriac versions:
Old Syriac (1st century)
Syriac Peshitta (3rd century)

Latin versions:
Old Latin (1st century)
Latin Vulgate (400 AD)

Coptic versions:
Sahidic (Upper Egypt) 3rd century
Boharic (Lower Egypt) 4th century

Ethiopic version (4th century)

Armenian version (5th century)

Arabic version (8th century)

700 300 200 100 0 100 200 300 400 600 800 900 1000

and the classification of biblical manuscripts into textual groups based on their geographic origin by Johann Jakob Griesbach (1745–1812).

The science of textual criticism, when properly applied, has brought each successive generation closer to the goal of recovering the text of the Original Bible. As Paul D. Wegner, author of *A Student's Guide to Textual Criticism of the Bible,* has affirmed,

> Careful examination of these manuscripts has served to strengthen our assurance that our modern Greek and Hebrew critical texts are very close to the original autographs, even though we do not have those autographs.[15]

It is also important to realize that we have more information available to us today regarding the text of the Bible than anyone in history has ever had. At this stage in time, having acquired such an amount of data, and having the technology to manage this data, it is incumbent upon biblical scholarship to recover, within our ability, the text of the Original Bible.

What Are We Trying to Recover?

The commonly understood goal of textual criticism is

> the study of copies of any written work of which the autograph (the original) is unknown, with the purpose of ascertaining the original text.[16]

While it might be desirable to be able to trace the path forward from the original to the textual tradition, as Maurice Robinson has noted, "At best, the text-critical 'quest for the autograph' can only work backward from the extant evidence to what might be termed the earliest regularly transmitted form of the text."[17] In Old Testament textual criticism, this means basically the "canonically transmitted form" of the text, since the earliest period up to 300 BC has left us no witnesses.

Therefore, a better understanding of the achievable goal of Old Testament textual criticism would be "to determine the most reliable wording of the biblical text."[18] A secondary goal of textual criticism is to establish the history of the transmission of the text through the centuries.[19]

In New Testament textual criticism the situation is much improved, though there is the question of whether the earliest transmitted form of the text is the *autograph* or the *archetype* (see sidebar on next page).

Autographs and Archetypes

An *archetype* is the most recent common ancestor of all extant manuscripts in a textual tradition. A number of scholars have argued that we cannot assume, as has traditionally been done, that the archetype is the original. It may be in some cases that the two are identical but such a conclusion ought to be argued rather than simply assumed. Nonetheless, since the archetype is the earliest recoverable form of the text on the basis of the textual witnesses that have survived, it can be assumed that in most cases it is the autograph or that the form of the text is so near the autograph as to represent its exact wording.[20]

Still, it must be conceded that since the archetype is not necessarily the autograph, variant readings *could* have been inserted sometime between the autograph and the archetype. For this reason Bart Ehrman and others, such as David Parker and Eldon Jay Epp, have argued that the goal of determining the wording of the original cannot be achieved and therefore should no longer be the goal of biblical textual criticism. In addition, they argue for this point because the New Testament's history of manuscript transmission was influenced by the history of the early church, a history in which intentional changes to the text were made. For them, this in turn raises all-but-insurmountable questions concerning the accuracy of textual transmission (see chapter 7), and makes the attempt to reconstruct the text unattainable. For this reason, Bart Ehrman has declared that

> it is by no means evident that this [reconstructing the original text] *ought* to be the ultimate goal of the discipline....In recent years, however, some scholars have recognized that it is important to know not only what an author wrote (i.e., the autograph), but also what a reader read (i.e., in its later transcriptions)...since throughout this history, virtually no one read the NT in its original form.[21]

However, as we have shown, there is far more evidence for the reliability of textual transmission than there is evidence to the contrary, especially when it is recognized that even the intentional changes are relatively insignificant and do not affect the meaning of the text.

And the extant form of the text is necessarily one that was regularly transmitted (at least in the opinions of the scribes who produced it). If there is no evidence that a Greek manuscript had a text that differed from what is in our critical editions, it can be assumed that it represents the archetype of our textual tradition. While it cannot be proved that this archetype is the original, neither can it be proved that it is not. Therefore, skepticism about the ability to recover the original text is at best a preference—which may in turn be determined by other, external presuppositions.

The majority of scholars, however, believe it is certainly possible to produce a critical edition of the New Testament that very closely resembles the original. Let us now consider the methods by which textual critics weigh the material evidence for both testaments and make the necessary decisions to recover the "original text."

How We Recover the Text

Certain rules are followed by the textual critic in recovering the texts of the Hebrew Bible and Greek New Testament. These rules of textual criticism fall into one of two categories:

- *external evidence*—pertaining to the evidence from *outside the text* such as manuscripts or versions

- *internal evidence*—evidence *in the text itself* that pertains to the logic of readings

While some textual critics elevate one category over another, others believe they should be given equal weight in the process of textual decision-making. Most textual critics, however, "argue that both internal and external evidence are subjective in varying degrees, and that skillful wrestling with both considerations is the surest way to recover the wording of the original text."[22] Whatever the critic's view, *the goal is to use the available data to determine the most plausible reading that restores the original text.*

External Evidence

The basic criterion for external evidence is that manuscripts are to be weighed and not counted (since these sources are not equal in quality). Certain rules have been developed for both the Old and New Testament critic in evaluating what evidence is more or less important.

For the *Old Testament,* the external evidence, in order of importance, is as follows:

1. The language of the witnesses. The priority is always given to Hebrew texts since that is the language of the original. In the case of the versions (translations), each must be examined in order to understand how a copyist translated specific Hebrew words and used grammar and sentence structure. From this comparison it can be demonstrated how a certain translation developed and how close it is to the manuscript from which it was translated (the *Vorlage*—see page 99).

2. The date of the witnesses. The general rule is this: The earlier the manuscript, the less it has been copied—and therefore the less it should have been corrupted by variants. Because the Hebrew text was standardized around the first century AD, beginning the Masoretic tradition, earlier texts may have variant readings that were removed in the process of standardization. Since we lack the earliest copies, the biblical manuscripts of the Dead Sea Scrolls furnish the majority of these proto-Masoretic variants, as do also the major versions (the Septuagint, the Samaritan Pentateuch, and the Peshitta—see chapter 4).

3. The reliability of the manuscript. This judgment is based on a manuscript's textual tradition and how many variants it may contain. While some variant traditions are preferred, the witness of the Dead Sea Scrolls is that the Masoretic Text has the most reliable textual tradition, and therefore it is favored.

4. The provenance and purpose of the text. Where and why a text was written can often help determine the authenticity of a particular reading.

For example, the Samaritan sect's belief that Mt. Gerizim and not Mt. Sinai was the sacred mountain of God led them to substitute "Mt. Gerizim" in Deuteronomy 12:5 in the Samaritan Pentateuch.

5. The interdependence of witnesses. Most of the later versions (Peshitta, Old Latin, Vulgate, Sahidic, Bohairic, Ethiopic, Armenian, Arabic) are dependent upon the Septuagint. However, in those places where the later versions disagree with the Septuagint, there may be seen an original, independent variant.

In the case of the *New Testament*, three criteria of external evidence are used to judge the variant that is closest to the original reading:*

1. Date and character. As is the case for the manuscripts of the Old Testament, those of the New Testament that are closest in date to the originals are most likely to have the original reading. Just as the Hebrew tradition is more important than the versions for the Old Testament, so the Greek tradition is more important than the versions (translations) for the New Testament.

Fortunately, there are reliable manuscript traditions that date close to the original (early second to early third century AD) and are to be preferred. In this light, certain text families are considered to be superior to others (for example, Alexandrian over Byzantine). However, in some cases a later manuscript that was carefully copied is to be preferred to an earlier one in which less care was taken by the scribe. The character of any given manuscript is first judged by its text type. This is the best way to test reliability for the New Testament texts, since the means of getting to the wording of the original is through the different families of texts.

2. Genealogical solidarity. A text type is a specific pattern of variant readings that are shared among a distinct group of manuscripts. Manuscripts belonging to a particular text type are thought to be from the same locality, and they contain traditional variants that have been repeated and thus agree on a certain reading.* Three text types or families have been identified:[23]

---

* See also the chart on page 84.

1. *Western:* the local text typical of the Latin-speaking portions of the Roman Empire (subdivided into European and North African subtypes)

2. *Alexandrian:* the local text of the Egyptian region, heavily influenced by the Coptic language

3. *Byzantine:* a later-developed text type that is based primarily on Western and Alexandrian manuscripts. It has the largest number of surviving manuscripts (especially owing to the invention of the minuscule in the ninth century), and it forms the basic text of the Greek Orthodox New Testament.

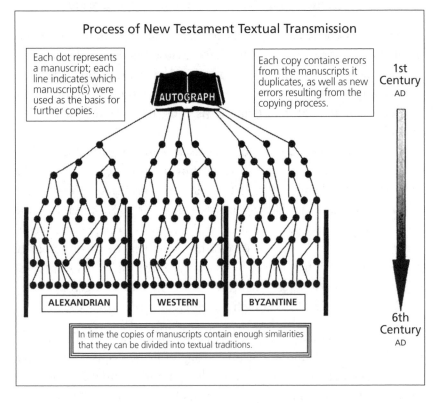

Process of New Testament Textual Transmission

Each dot represents a manuscript; each line indicates which manuscript(s) were used as the basis for further copies.

Each copy contains errors from the manuscripts it duplicates, as well as new errors resulting from the copying process.

AUTOGRAPH

1st Century AD

ALEXANDRIAN   WESTERN   BYZANTINE

In time the copies of manuscripts contain enough similarities that they can be divided into textual traditions.

6th Century AD

Even so, the manuscripts within a group are not the same, since each manuscript will have its own peculiar readings, as well as some mixture from readings of other text types. In other words, the text itself is a separate concept from the manuscripts which make it up.

An undisputed reading in these text types points to a common preexisting regional archetype, even if the local original is no longer extant (see sidebar on pages 224-225 for more detail on *archetypes*). By pushing a given set of readings within a text type back to their points of origin, it can be determined which reading is earlier (predates others). This is helpful, though not determinative by itself, in proving a reading is genuine.

3. Geographical distribution. Just as on the witness stand a consistent testimony from multiple witnesses makes a stronger case, so manuscripts from diverse geographical locations that contain the same variant reading are more likely to be original. This, however, is true only of manuscripts from the first four centuries of New Testament transmission, since after Constantine legalized Christianity there was greater circulation of manuscripts. As Christians began to realize there were differences among manuscripts, they began to bring them into greater agreement by making changes in them as they were copied. Thus, in the later manuscripts, there was more mixture of variants from the various text types.

Internal Evidence

The basic criterion for internal evidence is, "That reading is best which explains the rest." There are also rules and principles that govern the internal evidence (see chart on page 230). For the Old Testament these are what the text itself reveals, as well as scribal habits and the types of variants (intentional and unintentional) that were made in the manuscripts. These scribal habits tell us what a scribe was likely to do in altering a text, what mistakes a scribe commonly made (see the chart on pages 217–218, "Scribal Tendencies that Produced Textual Variants"), and what the original biblical author probably wrote (which variant fit his style).

Examination of these causes of textual variation can help textual critics decide which reading is the most genuine. However, only by weighing both the external and internal evidence together can the most plausible reading with respect to the original be determined. In fact, the general rule is, *only the reading that best satisfies the external and internal criteria can be original.* That is, only the oldest *and* best attested reading can be original.

The Principles (Canons) of Internal Criticism

1. There can be only one original reading.
2. Variations between texts have a cause.
3. The cause can be either intentional or unintentional.
4. Manuscripts must, therefore, be examined so that the most difficult reading outweighs any effort of clarification (for scribes are more likely to simplify and clarify than they are to make a text difficult).
5. Manuscripts must be *weighed,* not *counted* (there is no majority rule in textual criticism).
6. The harder reading is to be preferred. These readings contain variants with rare words or other discrepancies that mark them out as ambiguous and therefore original (since an easier reading was most likely to result from a scribe correcting or smoothing out the text to eliminate a discrepency or aubiguity).
7. The shorter reading is to be preferred. Scribes almost never intentionally omitted words, but sometimes they tried to harmonize difficulties by adding words or phrases, indicating the longer wording is likely not original.
8. Determine which reading is more appropriate in its context. The author's use of grammar, vocabulary, theology, and context must be compared.

Recovering the Text of the Old Testament

The history of the knowledge concerning the text of the Hebrew Bible has been a gradual one. In the view of Julio Trebolle Barrera, Professor of Hebrew and Aramaic at the Universidad Complutense of Madrid,

> First, [there was] recovery of the vocalized text, which reached a state of equilibrium towards the end of the tenth cent. CE [AD]; next of the consonantal text, which was fixed towards the end of the first cent. CE [AD]; and lastly, recovery of the texts known in the third and second cents. BCE [BC], i.e., before and after the translation of the Bible into Greek.[24]

As we have discussed, the text of the Old Testament has come down to us as a unified text whose transmission has been verified as accurate (see chapter 6). Although higher critical scholars continue to question the transmission accuracy of certain matters, such as the large numbers in the historical books and certain recorded details in historical events, these are interpretive issues for which plausible explanations have been given. However, for lower criticism, as mentioned, the goal is recovering the best and most reliable text possible. Following are two basic steps necessary to reconstruct the original reading of the Hebrew text.

1. Consulting the Masoretic Text

For Old Testament textual critics the Masoretic Text is the starting point, since it is the standard and authoritative text. While the text it represents was not the only text available to Jews in the past, it has been established as a stable and superior text by comparison with the extant manuscripts and versions. (For details, see chapter 6.)

2. Consulting the Versions and the Dead Sea Scrolls

Then the versions (translations) must be consulted. Especially, the evidence from the Dead Sea Scrolls must be examined and given preference unless the scrolls' reading is simply impossible. With the Dead Sea Scrolls as a basis for comparison, the textual critic does not have as great a dependence on the versions as in the past. However, the versions are still of significance in determining crucial questions about variants in the text and assisting the reconstruction of certain texts. However, the biblical Qumran texts have also lent support to the Septuagint and Samaritan Pentateuch versions, confirming the antiquity of the latter and affirming the textual authority of the former.

How critics are helped by the Dead Sea Scrolls. Many of the variants in the scrolls that support the Septuagint and the Samaritan Pentateuch where they depart from the Masoretic Text are worthy of note. In certain cases they may offer significant clarifications and insights for our traditional translations.[25] For example, the scrolls are of help with the longer and shorter versions of Jeremiah, the unexplained action of Nahash in

1 Samuel 11, and minor textual variants such as those related to names, numbers, vocabulary, and sequence.

One example of a textual problem long debated by Jewish and Christian interpreters is found in Psalm 22:16 (Hebrew verse 17). Christian tradition accepted the reading of the Septuagint: "*They pierced* my hands and my feet." This reading appeared to justify a messianic interpretation of the Psalm, seeing a prophecy of Christ's crucifixion in the description of David's suffering.

However, the Masoretic Text read quite differently: "*Like a lion are* my hands and my feet." This difference arose because in Hebrew the unpointed consonants could be read either as a noun ("lion") or a verb ("pierced"). There were no pre-Masoretic manuscripts to justify the Septuagint's translation, and so the Masoretes, after a millennium of disputation with the Christian interpretation, preferentially pointed the consonants as a noun. They did have some internal support since the immediate context did mention other wild animals in the imagery of suffering. It was also difficult to decide which reading was the more difficult (harder) reading, since both fit the style of the writer and made sense in the context.

However, the Psalms Scroll discovered at Nahal Hever (5/6HevPs), textually close to the Masoretic Text, clearly indicated (by the addition of a consonant) that the word was to be read as a verb instead of a noun. Therefore, on the basis of the witness of the oldest Hebrew text the agreement of this verse is with the Septuagintal text, and the preferred reading is "they pierced."

How Critics Struggle with Variant Readings

A significant variant from the Masoretic Text is found in Exodus 12:40:

> Now the time that the sons of Israel lived in Egypt was four hundred and thirty years.

The Dead Sea biblical text of 4QExod[c] agrees with the Masoretic Text, but both the Septuagint and the Samaritan Pentateuch depart from it by adding extra words. The Samaritan Pentateuch and the Septuagint (LXX[A]) add the word "and their fathers" to the words "the sons of Israel" and add the phrase "in the land of Canaan and in the land of Egypt" (Samaritan Pentateuch, reverse order for the Septuagint).

If the Masoretic Text is correct, the length of Israel's bondage in Egypt was 430 years, a time period that has chronological (though not irreconcilable) difficulties. Therefore, on the grounds of both the internal and external evidence, many scholars argue for an Egyptian sojourn of 215 years. This length of time finds support in the writings of the first-century Jewish historian Flavius Josephus, who wrote that the Israelites

> left Egypt in the month of Xanthicus, on the fifteenth day of the lunar month; four hundred and thirty years after our forefather Abraham came into Canaan, but two hundred and fifteen years only after Jacob removed into Egypt (*Antiquities of the Jews* II. 15.2).

Josephus understands the Egyptian sojourn to be 215 years, but sees it as *part* of the 430 years, which also includes the prior sojourn in Canaan (215 + 215 = 430). This view also seems to be the one understood by the apostle Paul in Galatians 3:17:

> What I am saying is this: the Law, which came four hundred and thirty years later, does not invalidate a covenant [with Abraham] previously ratified by God, so as to nullify the promise.

Perhaps an ancient Hebrew scribe who also struggled with this problem added the words to his copy to harmonize the text and resolve the apparent difficulty. This variant ("in the land of Canaan"), reflected in the proto-Masoretic Dead Sea text (4QExod^c), served as the basis for the translation in the Septuagint and in the Samaritan Pentateuch.[26]

On the other hand, it is also possible that, in the process of transmission between the time of the Septuagint and Samaritan Pentateuch and that of the Masoretic Text (over 1000 years), a scribe edited out the words referring to "the fathers" and "the land of Canaan," either through error or to harmonize the text with Genesis 15:13 (see also Acts 7:6):

> God said to Abram, "Know for certain that your descendants will be strangers in a land that is not theirs, where they will be enslaved and oppressed four hundred years."
>
> However, even if the reading in the Masoretic Text is the original, the period of Israel's oppression and ill-treatment under Egypt could still be understood to go back to the time of Abraham's call and entrance into Canaan, since from this time until the Exodus, the Patriarchs went in and out of Egypt and suffered variously under Egypt's influence (see Genesis 12:10-20; 16:1-16; 21:9-21; 25:18; 26:1-2; 37:25–50:26).[27] Therefore, while the variant is significant, it does not result in a textual contradiction and does not affect a historical or doctrinal understanding.

Recovering the Text of the New Testament

A fundamental issue for the textual critic of the New Testament is to decide what kind of critical text to use. Should it be a critical text based on only one text type, such as the Byzantine (and its derived *Majority Text*); or should it be one that is a careful combination of readings resulting from weighing the evidence from all text types, an eclectic text (such as the United Bible Societies or Nestle-Aland critical editions of the Greek text)? The use of a single family text, assuming it is superior to all others, would seem to make the work of the textual critic simpler because the guiding principle is to weigh the transcriptional evidence by finding texts that have the majority of readings with a particular variant.

However, while most scholars have agreed that some text families are superior to others (the Alexandrian having earlier and better manuscripts), they have not agreed that one should be elevated to the exclusion of all others. Therefore, it is better to choose the most accurate readings from all of the available data, since transcriptional errors have been incorporated into every text since the first copy of the original was made. As Paul D. Wegner explains,

A text that combines the most plausible readings will probably read closer to the original Greek than any single text. An eclectic text weighs and compares the various readings, incorporating them into one text.[28]

This approach also takes advantage of the thousands of manuscripts and versions and recognizes the importance of geographical distribution in making a decision about the authenticity of a variant reading.

Weighing the Evidence

In recovering the New Testament text, the textual critic faces several steps:

1. All of the available textual evidence must be diligently collected, which critical editions of the Greek text have done (for the most part) in the printed apparatus at the bottom of each page.

2. This evidence must be meticulously evaluated according to the principles and guidelines previously discussed.[29]

3. The final step is to determine which reading is the most plausible, based on the internal and external evidence and the rules governing them. This of course includes examining the Greek text as it appears in the manuscripts to determine whether a variant was intentional or accidental. This can be done by looking at the shape of the letters in those manuscripts in which a script was written continuously and without word divisions. The close proximity of certain similarly shaped letters increases the probability that a letter or even a word could have been accidentally omitted.[30]

One example of a textual variant that fits the above description under number 3 and is of interest to Christians is the famous announcement made by the angelic multitude at Jesus' birth in Luke 2:14.[31] One variant reads, "peace on earth, goodwill toward men." This is the reading of the King James version and the one that is found on most Christmas cards. However, another variant reads, "on earth, peace among men of good will."

The difference between these two variants is only one letter, the Greek letter *sigma* (equivalent to our letter "s"). If the final word in the

Greek phrase ends in "s," the translation is the latter; if it omits the "s," the translation is the former. Which ending did Luke write in his Gospel?

Applying the methods of textual criticism we begin by considering the external evidence of how a scribe might have produced such a difference in spelling, which reading is the most difficult, and which reading would have more easily occurred. The form without the "s" ("goodwill toward men") is the easier reading, and a scribe would likely not have changed it intentionally. However, if the "s" was original, the reading would be harder ("among men of goodwill"), and so the scribe might have dropped the "s" intentionally to make it easier to interpret. Or, he might have omitted it accidentally since the Greek "s" was sometimes written at the end of a line as a tiny raised letter.

When we compare the manuscript evidence we discover that the form ending in "s" is supported by the Alexandrian and Western text types and the form without the "s" is supported by the Caesarean and Byzantine text types. If we follow the convention that the former have earlier and better manuscripts (the best of which do support this reading), then the form with the "s" is preferred on the external evidence of the manuscripts. Therefore, both the internal and external evidence favors the reading "on earth, peace to men of good will."

Now, this must be interpreted to give it a proper meaning. Does it refer to people who have an attitude of good will toward others, or to people who are the objects of God's good will? The latter makes better sense, and therefore we find it is translated in a version such as the New American Standard as "on earth peace among men with whom He is pleased."

While this may not agree with our "Christmas card theology," it appears to be what the original text read. Therefore we are to acknowledge God's gracious revelation of His Messiah to those for whom He was sent, especially those Jewish believers who were anxiously awaiting His advent. However, it should be apparent that whichever variant we choose, no doctrinal teaching is affected.

We have seen that the methods of textual criticism enable scholars to determine the most likely reading among the varying readings in the manuscripts. However, is this discipline reserved only for scholars? Not at all. With the proper resources and training any teacher or student of the Scriptures who has a little knowledge of the original languages should be able to begin to exercise these guidelines and decide for himself or herself the issue of questionable texts. Certainly any pastor with a Bible college or seminary background can apply the methods of textual criticism as part of his preparation in exegeting the text for his sermon.

However, even if this is asking too much of busy pastors and teachers, it is not asking too much for them to *understand the issues* involved with the need for textual criticism. As the first chapter of this book has pointed out, people today—and church people in particular—are being assaulted by critical scholars and skeptics who reveal to them the "thousands of errors" in the Bible and undermine their confidence in the accuracy of the biblical text. It is for those who know the truth to make it known and to assure their fellow believers that most variants are insignificant, and those that are significant can be resolved through a careful evaluation of the textual evidence.

At any rate, God has given godly people to His church who have both the knowledge and the skill to restore the readings of the text to as close to the original as possible. In this we should rejoice, and we should encourage more people to consider joining their ranks to ensure the accuracy of the text for the next generation.

With that in mind, we must move in our final chapter to consider what else we should know in this search for the Original Bible.

Chapter 14

What Should We Believe About the Original Bible?

If God supervised the writing of Scripture to the degree that people could produce absolutely inerrant, flawless writings beyond their own capability to do so, why could God not have, or why *didn't* he, just as easily superintend the transmission of that text so that it would *remain inerrant* as it was copied through the centuries. What is the purpose of having inerrant *originals* if that inerrancy is not to be maintained in some way? What purpose is served in allowing a perfect text to deteriorate?

—Dennis Bratcher,
"The Problem with Autographs"

The above quote argues that if God gave to His people an inerrant Original Bible, there is no reason why He should not have guaranteed its continuing inerrancy during transmission. Moreover, the view expressed implies all of our attempts to recover the original text of the Scripture are in vain since we do not, in the final analysis, produce an inerrant copy. In a further twist, such arguments contend that the fact of errant copies forces believers to project inerrancy onto the originals—when in fact there is no logical reason to assume those originals were inerrant. Just such a path of thinking led New Testament scholar and author Bart Ehrman to reject the concept of inerrancy in the originals. As he explained,

> For me, [the loss of the original manuscripts] was a compelling problem. It was the words of scripture themselves that God had inspired. Surely we have to know what those words were if we

239

want to know how he had communicated to us, since the very words were his words, and having some other words (those inadvertently or intentionally created by scribes) didn't help us much if we want to know his words....The Bible began to appear to me as a very human book...from beginning to end.[1]

Once such a line of reasoning is embraced, the Bible becomes just another piece of historical literature, and therefore it cannot any longer be the basis for faith. Consequently, Professor Ehrman, once a professed "fundamentalist" and a student at two of the leading evangelical Christian schools (Moody Bible Institute and Wheaton College) now considers himself an "agnostic." For Ehrman, the lack of original texts and the presence of errors in the copies led him to deny inspiration and inerrancy in the Original Bible, and finally to doubt its message and discard his faith.

Whose Error?

Critics like Ehrman assume that the source of errors always lies outside of themselves. Instead, it lies with scribes who copied the texts; the early church, who tampered with the texts; or even the original text itself. In fact, in his book *Misquoting Jesus*, Ehrman credits the cause of his spiritual doubt and declension to a moment of realization that occurred in an exegetical course at Princeton Theological Seminary.

Ehrman discovered that Mark appeared to have made a historical error in his Gospel when he had Jesus state that David went to "Abiathar the high priest" (Mark 2:26). However, according to 1 Samuel 21:1-6 Abiathar was not yet the high priest—his father Ahimelech was. Ehrman, then still clinging to his belief in inerrancy, tried in a course paper to harmonize the two texts and explain the error. He next describes the "turning point" that moved him away from a belief in inerrancy:

I was pretty sure Professor [Cullen] Story would appreciate the argument, since I knew him as a good Christian scholar who obviously (like me) would never think there could be anything like a genuine error in the Bible. But at the end of my paper he made a simple one-line comment that for some reason went straight through me. He wrote: "Maybe Mark just made a mistake." I started thinking about it, considering all the work

I had put into the paper, realizing that I had to do some pretty fancy exegetical footwork to get around the problem, and that my solution was in fact a bit of a stretch. I finally concluded, "Hmm...maybe Mark *did* make a mistake."[2]

Now it is strange to me that a professor of Cullen Story's stature, and a proficient and seemingly committed evangelical student like Bart Ehrman, could give and succumb so easily to the simple answer "Mark made a mistake." After all, one of the rules in textual criticism is that the more difficult reading is to be preferred as genuine. Though this was a historical rather than strictly textual problem, still to be able to admit "Mark made a mistake," one must have already adopted a view of limited inerrancy or have accepted a presupposition that the Bible is only a "human book."

The ease with which this viewpoint is adopted by nonevangelical scholars first came home to me when I was reading Anders Nygren's commentary on Romans. Dealing with the controversial section in chapter 9 on divine sovereignty and election, Nygren stated that "the Apostle Paul clearly taught that God was sovereign with respect to election." And then he added, "but Paul was wrong." Nygren easily recognized the truth of the text, and just as easily rejected it...because Paul's words, like the words of the rest of the Bible, were only human.

Ehrman, knowing that he was working on a classic "problem passage" and that scholars for centuries had dealt with its interpretation without "losing their faith," nevertheless came to accept the "easier" verdict that Mark was wrong—which ultimately meant discarding the doctrine of inerrancy. With this as his point of departure, the end result was predictable:

> Once I made that admission, the floodgates opened. For if there could be one little, picayune mistake in Mark 2, maybe there could be mistakes in other places as well.

In other words, if Mark erred, and Mark is part of the New Testament, then the New Testament contains error and cannot be inspired nor taken as authoritative, concluded Ehrman. Worse, if Mark erred, then Jesus erred, since Mark was only reporting His words.

It seems to me, however, that real scholarship would use its training to resolve textual difficulties rather than dismissing them as "mistakes."

A liberal mind-set might convince itself that in doing so it has absolved God of error by blaming it on His "reporters," but since Scripture claims to be "inspired by God," in the final equation it is impossible to exonerate the Almighty. For this reason, those scholars who respect the divine origin of the Bible do not jump to the easier conclusion that the Original Bible simply contained errors. They also consider human limitations in understanding, as well as human liability in the transmission of the text.

Where Does the Mistake Lie?

If we look more closely at what Mark actually wrote in chapter two, we find he did not say, "*when* Abiathar was the high priest," as Bart Ehrman quotes it, but "*in the time of* Abiathar the high priest." It was this very argument that Ehrman had made to his professor—a rational and reasonable argument, within the context, that follows a proper principle of interpretation.

What is ironic is that in Ehrman's account in *Misquoting Jesus* he unwittingly makes the very same "mistake" (twice) he came to believe Mark had made. On page 9 he writes of "what the great King David had done when he and his men were hungry, how they went into the Temple 'when Abiathar was the high priest'...." However, David was not yet *king* when this occurred and no *Temple* yet existed, only the Tabernacle![3]

Now, if a world-class scholar like Ehrman can make anachronistic statements like this and expect his readers to understand what he *really* means without accusing him of error, why couldn't Mark (actually, Jesus) do the same?

Having come to the end of our study of the origin of the biblical text and how it has been transmitted to us over time, what finally should we believe about the Original Bible? Will what we believe be sufficient to save us from the disillusionment and despair experienced by some scholars?

The answer to this question must consider both the question of the inerrancy of the Original Bible and the question of whether the loss of the original texts was a necessary part of the divine plan.

What Should We Believe About the Inerrancy of the Original Bible?

In the 1880s two scholars at Princeton Seminary, A.A. Hodge and B.B. Warfield, argued that only the original autographs of the Bible were inerrant. Critics claimed that these scholars retreated to this thesis because the mounting pressures of higher biblical criticism and the impact of textual criticism in their day made it impossible to ignore the large amount of variants in the available manuscripts. They further claimed that the "rationalistic theology" of these Princeton scholars shaped fundamentalism's perspectives on the Bible and later those of evangelicalism.[4] However, Hodge and Warfield were simply emphasizing the position traditionally held through the ages—that only the biblical authors, not the copyists, were inspired.

Rehashing this argument for a postmodern culture, Bart Ehrman contends that the issue of inspiration in the Original Bible is irrelevant because no original exists:

> It is one thing to say that the originals were inspired, but the reality is that we don't have the originals—so saying that they were inspired doesn't help me much, unless I can reconstruct the originals. Moreover, the vast majority of Christians for the entire history of the church have not had access to the originals, making their inspiration something of a moot point.[5]

Here, however, Ehrman misses the point concerning inspiration of the original text. It is not necessary that we have an original text to believe in inspiration or inerrancy, since the text that we have affirms this for itself (see next page). It was a help to the early church to recognize that revelation and instructions received from the apostles and their associates carried divine authority and were orthodox. Otherwise the church could have just as easily listened to any heterodox voice and become something different than it became. It is likewise a help to believers today to know that the text as it left the pens of its human authors was in reality the Word of God.

Therefore, if the whole of the Bible is the Word of God, then despite the loss of the originals and "the corruption of the text," the text we have is still sufficient to help believers discern the Will of God. We must trust that God has given us the verbal revelation He wanted us to have, and that this revelation is true. To ignore this fundamental belief (especially with a book that declares itself to be divine truth) in some intellectual pursuit is to guarantee a false conclusion.

However, as we saw in chapter 6, there is no reason to adopt Ehrman's skepticism toward the present state of the New Testament text (or the Old Testament text).[6] If we have 99 percent of the original of the New Testament (and some 95 percent of the original Old Testament) in our critical editions, there is no reason to doubt what the Bible says about itself. The believer has both the internal witness of the text as the Word of God and the subjective witness of the Holy Spirit as the Word guides his life and confirms his faith.[*]

Principles for Understanding Inerrancy

The need to understand what we mean by inerrancy can be seen from a poll taken back in 1994 in which, according to George M. Marsden, 85 percent of the students in one of America's largest evangelical seminaries declared they did not believe in inerrancy. In addition, a poll taken in 1987 by sociologist Jeffrey Hadden of 10,000 American clergymen (of whom 74 percent replied) documented denominational belief and the shift in evangelical commitment to the doctrine between 1987 and 1994. The poll asked if the clergymen believed that the Scriptures are the inspired and inerrant Word of God in faith, history, and secular matters. Among those denying this doctrine were 95 percent of Episcopalians, 87 percent of Methodists, 82 percent of Presbyterians, 77 percent of American Lutherans, and 67 percent of American Baptists.[7]

These statistics, of course, do not tell the whole story, and may not give an accurate accounting of what individual respondents thought was being asked of them. For example, did they perceive they were being asked

---

[*] Psalm 19:7-11; 119:9-11,15,25-28,49-50,98-101,105.

to define themselves as fundamentalists by accepting a fundamentalist's statement on inerrancy? Most, perhaps, might have agreed the Bible was the Word of God in matters of faith, but not history and secular matters; or some might even have believed it was "inspired and inerrant" in some historical details, but not others (for example, Genesis 1–11). However, the point here is that if almost two decades ago clergymen and seminary students were confused about or outright denying inerrancy, then matters today cannot have expected to have improved, even among evangelicals.

For example, at the Evangelical Theological Society's annual meeting in 2006, a resolution was considered to clarify the society's understanding of what its doctrinal statement meant by inerrancy. The proposed method of clarification was the adoption of the meaning as given in The Chicago Statement on Biblical Inerrancy, a document designed to represent evangelicals on this issue (see more on pages 34–35). But there was considerable debate on using this document, primarily because of its statement that the autographs were inerrant. As a case in point, one friend of mine says that when he receives the doctrinal statement to sign each year, he simply crosses out the word "autograph" and writes in the word "Jesus."

Regardless of the reasons some have felt uncomfortable with this statement, the lack of consensus within the largest body of professional evangelicals (representing university, seminary, and college professors as well as pastors) on such a defining doctrine of evangelicalism indicates that there continues to be confusion on this matter. And as the old saying goes, "If there is mist in the pulpit, there is fog in the pews."

For this reason, let us consider some principles for understanding inerrancy with respect to the original autographs.

Verbal inspiration and verbal inerrancy. First, it should be understood that *there is a difference between verbal inspiration and verbal inerrancy.* Inspiration concerns the *words* of the text (2 Timothy 3:16; 1 Peter 1:12), while inerrancy concerns the *truth* or *trustworthiness* of the statements they make (Luke 1:1-4; John 17:17; 2 Peter 1:16). Certainly the recognition that copies of the Bible were "errant" led evangelicals to agree that inspiration and inerrancy extend only to the originals, and that God was not required to preserve the text without error through the ages and through translations. While only the words were *inspired,* it is possible that one of our *copies* of the originals was copied *inerrantly*. (While human beings may and do make mistakes, it does not logically follow that they *must* make them.)

Even so, to admit that human error was possible in the transmission does not mean that it was equally possible in the original writing. This is a non sequitur, a logical error. A human scribe or translator working with human skills is expected to make errors. A human author working under divine superintendence is not. Nonetheless, even though we have errors in our copies, *somewhere* the original still exists within the mass of manuscripts we possess—and it is that original that is inerrant.

Are what *we* call "errors" what *they* would have called errors? Second, it should be understood that *much of what critics call "errors" would never have been interpreted as such by the original authors.* What the ancients regarded as a form of narrative art, within which precision could acceptably be compromised, is regarded as an "error" today.

For example, God said to Abram,

> Know for certain that your descendants will be strangers in a land that is not theirs, where they will be enslaved and oppressed four hundred years (Genesis 15:13).

This was repeated verbatim in Acts 7:6, even though both Stephen and his Jewish audience knew that Israel had been in Egyptian captivity "four hundred and thirty years" (Exodus 12:40-41), a figure precisely cited by the apostle Paul in Galatians 3:17.[8]

That Luke, who wrote Acts and claimed to have "investigated everything carefully" (Luke 1:3), would allow Stephen's 30-year "error" to stand without correction seems remarkable to our mathematically exact way of thinking. However, it did not bother the ancient audience, who accepted both a general figure of 400 years and a specific number of 430 years; nor did it bother the New Testament writers, who could cite either text without the need of explaining the other. They accepted both rounded and exact figures as part of the inerrant Scripture.

Keeping the text inerrant. Third, it should be understood that *it was impossible to maintain an inerrant text through the ages.* We will remember from chapters 3 and 4 that most manuscripts of the Bible were written on perishable materials, and that conditions in the ancient world were not favorable to preservation. It was for this reason that copies were made, and with the production of copies it was possible for variants (errors) to be introduced. The very need to preserve the written text and distribute it to synagogues and churches meant the creation of an errant text. (However, as we will see below, this was a necessary and providential act.)

This fact also refutes the idea that, because a version was cited in the original inerrant text, it also must be inerrant. For example, the use by the authors of the New Testament of the Septuagint does not mean it was inerrant, or even inspired, even though many in the early church thought so and the Greek Orthodox Church still thinks so today.[9] These authors also made use of different Hebrew texts and the Aramaic Targums. Nevertheless, whatever source they used was already errant by virtue of the fact that it was not the original but had been produced by scribes, translators, and expansionists.

The grounds for biblical faith. Fourth, it should be understood that *biblical faith rests on historical facts for validation and not on an original inerrant text.* For Judaism, this is the defining event of the Exodus, and for Christianity, the Resurrection of Jesus. If these events did not happen, then our faith is in our faith (it is purely subjective), not in objective reality. Then the Bible is just a collection of stories still evolving in the modern dramas of Judaism and Christianity, and God is an idea best defined by the experience of each person.

But if these miraculous historical events did happen, as the Bible declares they did, then the biblical text is an accurate and contemporary witness to them.* Nevertheless, the events themselves attest to the truth that is the basis for faith, apart from the text that records them. While we should believe the Bible and desire as accurate a text as possible, the object of our faith (and worship) is not the Bible but God, and for Christians, "our great God and Savior, Christ Jesus" (Titus 2:13).

Divine *inerrancy* vs. divine *preservation*. Fifth, *we must separate the concept of divine inerrancy from the concept of divine preservation of the text.* Recall that we have all of the variants that make up the Original Bible somewhere in our vast number of manuscripts, and that textual criticism has so far been able to bring our state of the text very close to the wording of the original (95 percent for the Old Testament and 99 percent for the

---

* Acts 7:30-38; 1 Corinthians 15:3-4.

New Testament). This clearly indicates Divine Providence has preserved the text for us to an amazing degree. By comparison with secular literature, we have in the Bible, hands down, the best and most complete text in all of human history. That cannot be by random chance!

However, it is unwarranted to connect this preservation with verbal inspiration and inerrancy. We cannot claim that the very words that comprise our Bibles today are the very words God originally gave and that there has been no alteration at all—"else God would not be God and His Word would not be His Word" as some have put it.

Such people have often appealed for their understanding to Matthew 5:18: "Truly I say to you, until heaven and earth pass away, not the smallest letter or stroke shall pass from the Law until all is accomplished." This verse from the lips of Jesus has been used by both friends and foes of the Bible to prove, respectively, that the Bible is true and false. In the first instance, some friends of the Bible have declared on the basis of this verse that no errors of any kind, especially of a textual nature, could ever exist in the copies or translations of the Bible. In the second instance, some foes of the Bible, recognizing that copies and translations differ, argue that this verse does not hold true—and therefore, since it is a word of Jesus, He and His Bible are not infallible.

Both of these interpretations misunderstand the use and intent of Jesus' words. These words refer to the fulfillment of all that the Old Testament ("Law and Prophets," verse 17) predicted—not that every single letter of every single word must be preserved as given. If this were so then the change from paleo-Hebrew script, in which most of the Old Testament was written, to the Aramaic script (in which all of our manuscripts are written), let alone to another language, would have violated this understanding.

Inerrancy and the Original Bible

Inerrancy is simply the belief that God, not man, is the ultimate author of the Bible. If God is without error,* then so is the revelation that comes from Him,† even when it comes through men.††

---

* See Numbers 23:19; Psalm 19:9; 25:5,10; 31:5; 89:14; 111:7-8; Isaiah 32:6; 65:16: Daniel 4:37; John 3:33; 8:26; 14:6; Romans 3:4; Titus 1:12; 1 John 5:7; Revelation 6:10; 19:11.

† See Joshua 21:45; 23:14; 2 Samuel 7:28; 1 Kings 8:56; Psalm 119:142,151,160; Proverbs 30:5; John 10:35; 17:17; Romans 2:8; 9:6; 2 Corinthians 13:8; Galatians 2:5,14; Ephesians 1:13; Colossians 1:5; 2 Thessalonians 2:13; 1 Peter 1:23; James 1:18; 3 John 3.

†† See 1 Kings 17:24; Jeremiah 23:28; Luke 21:22; 24:44; John 5:33; 16:13; Romans 9:1; 1 Corinthians 2:13; 1 Thessalonians 2:3,13; 2 Peter 1:20-21; 1 John 2:21; 4:6.

Therefore, the Original Bible was inerrant because it came to men from God. All subsequent copies and translations are errant because they came to men from men. Even so, the message is unchanged and is therefore the same Word of God as revealed to the original authors. The difference here is that, while the Word of the Bible is from God and cannot change, the transmission of its text is by man, who has introduced changes.

There should be no problem in acknowledging that only the autographs were inerrant, for this is merely to testify that Scripture is a divine revelation. Likewise, to accept that copies and translations are errant is only to affirm the truth that man is errant and cannot duplicate God's act of inerrancy as he transmits His Word. While it is a worthy endeavor to try to recover the original wording of the Bible through textual criticism, it would be unworthy to accuse God of not empowering every copyist and translator with His exclusive divine ability to preserve the text from error. Old Testament scholar Walter C. Kaiser Jr. sums up the matter:

> Believers have always seen a single hand and a superintending mind that guided the whole process: the hand and mind of God….But this is all too frequently dismissed simply out of hand by modern scholarship before the texts are shown to be guilty. If we use the American system of jurisprudence, the claims of the text must be held to be innocent until proven guilty by evidences to the contrary. Unfortunately, the reverse system seems to be in vogue in scholarship at the present moment: the text is guilty by virtue of its divine claims, miracles and talk about God. The scholar is judged in this case, to be innocent of any false motives, but the text is impugned as full of all sorts of impossibilities due to its very nature of claiming to be from God himself. In an indictment of this so-called objectivity, the judgment of history has caught up with that bit of Enlightenment hubris and has exposed such claimants to objectivity as a plurality of subjective relativizers.[10]

As Shakespeare wrote in his play *Julius Caesar*, "The fault, dear Brutus, is not in the stars, but in ourselves." Only God is inerrant; only an inerrant God can produce an inerrant Bible. The fact that errant men are converted by errant copies and come to acknowledge the Bible's supernatural effect in their lives is sufficient evidence that it remains, as always, the Word of God.

Did God *Promise* to Preserve the Original Word?

There are many believers who have never thought about this question. They assume God has preserved the original word and therefore it is unnecessary to question it. However, even though we have, through the science of textual criticism, brought the state of our present text very close to the original, we do not have exactly that original. Thus the issue at hand is whether or not God promised to preserve His Word exactly as it was revealed in the original.

For some people this must be undeniable, and they will defend a textual tradition (such as the Majority Text) or a translation (such as the King James version) because they believe it is what they seek—the unchanged and unchangeable Word of God. It is only the modern translations that are corrupt because they are based on inferior manuscripts.

Others contend it is a dogma that is supported by Jesus' own words: "Heaven and earth will pass away, but My words will not pass away" (Matthew 24:35; Mark 13:31; Luke 21:33). To rightly understand this statement of Jesus we must consider its context. It is spoken as a promise of confirmation at the conclusion of Jesus' Olivet Discourse, in which He declares the coming future events that will be climaxed by His personal return to earth (Matthew 24:30; Mark 13:26; Luke 21:27) for both judgment (Matthew 24:39; Mark 13:20; Luke 21:26) and restoration (Matthew 24:31; Mark 13:27; Luke 21:28). His words contain allusions to two Old Testament passages in prophetic contexts where God Himself confirms that what He has prophesied (both passages contain messianic prophecies) will be fulfilled (Isaiah 40:8; 55:10-11).

Therefore, in the Gospels Jesus in like manner and authority is declaring the certainty of His own prophecies. He could not have been speaking about the *preservation* of His own words, since John 21:25 states that Jesus said much more than what was recorded in Scripture. What was recorded in the Gospels was only a small portion of what Jesus said in less than a two-month period of time, although we have one statement at one instance in His young adulthood (age 12) in Luke 2:49.

Still, all of Jesus' words recorded in the Gospels amount to less than 5 percent if Jesus' ministry lasted three years in duration. If we insist that "My words" in this text refer to *all* of Jesus' words, then we would have to admit that this word of Jesus failed. However, if "My words" refers to His prophetic promises (just before given in the context), then we have a statement that the certainty of fulfillment is more stable and enduring than the creation ("heaven and earth") itself.

Having said this, does Scripture speak of its own preservation? Not in the sense that it promises that each and every word will be preserved exactly as they were in the original, but certainly in the sense that what was originally promised will be fulfilled (which implies that the *words* of promise would be preserved so that fulfillment can be recognized). What is a dogma is that the divine revelation has been mediated through the manuscripts to us. The Reformation affirmation of *sola scriptura* is the confession that this special revelation can be found nowhere else than in Scripture, and to find it we must start with the manuscripts that God has preserved for us.

For this reason we have God's Word, even in our translations, that remains a witness to us of His promise and a testimony of His truth in past and future fulfillment. If this is the case, then perhaps we have a reason for understanding why the Original Bible itself was not preserved, even though we have it essentially in the textual tradition that has come down to us. There are, in fact, formidable reasons why we did not need the Original Bible in the form of the autographa.

Ten Reasons Why We Don't Need the Original Bible

We moderns lament the loss of the past and try to preserve as much of it as possible in museums, archives, libraries, and on computer disks. However, people did not think like this in the ancient world. The remains of a previous civilization were usually harvested for materials that could be used in the present civilization. When a builder surveyed such a scene and saw perfectly good pre-cut stones lying on the ground, he saw no reason, as we say, to "reinvent the wheel"!

For this reason archaeological sites often reveal much earlier original monuments, columns, inscriptions, statues, and so on in "secondary use" in newer constructions. Not everything can or needs to be preserved in its original state.

While the production of inerrant originals was the necessary result of divinely inspired authors, their providential loss may also be seen as a divine necessity. As difficult as it may be to believe, it seems that it was not expedient, nor even preferable, that the originals were preserved. Below are ten reasons why we do not need the Original Bible. Some points are stronger, some are weaker, but it will be profitable for us to consider them.

1. We already have most of the Original Bible in our manuscript copies. As this book has attempted to show, our present critical texts of the Bible are very close to the originals. The science of textual criticism has attained an extremely high degree of accuracy in the Old Testament and in the New Testament. This accuracy is such that textual variants (usually exceptionally minor) occur in only about 40 pages out of some 830 in our modern translations of the Old Testament and in only three pages out of some 200 in the New Testament.

Even so, scholars are still working at restoring the text further, and more manuscripts are sure to be discovered that will add to our knowledge and to textual accuracy. Having said this, it must be stated again that not having the original does not mean we do not have God's Word.

2. If we found the original, we could never be certain it *was* the original and not a copy. The only way there could be certainty of originals would be if the originals had never been lost. If tomorrow a hidden cache of ancient Hebrew or Greek documents were discovered that *could* be autographs, it would be possible to identify the texts as the earliest and best copies, or the closest to the originals that we possess, but there would be no way, even with author signatures (which could be faked), to guarantee that what had been discovered was *the* original. Even if many of the experts were convinced, there would always be room for doubt, especially if anything in the original differed with an accepted belief (such as one sourced from the ending of the Gospel of Mark).

3. God sovereignly determined that we did not need the Original Bible. The fact that the Original Bible has not been preserved in the original manuscripts forces us to accept that, if God is sovereign over history, and particularly the history of textual transmission, it was His will we did not need the originals. However, could God sovereignly have done otherwise and preserved the transmitted text without error? Can it be imagined that He would, against their own wills, so control the minds, eyes, and hands of every scribe (many of whom were not believers) as well as of every typesetter (and their printing presses) so as to produce inerrant copies exactly matching the originals?

Moreover, how in the case of translations (see number 9 below) would He overcome the inherent differences among languages (which He instituted—see Genesis 11:7) so as to avoid any variation that might be perceived as an error in comparison with the originals? The obvious answer is that God could not do this because He *would* not do this, and therefore He determined that the inerrant originals would give way to errant copies and translations.

4. If we had the originals, we would not labor in the same way over the text. Solomon wisely said, "In all labor there is profit" (Proverbs 14:23), and there is no greater profit than that which comes from laboring over Scripture. Doing textual criticism causes us to more diligently search the Scriptures in order to understand the text and make exegetical decisions necessary for exposition.

Granted, if we had the originals we would still have to do exegesis in the languages of the originals and make interpretive decisions, but we would not have to labor in the same way over the text. Because textual variants were made by men, it may be that God has given men the opportunity to make corrections and restore the text to greater purity. Having textual variants that result in disputed passages also forces the student of the Word to a greater dependence on the Lord and on the rest of Scripture to resolve questions and find the truth.

5. The originals would most likely acquire the status of relics. The testimony of history is that most people have not been able to resist according some special worship to supposedly sacred relics. Today one can observe an endless procession of the faithful visiting the reliquary of the Vatican in

Rome, believing that as a result they have accrued some sense of merit. If an Original Bible still existed and had sacred status for billions of people, it would be the most carefully guarded document in the world. For example, I used to work at the Shrine of the Book in Jerusalem, where some of the most famous of the Dead Sea Scrolls are housed. In this specially designed underground building the scrolls are guarded day and night in humidity-controlled cases and in extremely dimmed light. The very best of the scrolls, such as the Great Isaiah Scroll, are kept away from public view, and only facsimile copies put on display. If our most ancient copies of the Bible are treated in such a manner, can it be imagined how the original manuscripts themselves would be treated?

God, however, wants His people to worship Him alone. While the Bible is His word and a revelation of His will, it is not a substitute for Him. It is *through* the Word that we come to know God and learn how to please and worship Him. The Bible, therefore, even in the original, was simply the means by which people came to faith and through which they directed their worship to its divine Author. If the Original Bible had continued to exist down through history, it would have been impossible to prevent believers from the sin of bibliolatry.

In the Scripture, such misplaced devotion was not tolerated. King Hezekiah destroyed the bronze serpent made by the hands of Moses (2 Kings 18:4). It had served as a conduit of faith to those bitten and perishing from the deadly vipers (Numbers 21:6-9). As such, it had been the only means to physical salvation from a temporal judgment of God. For this reason, Jesus used it to illustrate His death on the cross as the greater means of spiritual salvation from the eternal judgment of God (John 3:14).

This relic, kept by the sons of Israel for another 700 years, was given the name *Nehushtan* ("copper"), and became an illegitimate object of Israelite veneration (2 Kings 18:4c). Had it continued to exist, it no doubt would have also been an object of veneration by the church. However, King Hezekiah recognized the basic principle that when that which once demonstrated faith becomes that which destroys faith, those with faith must destroy it. Even though by Hezekiah's time it was a priceless antiquity, connected directly to Moses and a miracle, it had to be "broken in pieces" in order to honor God's first commandment: "You shall have no other gods before Me" (Exodus 20:3).

Having the Original Bible would also have created political problems for people of faith down through history. After all, what one people or nation could be entrusted with such a treasure? It would also have created political problems for people without biblical faith. Superstitious people have often endowed imagined relics with magic power with the hope they would offer supernatural advantage over enemies.

Moreover, nations have even gone to war against other nations in order to possess or to destroy holy relics. The Romans destroyed the religious structures of those peoples they conquered, such as the Jewish Temple, not to mention sites of Christian veneration, such as the birthplace of Jesus in Bethlehem and those of the crucifixion and resurrection in Jerusalem. A nation with a rival religion that wanted to supersede Judaism and Christianity would certainly target the Original Bible as the greatest symbol of those religions on earth.

6. Having the original would neither increase faith nor reduce the differences in interpretation that divide Christians. For the first 10 to 15 years of the existence of the church, not one book of the New Testament (original or copies) was in existence, yet the church experienced tremendous growth. In fact, for most of its history, most people never read (nor could read) a Bible. Therefore, the lack of the Original Bible (and issues of interpretation based on variant readings in the available versions) never crossed their minds. This suggests that having or not having an Original Bible would have made no real difference to the masses because the facts of the faith were communicated orally by parish priests or local pastors.

Likewise, the differences in interpretation that have divided Christians in the past—and present—have had little to do with textual matters (lower criticism). The differences that divide are usually based on conflicting hermeneutical principles, different traditional or confessional positions, political interference and, since the nineteenth century, the disparaging attacks of higher criticism.

In short, the problem has not been lack of an original text, but the lack of any text, and disinformation concerning and division over what text there was. The problem of differences in Judaism is similar. Talmudic study consisted largely of discussions (debates) between rabbinic authorities. In such discussions the problem was not the lack of an original text, since the Masoretic Text was considered to be the same as the original handed down from Mt. Sinai. The problem was usually a difference over what a text meant and how it should be applied.

7. Since the originals could not be distributed without suffering damage, it has always been necessary that copies exist to spread the Word. While the religious situation in ancient Israel did not require the distribution of copies of the original text, it was nevertheless distributed to kings, foreign rulers, the Jewish community in Exile, and to Jews who remained in the Diaspora.

The New Testament was created for the church, and from the beginning of the spreading of the church there had to be the spreading of the Scripture. We cannot know if the original Gospels were circulated or copies of them were made for the local churches that desired them. We do know that epistles by design were original letters sent to local churches or communities. (Even though carefully handled, papyrus scrolls can only go so far and last so long.)

If the important thing was teaching the word of truth by local pastors (2 Timothy 2:2), then it could only be done as they had copies of the Word to study and to preach. Such a need could not be met by a single original, but only by multiplied copies.

8. The copies were in many cases better than the originals—the script was clearer, the materials were better. As we observed earlier, Orthodox Judaism has always preferred, and held to be superior and more valuable, newly produced copies rather than old and worn ones. This is not to say they would not have a higher regard for originals; they did, and they had them placed within the Ark or the Temple archives. (These, of course, were lost or may have been destroyed when the Temple was destroyed.)

However, the Jewish people have never thought that the copies their scribes continually transcribed were inferior to the originals, even when those originals were available in storage. Since all of the authors of the New Testament (Luke may be an exception) were Jewish, and the early church began with Jewish leadership centered in Jerusalem, there is every reason to believe they felt the same as the Jewish community did about the greater value of the copies.

The originals of New Testament books, especially the epistles, would have been written on poorer-quality papyrus and would have probably been written without regard to widespread publication, since most were private correspondence. Daniel B. Wallace describes the quality of the autographs in comparison to the apographs (copies):

> The originals were not always neat. I believe there were a few places in which words were marked out and the text was rewritten [and] words were added in the margins, etc. For this reason, the copies, if done carefully, would be easier to read. As illustrations of the messiness of the originals, consider the following passages that have important variant readings: Romans 5:1, 1 Corinthians 14:34-35, 1 Thessalonians 2:7. On the other hand, I do not believe the originals would have been left uncorrected as Metzger suggests for Romans 5:1. Paul in particular would have read through his manuscript carefully before signing off on it (see 2 Thessalonians 3:17); this was his customary practice.[11]

Therefore, if parchment could be exchanged for papyrus, and the clear neat uncial script of a professional scribe used instead of an individualistic and possibly unclear script, then on this basis the manuscript copies would prove to be superior to the autographs.

9. Even if we had the originals, we would still have differing translations based on them. The divine mandate for the church from its outset was to spread the gospel "to the remotest part of the earth" (Acts 1:8) and "to make disciples of all the nations…teaching them to observe all that I [Jesus] commanded you" (Matthew 28:19-20). In order to fulfill this command of the risen Lord, the gospel had to be communicated outside the Jewish world (which preserved its traditions in Hebrew and Aramaic).

For this purpose the New Testament was written in Greek, which at that time linguistically united Jew and Gentile. This had already occurred some 300 years earlier for the Hebrew Bible with the Septuagint translation. However, it was only a matter of time before there was a need to communicate both the Old and New Testament in other languages, such as Latin and Syriac.

Each act of translation, necessary in the purpose and plan of God to fulfill the Great Commission (Matthew 28:19), required that the Hebrew and Greek originals be replaced by ones that made it possible for the word to be understood by a new audience. Even if God had preserved the Original Bible and every translation had been made directly from it, differences in the text would still occur (not to mention human errors) by virtue of the fact that it is impossible for any translation (receptor language) to exactly reproduce the original language. This results from matters of sentence structure, grammar, syntax, and idiomatic and cultural nuances of the original and its social context (words mean different things at different times and places) as well as the language interference (complications in usage between tongues) normal to bilingualism and more pronounced for translators.[12] This problem is increased when translating ancient texts, as James Patrick Holding illustrates with respect to the Septuagint:

> Have you ever read Chaucer...in the original? Most of you would look at that Old English and understand a few words of it, but unless you were a scholar of that time period, or had Cliff's Notes, you would miss most or all of the puns, political references, etc. peculiar to that time. Now if we have such trouble with [600]-year-old English, imagine what trouble the Septuagint translators had with even older Hebrew![13]

10. Because of constant use and the effects of time, copies were necessary to preserve the biblical texts. The autographs of the Old Testament books were put in storage in the Temple, and only copies of texts were available to those outside (such as those Jewish scribes that translated the Septuagint or a sectarian group like those at Qumran). The autographs of the New Testament, however, were written to particular communities or churches. According to the Church Father Tertullian, the original recipients of these autographs would have kept them most of the time. This meant that they potentially suffered damage from the day they left the hands of the apostles.

It is reasonable to suppose that the authors of the New Testament or recipient churches would have made copies of the autographs, as was customary for important documents in Greek. This would have caused further wear and tear as scribes constantly handled them. Once they had become old, worn, or in any way imperfect (in terms of their quality), according to Jewish law they would have to be consigned to a *genizah* (storehouse for old manuscripts), which would have meant they could have no longer been used.

Therefore, if the early church followed Jewish custom, as did the Jerusalem church and Paul,* then the New Testament autographs might have been stored in a sympathetic synagogue's *genizah*. The point here is, if the Original Bible had not vanished, it still could only have been practically preserved for use by means of copies.

Therefore, for all of these reasons we do not have the Original Bible. What we do have is an abundance of faithfully transcribed manuscripts that have preserved God's Word and have been used to give us, through the labors of textual critics, the most accurate copies of the originals possible. For this we should continually thank God, for by divine Providence, our Bible is the best preserved book in the world!

Belief and the Bible

At the heart of the question of what to believe about the Original Bible is the question of whether or not we can believe the Bible. After all, if the Bible can be thought to have been changed or lost in part, or to be missing parts that tell a different story, why should it be believed? Faith is the absence of doubt, so if the Bible is in doubt, faith in its message is conflicted, if not constrained. However, even if the choice of some words in the Bible or the understanding of some events in the Bible are difficult for scholars to decide, this does not discount the whole of the Bible. To avoid such a pitfall, we must be careful that our faith is not the kind once described by a little boy. When asked to define "faith" he said, "It's believing things you know aren't so!" Tübingen professor and scholar Martin Hengel once cautioned about the parallel dangers of "an uncritical, sterile apologetic fundamentalism...[and a] no less sterile 'critical ignorance' of radical liberalism. At bottom, the approaches are the same; the only differences are the presuppositions."[14]

---

* See Acts 15:21; 21:20-26; 24:17-18; 25:8; 28:17,19.

Affirming a Proper Perspective of Scripture

In his chapter on the uses and abuses of textual criticism in formulating an evangelical doctrine of Scripture, John J. Brogan makes the following assertion:

> Any adequate doctrine of Scripture must be able to make positive claims about the entire phenomena of Scripture, not just the original autographs.[15]

He makes a twofold plea for a more positive perspective of the Bible—one that acknowledges both the divine inspiration inherent in the Original Bible and the divine authority contained in the Bible as it has come to us.

- First, Brogan asserts that "our doctrine of Scripture must adequately explain the origin of Scripture and affirm that God, through the Holy Spirit, spoke his word to humanity through the human authors of Scripture (Acts 1:16; 2 Peter 1:21)." The result of this explanation should uphold that the Bible, as a product of divine and human authorship, is the unique, inspired Word of God.

- Second, "our doctrine of Scripture must adequately explain the entire 'phenomena of Scripture.' It must address not only the historical nature of the writing of Scripture, but also the editing, transmission, canonization and translation of Scripture."[16] Thus, the superintendence of the Holy Spirit must be seen to have accompanied the editorial development of certain biblical texts so that they remained the Word of God at every stage of the process.

In a word, despite the loss of the original and the presence of scribal variants in the copies, an authoritative Word of God has always been accessible. Brogan expresses the guiding principles for textual critics who hold to a high view of inspiration. Brogan also suggests that our doctrine of Scripture has "made too sharp a distinction between ancient inspiration and contemporary illumination." However, this may move us too close to the postmodern concept of "reader-inspiration," and it is best to leave inspiration and its concomitant doctrine of inerrancy with the original text.

Nevertheless, recognizing, as we have, that 1) the text has been transmitted accurately, 2) we have a text very close to that of the Original

Bible, and 3) the goal of recovering all of the original text is achievable should give us confidence that we have the "Word of God"—and that it is, as it has always been, authoritative for faith and practice to those who believe.

In conclusion, we moderns need to have a greater respect for the ancient texts that have been transmitted through time and have contributed to the text of our Bible (whatever translation we may use). Although we have more manuscripts and versions than ever before and have developed methods of textual criticism that have made our texts more accurate than any in the previous history of the Bible, it is the Bible itself, not our materials and methods, that carries the imprint of inspiration that surely resided in the originals.

We are not that far from those originals at this juncture in time, though there remain a number of unsolved problems in our understanding of the text, in its transmission history, and in variants that defy our best attempts at recovering the correct reading. In such cases we should remember the words of Deuteronomy 29:29: "The secret things belong to the LORD our God, but the things revealed belong to us and to our sons forever, that we may observe all the words of this law." What we do not have is not as important as what we do have; further, we cannot know whether or not the God of the Bible has prevented us from answering all our questions for His greater purpose.

In the end, it is our "observing all the words of this law" that honors the purpose for which the Original Bible was given and for its preservation in our Bibles today. A fitting conclusion to this matter has been made by Sir Frederic G. Kenyon:

> It is reassuring at the end to find that the general result of all of these discoveries and all this study is to strengthen the proof of the authenticity of the Scriptures, and our conviction that we have in our hands, in substantial integrity, the veritable Word of God.[17]

Notes

Chapter 1—Why Does It Matter?

Epigraph: Daniel B. Wallace, "The Gospel According to Bart: A Review Article of *Misquoting Jesus* by Bart Ehrman," *Journal of the Evangelical Theological Society,* 49:2 (June 2006), p. 337.

1. For a recent concise rebuttal to the supposed links between Christianity and the pagan religions, see chapter 16 in J. Ed Komoszewski, M. James Sawyer, and Daniel B. Wallace, *Reinventing Jesus: What the Da Vinci Code and Other Novel Speculations Don't Tell You* (Grand Rapids, MI: Kregel Publications, 2006), pp. 219-237.

   The "new school" refers to those scholars whose interpretation of the origin and early history of the church rejects the old model of orthodoxy versus heresy and instead holds that there were varieties of Christianities—until one (now called "orthodoxy") overpowered the others in the second century AD using the political power of the Roman church and deliberately distorted the teachings of the "alternate Christianity" in its own teachings. The roots of the "new school" are the theories of the German New Testament scholar and historian Walter Bauer, whose first influential work on this subject—*Orthodoxy and Heresy in Earliest Christianities*—was published in 1934 and is still in print. For more information and a critique of Bauer's views, see Darrell L. Bock, *The Missing Gospels: Unearthing the Truth Behind Alternative Christianities* (Nashville, TN: Nelson Books, 2006), pp. 44-55.

2. A method of biblical criticism that classifies written documents based on their perceived literary form in order to determine their source or prehistory. On this basis some New Testament form critics have denied that the Gospels are the product of eyewitnesses, but assert they are the later creation of the church based on collected oral sayings and stories and even myths about Jesus.

3. The Jesus Seminar is a "fellowship" of some 80 scholars that was founded in 1985 to assess all sayings attributed to Jesus from both canonical and noncanonical sources according to the probability of their authenticity. Voting on the sayings on a scale of 1 (authentic) to 4 (unauthentic), they drastically reduced what they believed to be authentic information about Jesus in the four canonical Gospels (to

18 percent). They also elevated as authentic many of the sayings in the Gnostic Gospels. Their methods and research have been widely criticized, and they are considered radical even by other critical scholars.

4. The television special "The Gospel of Judas," produced by National Geographic, was aired on their cable channel in tandem with the release of the book by Herbert Krosney, *The Lost Gospel: The Quest for the Gospel of Judas Iscariot* (Washington, DC: The National Geographic Society, 2006).

   The 90-minute program "The Lost Tomb of Jesus" was produced by *Titanic* director James Cameron and was aired on the Discovery Channel on March 4, 2007. See also Simcha Jacobovici and Charles Pellegrino, *The Jesus Family Tomb: The Discovery, the Investigation, and the Evidence That Could Change History* (San Francisco: Harper-Collins, 2007).

5. John Barton and Julia Bowden, *The Original Story: God, Israel, and the World* (Grand Rapids, MI: Eerdmans, 2004), introduction.

6. As quoted in "Church 'will be dead in 40 years time,'" Independent.co.uk, April 16, 2003.

7. Barna Group poll, as reported in "Young Adults in the U.S. Abandoning Biblical Faith," *Whistleblower* magazine, December 2006, p. 33.

8. Chuck Colson, *Against the Night* (Ann Arbor, MI: Vine Books, 1989), pp. 107-108.

9. Gary L.W. Johnson, in Gary L.W. Johnson and R. Fowler White, eds., *Whatever Happened to the Reformation?* (Grand Rapids, MI: Baker Books, 2005), p. 1.

10. Johnson, citing Richard Cimino and Don Lattin, *Shopping for Faith: American Religion in the New Millennium* (San Francisco: Jossey-Bass, 1998), p. 2.

11. David Noebel, "What Is Postmodernism?" paper presented to the Fifteenth Annual Meeting of the Pre-Trib Study Group, Sheraton Grand Hotel, Fort Worth, Texas (December 4-6, 2006).

12. Edwin M. Yamauchi, "Gnosis, Gnosticism," in Gerald F. Hawthorne, Ralph P. Martin, and Daniel G. Reid, eds., *Dictionary of Paul and His Letters* (Downers Grove, IL: InterVarsity Press, 1993), p. 352.

13. For the media's perspective on this "unlikely bestseller," see Neely Tucker, "The Book of Bart: In the Bestseller 'Misquoting Jesus,' Agnostic Author Bart Ehrman Picks Apart the Gospels That Made a Disbeliever Out of Him," *Washington Post* March 5, 2006; accessed at: www.washingtonpost.com/wpdyn/content/article/2006/03/04/AR2006030401369.html.

Chapter 2—What Do We Mean by the "Original Bible"?

Epigraph: John J. Brogan, "Can I Have Your Autograph?: Uses and Abuses of Textual Criticism in Formulating an Evangelical Doctrine of Scripture," *Evangelicals and Scripture: Tradition, Authority and Hermeneutics,* ed. Vincent Bacote, Laura C. Miguélez, and Dennis L. Okholm (Downers Grove, IL: InterVarsity Press, 2004), p. 103.

1. Jaroslav Pelikan, *Whose Bible Is It?: A History of the Scriptures Through the Ages* (New York: Viking, 2005), pp. 3-4.

2. For a summary of these arguments see the introduction to my commentary on Daniel in *The Popular Bible Prophecy Commentary,* eds., Tim LaHaye and Edward Hindson (Harvest House Publishers, 2007), pp. 220-222, and my *Secrets of the Dead Sea Scrolls* (Harvest House Publishers, 1996), pp. 157-163.

3. This was first observed in relation to 2 Samuel and the book of Kings by Gerhard von Rad, *Studies in Deuteronomy* (Chicago: Henry Regnery, 1953), pp. 74-91.

4. For further study on this problem in relation to the subject of this book, see J. Daniel Hays, "Jeremiah, the Septuagint, the Dead Sea Scrolls and Inerrancy: Just What Exactly Do We Mean by the 'Original Autographs'?" *Evangelicals and Scripture: Tradition, Authority and Hermeneutics,* eds. Vincent Bacote, Laura C. Miguélez, and Dennis L. Okholm (Downers Grove, IL: InterVarsity Press, 2004), pp. 133-149.

Chapter 3—What Happened to the Original Bible?

Epigraph: F. F. Bruce, *The Books and the Parchments: Some Chapters on the Transmission of the Bible,* 3rd rev. ed. (New Jersey: Fleming H. Revell Company, 1963), p. 14.

1. *The Ante-Nicene Fathers,* eds. Alexander Roberts and James Donaldson (Peabody, MA: Hendrickson Publishers, Inc., 1994), vol. 3, p. 260.

2. Michelle P. Brown, ed., introduction to *In the Beginning: Bibles Before the Year 1000* (Washington DC: Freer Gallery of Art and the Arthur M. Sackler Gallery, 2007), p. 5.

Chapter 4—Witnesses to the Original Old Testament

1. For a complete listing of these see Eugene Ulrich, "An Index of the Passages in the Biblical Manuscripts from the Judean Desert (Genesis–Kings), *Dead Sea Scroll Discoveries* 1:1 (April 1994), pp. 113-129; and "An Index… (Part 2: Isaiah-Chronicles)," *Dead Sea Scroll Discoveries* 2:1 (April 1995), pp. 86-107.

2. Emanuel Tov, "A Modern Textual Outlook Based on the Qumran Scrolls," *Hebrew Union College Annual* 53 (1982), pp. 11-27; and *Textual Criticism of the Hebrew Bible* (Minneapolis: Fortress Press, 1992), pp. 114-17. Tov sees only a 60 percent agreement; however, he excludes from this count (20 percent) scrolls he considers uniquely Qumranic because of grammatical differences, such as *1QIsa^a*. If we instead include these because of their textual alignment to the Masoretic Text we arrive at our figure of 80 percent.

3. Interview with Emanuel Tov, Hebrew University, Jerusalem, November 7, 1995.

4. For a further discussion on the Ezekiel fragment as well as the other Dead Sea texts see my *Secrets of the Dead Sea Scrolls* (Harvest House Publishers, 1996).

5. Abraham and David Wasserstein, *The Legend of the Septuagint: From Classical Antiquity to Today* (Cambridge: Cambridge University Press, 2006), suggest that the miraculous element in the legend was borrowed by the Church Fathers from a story fashioned by rabbinic *aggadah* for the purpose of encouraging Christians who could not read Hebrew to accept and use the Greek Old Testament. These authors may be correct that the source of the legend is Jewish, since both Josephus and Philo embellished Aristeas's account in their writings in the first century AD. However,

to my mind, it impugns the character of the Fathers to believe they willingly or unwittingly accepted an extrabiblical tale of inspiration and then employed it to motivate the church.

6. Jerome states this in the introduction of his *Hebraicae Quaestiones in Libro Geneseos: Hieronymus I/I*, CChr. SL 72, as cited by Martin Hengel, *The Septuagint as Christian Scripture: Its Prehistory and the Problem of Its Canon* (Grand Rapids, MI: Baker Academic, 2002), p. 49, n. 78.

7. For more discussion concerning the use of the Septuagint in Judaism and its use in Christian studies, see Karen H. Jobes and Moisés Silva, *Invitation to the Septuagint* (Grand Rapids, MI: Baker Academic, 2000).

8. Bruce K. Waltke, "Samaritan Pentateuch," in the *Anchor Bible Dictionary*, ed. David Noel Freedman (New York, NY: Doubleday & Co., 1992), vol. 5, p. 935.

Chapter 5—Witnesses to the Original New Testament

Epigraph: Philip Wesley Comfort, *Early Manuscripts and Modern Translations of the New Testament* (Grand Rapids, MI: Baker Books, 1996), xv.

1. Peter M. Head, "Some Recently Published NT Papyri from Oxyrhynchus: An Overview and Preliminary Assessment," *Tyndale Bulletin* 51:1 (2000), pp. 1-16.

2. Peter M. Head, "Fragments of Six Newly Identified Greek Bible Manuscripts in a Cambridge Collection: A Preliminary Report" (Tyndale House, Cambridge), from *A Journal of Biblical Textual Criticism, 2003*, accessed at www.rosetta.reltech. org/TC/vo108/Head2003.html.

Chapter 6—Can We Trust the Text of the Old Testament?

Epigraph: From Loeb Classical Library edition.

1. Walter C. Kaiser Jr., *The Old Testament Documents: Are They Reliable and Relevant?* (Downers Grove, IL: InterVarsity Press, 2001), p. 41.

2. The Old Testament passages ascribing Mosaic authorship to the books of the Law (Pentateuch) are Joshua 1:7; 8:32-35; 14:10; 1 Kings 2:3; 1 Chronicles 6:49; 2 Chronicles 33:8; 34:14; 35:12; Ezra 3:2; 6:18; 7:6; Nehemiah 1:7-8; 8:1,14; Daniel 9:11,13; Malachi 4:4. The New Testament explicitly refers to Mosaic authorship, as well as doing so implicitly in its references to "the Law of Moses," in the following passages: Matthew 8:4; 19:7; Mark 1:44; 12:26; Luke 2:22; 16:29,31; 24:27,44; John 1:45; 8:5; 9:29; 19:7; Acts 6:14; 15:5; 26:22; 28:23; Romans 10:5; 1 Corinthians 9:9; Hebrews 9:19; 10:28.

3. See, for example, Peter Enns, *Inspiration and Incarnation: Evangelicals and the Problem of the Old Testament* (Grand Rapids, MI: Baker Academic, 2005), pp. 50-52.

4. Richard E. Averbeck, "Compositional and Theological Implications for the Pentateuch from the Early History of the Hebrew Language" (paper presented at the Old Testament as Historical Literature Study Group, 58th Annual Meeting of the Evangelical Theological Society, Washington DC, November 16, 2006), p. 8, emphasis in the original.

5. See Jerold S. Cooper, "Sumerian and Semitic Writing in Most Ancient Syro-Mesopotamia," in *Languages and Cultures in Contact: At the Crossroads of*

Civilizations in The Syro-Mesopotamian Realm, ed. K. Van Lerberghe and G. Voet, RAI 42, OLA 96 (Leuven: Peeters, 1995), pp. 61-77.

6. William H. Shea, "The Earliest Alphabetic Inscription and its Implications for the Writing of the Pentateuch," in *Inicios, Paradigmas Y Fundamentos*, ed. Gerald A. Klingbeil (Argentina: Editorial Universidad Adventista del Plata, 2004), pp. 45-60.

7. Because we know that the history of Old Canaanite extends back into the second millennium BC, biblical Hebrew as a dialect could have existed at that time. There were, of course, changes in the dialect from Moses' time to the biblical Hebrew of the first millennium (as we find it in the Hebrew Bible), but this did not affect the meaning, or scribal accuracy in the transmission of the language.

8. For a discussion of this, see Richard Averbeck, "Factors in Reading the Patriarchal Narratives: Literary, Historical, and Theological Dimensions," in *Giving the Sense: Understanding and Using Old Testament Historical Texts: Essays in Honor of Eugene H. Merrill*, eds. David M. Howard Jr. and Michael A. Grisanti (Grand Rapids, MI: Kregel Academic, 2003), pp. 115-137.

9. John Van Seters, *The Edited Bible: The Curious History of the "Editor" in Biblical Criticism* (Winona Lake, IN: Eisenbrauns, 2006), pp. 398, 400-01.

10. See David Noel Freedman, "The Earliest Bible," in *Backgrounds for the Bible*, eds. M.P. O'Connor and D.N. Freedman (Winona Lake, IN: Eisenbrauns, 1987), pp. 29-37.

11. Freedman, pp. 35-36.

12. See Emanuel Tov, "The Contribution of the Qumran Scrolls to the Understanding of the LXX," *Septuagint, Scrolls and Cognate Writings: Papers Presented to the International Symposium on the Septuagint and Its Relations to the Dead Sea Scrolls and Other Writings* (Manchester, 1990), eds. George J. Brooke and Barnabas Lindars. Society of Biblical Literature Septuagint and Cognate Studies Series 33, ed. Leonard J. Greenspoon (Atlanta: Scholars Press, 1992), pp. 21, 28-29.

13. Interview with Dr. Emanuel Tov, Hebrew University, Jerusalem, November 7, 1995.

14. This challenge is raised by J. Daniel Hays, "Jeremiah, the Septuagint, the Dead Sea Scrolls and Inerrancy: Just What Do We Mean by the 'Original Autographs'?" *Evangelicals and Scripture: Tradition, Authority and Hermeneutics*, eds. Vincent Bacote, Laura C. Miguélez, and Dennis L. Okholm (Downers Grove, IL: InterVarsity Press, 2004), pp. 133-147.

15. Bruce K. Waltke, "Aims of Old Testament Textual Criticism," *Westminster Theological Journal* 51 (1989), p. 71, as cited by Al Wolters, "The Text of the Old Testament," in *The Face of Old Testament Studies: A Survey of Contemporary Approaches*, eds. David W. Baker and Bill T. Arnold (Grand Rapids, MI: Baker Books, 1999), p. 36.

16. For a helpful sevenfold standard for identifying allusions (specifically in Paul's writings), see Richard B. Hays, "Criteria for Identifying Allusions and Echoes of the Text of Isaiah in the Letters of Paul," paper for the International Colloquy on Isaiah 53 and Christian Origins (Waco, Texas: Baylor University, February 23-25, 1996), pp. 6-13.

17. Jack R. Lundbom, "Haplography in the Hebrew Vorlage of Septuagint," paper delivered at the Jeremiah Program Unit: Textual Criticism of the Hebrew Bible (Society of Biblical Literature Congress, 2004).

18. Interview with Dr. Emanuel Tov, Hebrew University, Jerusalem, November 7, 1995.

19. Shemaryahu Talmon, "Textual Study of the Bible—A New Outlook," in *Qumran and the History of the Biblical Text*, eds. Frank M. Cross and S. Talmon (Cambridge, MA: Harvard University Press, 1975), p. 326.

20. For a survey of modern translations employing Qumran readings, see Harold Scanlin, *The Dead Sea Scrolls and Modern Translations of the Old Testament* (Wheaton, IL: Tyndale House Publishers, Inc., 1993).

21. Bruce K. Waltke, "Old Testament Textual Criticism," in *Foundations for Biblical Interpretation*, eds. D.S. Dockery, Kenneth A. Matthews, and Robert Sloan (Nashville, TN: Broadman & Holman, 1994), p. 157.

22. Poul Hoffmann, *Nattetanker i arken* (Copenhagen: Frimodt, 1961), p. 48. Translation in Jens Bruun Kofoed, *Text History: Historiography and the Study of the Biblical Text* (Winona Lake, IN: Eisenbrauns, 2005), p. 33.

23. For this evidence see Paul Connerton, *How Societies Remember* (Cambridge: Cambridge University Press, 1989).

24. Kofoed, pp. 58, 110-122.

25. Kofoed, pp. 89, 111.

26. Karl van der Toorn, *Scribal Culture and the Making of the Hebrew Bible* (Cambridge, MA: Harvard University Press, 2007).

27. Toorn, p. 224.

28. Toorn, p. 224.

29. Even so, with the much greater sources and resources at hand, it should be possible, through projects like the Hebrew University Bible Project, to produce an even better edition of the critical text.

30. The Eastern Church has continued to uphold the priority and infallibility of the Septuagint.

Chapter 7—Can We Trust the Text of the New Testament?

1. For the evidence from the ancient world concerning oral societies and the accuracy of memorization, see Richard Bauckham, *Jesus and the Eyewitnesses: The Gospels as Eyewitness Testimony* (Grand Rapids, MI: Eerdmans, 2006), pp. 271-86.

2. Bauckham, p. 277.

3. Bart D. Ehrman, *Misquoting Jesus: The Story Behind Who Changed the Bible and Why* (San Francisco: Harper San Francisco, 2005), p. 10.

4. Mark Minnick, "Let's Meet the Manuscripts," in *From the Mind of God to the Mind of Man: A Layman's Guide to How We Got Our Bible*, eds. James B. Williams and Randolph Shaylor (Greenville, SC: Ambassador-Emerald International, 1999), p. 96, emphasis in the original.

5. Daniel B. Wallace, "Can We Trust the New Testament?: The Quantity and Quality of Textual Variants," in J. Ed Komoszewski, D. James Sawyer, and Daniel B. Wallace,

Reinventing Jesus: What the Da Vinci Code and Other Novel Speculations Don't Tell You (Grand Rapids, MI: Kregel Publications, 2006), p. 60.

6. The parenthetical wording is taken from William L. Petersen, "Textual Traditions Examined: What the Text of the Apostolic Fathers Tells Us about the Text of the New Testament in the Second Century," in Andrew F. Gregory and Christopher M. Tuckett, eds., *Reception of the New Testament in the Apostolic Fathers,* vol. 1 (Oxford: Oxford University Press, 2005), pp. 40, 45-46.

7. For this and other criteria in deciding the correct reading of a text, see Paul D. Wegner, *A Student's Guide to Textual Criticism of the Bible: Its History, Methods and Results* (Downers Grove, IL: InterVarsity Press, 2006), pp. 231-248 (especially 248).

8. For an excellent critique of these "proof texts" and examples of Ehrman's overstating his case with the internal evidence, see Daniel B. Wallace, "The Gospel According to Bart: A Review Article of *Misquoting Jesus* by Bart Ehrman," *Journal of the Evangelical Theological Society* 49:2 (June 2006), pp. 335-348.

9. Kurt Aland and Barbara Aland, *The Text of the New Testament: An Introduction to the Critical Editions and to the Theory and Practice of Modern Textual Criticism,* tr. Erroll F. Rhodes, 2nd ed. (Grand Rapids, MI: Eerdmans, 1989), p. 69.

10. Eldon Jay Epp, "The Significance of the Papyri for Determining the Nature of the New Testament Text in the Second Century: A Dynamic View of Textual Transmission," in Eldon Jay Epp and Gordon D. Fee, *Studies in the Theory and Method of New Testament Textual Criticism* (Grand Rapids, MI: Eerdmans, 1993), p. 295.

11. David H. Warren, "Was the Text of the New Testament in a State of Flux During the First and Early Second Centuries?: An Evangelical Response to the Oxford 2004/2005 Study" (Paper presented to the 58th Annual Meeting of the Evangelical Theological Society, Washington, DC, November 17, 2006), pp. 14-15.

12. Warren, pp. 17-19.

13. For a list of these see Lee Martin McDonald, *The Formation of the Christian Biblical Canon,* rev. ed. (Peabody, MA: Hendrickson Publishers, 1995), pp. 240-42.

14. See *Magn.* 8.1-10.3; *Phld.* 6.1-3; 9.1-11.2; *Trall.* 12.3; *Smyrn.* 2.1-7.2. I am indebted for these references to Warren, p. 15, n. 45.

15. For example, the Gnostic Basilides cited (using the citation formula "it is written") both from the Gospels and from Paul (Hippolytus, *Heresies* 7.25.2; 7.27.8).

16. Bart Ehrman, *Lost Christianities: The Battles for Scripture and the Faiths We Never Knew* (New York: Oxford University Press, 2003), p. 170.

17. I am indebted for these references to the review article of *Lost Christianities* by Samuel Lamerson in *Journal of the Evangelical Theological Society* 48:1 (March 2005), p. 173.

18. Bauckham, p. 273.

19. For a defense of this characterization of the Gospels see Richard A. Burridge, *What Are the Gospels?: A Comparison with Greco-Roman Biography,* 2nd ed. (Grand Rapids, MI: Eerdmans, 2004).

20. Bauckham, p. 507.

21. As cited in Josh McDowell, *Evidence That Demands a Verdict* (San Bernardino, CA: Campus Crusade for Christ, 1976), pp. 50-51.

22. McDowell, pp. 50-51.

Chapter 8—Are Books Missing from Our Bible?

Epigraph: F.F. Bruce, *The Canon of Scripture* (Downers Grove, IL: InterVarsity Press, 1988), p. 283.

1. *The NIV Study Bible,* 10th anniv. ed., genl. ed. Kenneth Barker (Grand Rapids, MI: Zondervan Publishing House), p. 1528.

2. Islamic Web site "Answering Christianity," p. 3.

3. Bruce K. Waltke and Michael Patrick O'Connor, *Introduction to Biblical Hebrew Syntax* (Winona Lake, IN: Eisenbrauns, 1990), p. 16.

4. The standard English translation of these texts (of which 47 are listed in the table of contents) is James H. Charlesworth, ed., *The Old Testament Pseudepigrapha* (2 vols.) (Garden City, NY: Doubleday, 1983, 1985).

5. David A. deSilva, *Introducing the Apocrypha: Message, Context, and Significance* (Grand Rapids, MI: Baker Academic, 2002), p. 27.

6. John Van Seters, *The Edited Bible: The Curious History of the "Editor" in Biblical Criticism* (Winona Lake, IN: Eisenbrauns, 2006), p. 397.

Chapter 9—Who Decided What Books Went into the Bible?

Epigraph: R.C. Sproul, *Scripture Alone* (Phillipsburg, NJ: P&R Publishing, 2005).

1. Howard Vos, *Can I Trust the Bible?* (Chicago: Moody, 1973), p. 71.

2. Adapted definition of S.Z. Leiman, cited without reference in Alec Gilmore, *A Concise Dictionary of Bible Origins and Interpretation,* 3rd ed. (New York: T&T Clark, 2006), p. 33.

3. John W. Miller, *How the Bible Came to Be: Exploring the Narrative and Message* (Mahwah, NJ: Paulist Press, 2004).

4. For this material I am indebted to the discussion of "The Old Testament Canon" in the *NIV Archaeological Study Bible,* genl. ed. Walter C. Kaiser Jr. (Grand Rapids, MI: Zondervan Publishing Co., 2005), p. 1552.

5. David Noel Freedman, "The Earliest Bible," in *Backgrounds for the Bible,* eds. M.P. O'Connor and D.N. Freedman (Winona Lake, IN: Eisenbrauns, 1987), p. 29.

6. This statement is made by Jaroslav Pelikan, *Whose Bible Is It?: A History of the Scripture Through the Ages* (New York: Viking, 2005), p. 46. For scholarly discussion on this issue see Eugene Ulrich, "The Bible in the Making: The Scriptures Found at Qumran," in *The Bible at Qumran: Text, Shape and Interpretation,* ed. Peter W. Flint (Grand Rapids, MI: Eerdmans, 2001), pp. 51-66.

7. James A. Sanders, "The Dead Sea Scrolls and Biblical Studies," *Sha'arei Talmon: Studies in the Bible, Qumran, and the Ancient Near East Presented to Shemaryahu Talmon,* eds. Michael Fishbane, Emanuel Tov (Winona Lake, IN: Eisenbrauns, 1992), pp. 327-28.

8. For my discussion on this see my work *Desecration and Restoration of the Temple as an Eschatological Motif in the Tanakh, Jewish Apocalyptic Literature, and the New*

Testament (Ann Arbor, MI: University Microfilms Incorporated, 1993), pp. 343-354.

9. F. F. Bruce, *The Canon of Scripture* (Downers Grove, IL: InterVarsity Press, 1988), p. 40.

10. For additional support for this view see Jack P. Lewis, "What Do We Mean by Jabneh?" *Journal of Biblical Literature* 32 (1964), pp. 125-30.

11. David A. deSilva, *Introducing the Apocrypha: Message, Context, and Significance* (Grand Rapids, MI: Baker Academic, 2002) p. 30.

12. Stephen M. Miller and Robert V. Huber, *The Bible: A History: The Making and Impact of the Bible* (Intercourse, PA: Good Books, 2004), p. 7. This work was first published in Great Britain and subsequently in the U.S.

13. As quoted in and translated by Krister Stendahl, "The Apocalypse of John and the Epistles of Paul in the Muratorian Fragment," in *Current Issues in New Testament Interpretation*, ed. W. Klassen and G.F. Snyder (New York: Harper Publishers, 1962), p. 239.

14. A.C. Sundberg Jr., "Toward a Revised History of the New Testament Canon," *Studia Evangelica* 4 (1968): pp. 452-461.

15. This is the position of David L. Dungan, *Constantine's Bible: Politics and the Making of the New Testament* (Minneapolis, MN: Fortress Press, 2007), pp. 118-125.

16. See the account of this in Eusebius, *Ecclesiastical History* 8.2.4. For details of the destruction of Christian scriptures see Bruce M. Metzger, *Canon of the New Testament: Origin, Collection, Text, and Canon* (Oxford: Clarendon Press, 1987), pp. 106-108.

Chapter 10—Has the Truth About Jesus in the Original Gospels Been Lost?

1. My meeting with dealer Bruce Ferrini, also author of a book on illuminated manuscripts, took place in his home in Akron, Ohio, in March 2004. Mr. Ferrini had also acquired other manuscripts, including Dead Sea Scroll fragments, from a dealer in Zurich, Switzerland.

2. For the details of this discovery and the history of the modern interpretation of the documents from the new school perspective, see Marvin Meyer, *The Gnostic Discoveries: The Impact of the Nag Hammadi Library* (San Francisco: Harper San Francisco, 2005).

3. For example, the introductory note to 1 John in the popular *Ryrie Study Bible* (p. 1878) states, "The heresy of Gnosticism had begun to make inroads among the churches in John's day."

4. Antonía Tripolitis, *Religions of the Hellenistic-Roman Age* (Grand Rapids, MI: Eerdmans, 2002), p. 125.

5. Alastair H.B. Logan, *The Gnostics: Identifying an Early Christian Cult* (New York: T&T Clark, 2006), p. 71.

6. N.T. Wright, *Judas and the Gospel of Jesus: Have We Missed the Truth About Christianity?* (Grand Rapids, MI: Baker Books, 2006), p. 68.

7. Ben Witherington III, *What Have They Done with Jesus?: Beyond Strange Theories and Bad History—Why We Can Trust the Bible* (San Francisco: Harper San Francisco, 2006), p. 29.

8. Logan, pp. 28-29.

9. For positive discussion concerning the historical Jesus in the Gnostic material see Thomas R. Yoder Neufeld, *Recovering Jesus: The Witness of the New Testament* (Grand Rapids, MI: Brazos Press, 2007).

Chapter 11—What the New Gospels Say About the Christian Faith

Epigraph: Promotional copy inside front jacket of Marvin Meyer, *The Gnostic Discoveries: The Impact of the Nag Hammadi Library* (San Francisco: Harper San Francisco, 2005).

1. Hans-Josef Klauck, *Apocryphal Gospels: An Introduction,* tr. Brian McNeil (London: T&T Clark, 2003), p. 108.

2. See Klyne Snodgrass, "The Gospel of Thomas: A Secondary Gospel," *Second Century* 7 (1989-90), pp. 19-38. I am indebted for this reference and the next to Darrell Bock, *The Missing Gospels*, p. 6.

3. The only extant witness to the *Diatessaron* is the Greek text of 14 lines preserved on a 4-inch-square parchment fragment. For a comparison between the *Diatessaron* and Thomas see Nicholas Perrin, *Thomas and Tatian: The Relationship Between the Gospel of Thomas and the Diatessaron* (Leiden: E.J. Brill, 2002).

4. E.g., Craig Evans contends the evidence "strongly suggests" a date no earlier than this. Craig A. Evans, *Fabricating Jesus: How Modern Scholars Distort the Gospels* (Downers Grove, IL: IVP Books, 2006), p. 67.

5. The C-14 date given of the extant copy is within 60 years, plus or minus, of AD 280. See Bart D. Ehrman, *The Lost Gospel of Judas Iscariot: A New Look at Betrayer and Betrayed* (Oxford: University Press, 2006), p. 8. However, Ehrman recognizes a possible reference to it by the Church Father Irenaeus c. AD 180.

6. *The Gospel of Thomas,* tr. Stevan Davies (Woodstock, VT: Skylight Paths Publishing, 2002)., p. 33, lines 1-3; p. 35, lines 15-21.

7. *The Gospel of Thomas*, p. 56, lines 15-20.

8. Ehrman, p. 180.

9. N.T. Wright, *Judas and the Gospel of Jesus: Have We Missed the Truth about Christianity?* (Grand Rapids, MI: Baker Books, 2006), p. 137.

10. Elaine Pagels, *Beyond Belief: The Secret Gospel of Thomas* (New York: Random House Publishers, 2003), p. 75.

11. Ehrman, p. 179.

12. Evans, p. 203.

13. James M. Robinson, *The Secrets of Judas: The Story of the Misunderstood Disciple and His Lost Gospel* (San Francisco: Harper San Francisco, 2006), p. 75, emphasis in the original.

Chapter 12—Do We Have Now What They Had Then?

First epigraph: James VanderKam, *The Dead Sea Scrolls Today* (Grand Rapids, MI: Eerdmans, 1994), p. 123.

Second epigraph: J. Ed Komoszewski, M. James Sawyer, and Daniel B. Wallace, *Reinventing Jesus: What the Da Vinci Code and Other Novel Speculations Don't Tell You* (Grand Rapids: Kregel Publications, 2006), p. 122.

1. Altaf Ahmed Kherie, *Islam: A Comprehensive Guide-Book* (Pakistan, 1993), pp. 28-29.

2. Among many excellent resources, see *Inside Today's Mormonism* by Richard Abanes (Eugene, OR: Harvest House Publishers, 2007).

3. John A. Emerton, "The Kingdoms of Judah and Israel and Ancient Hebrew History Writing," in *Biblical Hebrew in Its Northwest Semitic Setting*, eds. Steven E. Fassberg and Avi Hurvitz (Jerusalem: Magnes Press, and Winona Lake, IN: Eisenbrauns, 2006), pp. 37, 33.

4. There is also archaeological evidence of the continuity of the scribal tradition from the period of Egyptian dominance in the second millennium BC down through the time of the Israelite monarchy.

5. For these rules see b. *Menah.* 29b-32b; *b. Meg.* passim; *b. Sabb.* 103a-105a; *J. Meg.* 1.71d-72a; *Masseket Soferim* (based on *Masseket Sefer Torah*).

6. The scribal rules for copying Torah scrolls and other ritual texts are given in the following post-Talmudic sources: Mishnah tractates *Soferim* 1-10; *Tefillin* 1-10; *Mezuzah* 1-10; Maimonides, *Mishneh Torah, Yad Ha-zakah* 1-10; *Shulchan Aruk, Yoreh De'ah* 270ff.

7. Emanuel Tov, "Scribal Practices Reflected in the Documents from the Judean Desert and in the Rabbinic Literature," in *Text, Temples, and Traditions: A Tribute to Menahem Haran*, eds. Michael V. Fox, Victor A. Hurowitz, Avi Hurvitz, Michael L. Klein, Baruch J. Schwartz, and Nili Shupak (Winona Lake, IN: 1996), pp. 383-403. Tov lists some of the practices *in agreement:* ruling of columns, sizes of margins, spaces between books, division into content units; and some practices that *disagree:* correction of errors, marking of cancellation dots (for omitting letter already written), reshaping letters, parenthesis signs, crossing out words, use of paleo-Hebrew script (although forbidden in Talmudic literature for biblical texts), writing on papyrus (as well as parchment), and scribal markings (unknown purpose).

8. For further confirmation of this see James Barr, *Comparative Philology and the Text of the Old Testament* (Oxford: University Press, nda).

9. See E.Y. Kutscher, *The Language and Linguistic Background of the Isaiah Scroll (1QIsa^a)* (Leiden: E.J. Brill, 1974), and Elisha Qimron, *Indices and Corrections* (1979).

10. R. Laird Harris, *Can I Trust My Bible?* (Chicago: Moody Press, 1963), p. 124.

11. Interview with Dr. Halvor Ronning, Jerusalem, November 9, 1995.

12. Bart D. Ehrman, *Misquoting Jesus: The Story Behind Who Changed the Bible and Why* (San Francisco: Harper San Francisco, 2005), p. 177.

13. Ehrman, p. 207.

14. Daniel B. Wallace, "Is What We Have Now What They Wrote Then? *Reinventing Jesus: What the Da Vinci Code and Other Novel Speculations Don't Tell You,* coauthors J. Ed Komoszewski and M. James Sawyer (Grand Rapids, MI: Kregel Publishers, 2006), pp. 104-105.

15. For this and additional statistics between the texts of secular literature with the New Testament documents, see F.F. Bruce, *The New Testament Documents: Are They Reliable?* (Downers Grove, IL: InterVarsity Press, 1981), p. 11.

16. Wallace, p. 109.

17. Kurt Aland and Barbara Aland, *The Text of the New Testament: An Introduction to the Theory and Practice of Modern Textual Criticism,* 2nd ed. (Grand Rapids: Eerdmans, 1989), p. 296. The Alands were the first directors of the Institute for New Testament Research in Münster, Germany.

18. For a discussion of the proper understanding of preservation in light of the English text and its textual authorities, see James R. White, *The King James Only Controversy: Can You Trust the Modern Translations?* (Minneapolis: Bethany House Publishers, 1995), pp. 47-48.

19. See such a statement by Charles C. Ryrie in his note entitled, "Is Our Present Text Reliable?" in *The Ryrie Study Bible* (Chicago: Moody Press, 1978), p. 1926.

Chapter 13—Can the Original Bible Be Recovered?

Epigraph: William David McBrayer, Maurice A. Robinson, and William G. Pierpont, eds., introduction to *The Original Greek New Testament According to the Byzantine/ Majority Textform* (Atlanta, GA: Original Word Publishers, 1991).

1. Lee. W. Woodard, *Kodex W: Old and Holy: Discovery that the Washington (Freer) Manuscripts of the Four Gospels Were Written and Dated in the First Century AD* (LASALLEMONUMENT.COM, 2002).

2. Lee W. Woodard and James Rutz, "Codex W Discovered to Be the Original First Century Gospels" (distributed announcement brochure, 2006).

3. *In the Beginning: Bibles before the Year 1000,* ed. Michelle P. Brown (Washington, DC: Freer Gallery of Art & Arthur M. Sackler Gallery, 2006), p. 6.

4. See Carl Nordenfalk, "The Beginning of Book Decoration," in *Essays in Honor of Georg Swarzenski.* ed. Oswald Goetz (Chicago: Regnery, 1951), and *Studies in the History of Book Illumination* (London: Pindar, 1992).

5. Dennis Haugh, "Was Codex Washingtonianus a Copy or a New Text?" in *The Freer Biblical Manuscripts: Fresh Studies of an American Treasure Trove,* ed. Larry W. Hurtado (Atlanta, GA: Society of Biblical Literature, 2006), p. 180.

6. Lee W. Woodard, *Kodex W: Old and Holy,* pp. 164-172; pp. 150-151.

7. See Theodorus Lector (*Migne,* 86, 189); Severus of Antioch, in Assemani, *Bibliotheca Orientalis* 2.18; and *Vitae Omnium* 13 *Apostolorum.*

8. Jos. Dobrowsky, *Fragmentum Pragense Ev. S. Marci, vulgo autographi* (Prague, 1778).

9. See the rebuttal to this alleged autograph by Paul de Lagarde, *Aus dem deutschen Gelehrtenleben* (Göttingen, 1880), p. 117ff.

10. William Hugh Brownlee, *The Meaning of the Scrolls for the Bible* (New York: Oxford University Press, 1964), p. 45.

11. Personal correspondence with Daniel B. Wallace, October 14, 2006. Wallace is Executive Director of the Center for the Study of New Testament Manuscripts.

12. This statement made in contrast to textual criticism may seem strange to some, since the notion of ancient editors arose out of the very practice of textual criticism. However, the notion of "editors" and "redactors," as we have seen, is an anachronistic invention, and the evidence is against the existence of such in the ancient period.

13. John Van Seters, *The Edited Bible: The Curious History of the "Editor" in Biblical Criticism* (Winona Lake, IN: Eisenbrauns, 2006), p. 392.

14. David C. Parker, *The Living Text of the Gospels* (Cambridge: Cambridge University Press, 1997), p. 1.

15. Paul D. Wegner, *A Student's Guide to Textual Criticism of the Bible* (Downers Grove, IL: InterVarsity Press, 2006), p. 301.

16. J. Harold Greenlee, *Introduction to New Testament Textual Criticism* (Grand Rapids, MI: Eerdmans, 1972), p. 11.

17. Comments posted at www.evangelicaltextualcriticism.blogspot.com (March 2, 2006).

18. P. Kyle McCarter, *Textual Criticism: Recovering the Text of the Hebrew Bible*, (Philadelphia: Fortress Press, 1986), p. 18.

19. Richard N. Soulen and R. Kendall Soulen, *Handbook of Biblical Criticism*, 3rd ed. (Louisville, KY: Westminster/John Knox Press, 2001), p. 189.

20. For example, Maurice Robinson and others have argued, based on the Byzantine textual tradition, that after the church standardized this Greek text family and began a careful comparison (textual criticism) of the variants within this textual tradition, they produced a "universal text," which could only be one that would approach the common archetype lying behind all the local text forms. And for the Greek manuscripts, that archetype could only be the autograph form itself.

21. Bart D. Ehrman, "The Text as Window: New Testament Manuscripts and the Social History of Early Christianity," in *The Text of the New Testament in Contemporary Research: Essays on the Status Quaestionis*, eds. Bart D. Ehrman and Michael W. Holmes (Grand Rapids, MI: Eerdmans, 1995), p. 361, n. 1, emphasis in the original.

22. Daniel B. Wallace, "Laying a Foundation: New Testament Textual Criticism," in *Interpreting the New Testament Text: Introduction to the Art and Science of Exegesis*, eds. Darrell L. Bock and Buist M. Fanning (Wheaton, IL: Crossway Books, 2006), p. 44.

23. A fourth family, known as the *Caesarean* text type, was described by older books on textual criticism as a text type common to Israel and reflecting a local mixture of Alexandrian and Byzantine readings (since these are considered geographical neighbors textually). However, most textual critics today do not believe it was a separate text type, even though there may be some textual relatedness in the Gospel of Mark. For the argument against the Caesarean family see Bruce M. Metzger, "The

Caesarean Text of the Gospels," *Chapters in the History of New Testament Textual Criticism* (Grand Rapids, MI: Eerdmans, 1963), pp. 42-72.

24. Julio Trebolle Barrera, *The Jewish and the Christian Bible: An Introduction to the History of the Bible* (Grand Rapids, MI: Eerdmans, 1998), p. 268.

25. For a complete listing and discussion of these variants see Barrera., pp. 108-138.

26. However, it is also possible that the variant was introduced in the versions (the Septuagint contains longer readings and the Samaritan Pentateuch is particularly known for its harmonization and expanded text as compared with the Masoretic Text) and then influenced a Hebrew scribe who was familiar with these texts.

27. See Harold Hoehner, "The Duration of the Egyptian Bondage," *Bibliotheca Sacra*, 126 (October 1969), p. 309: "In conclusion, the 430 years went from Abraham's call to the Exodus. The first 215 years was their sojourn in Palestine and the last 215 years in Egypt. The 400 years was from the weaning of Isaac to the time of the Exodus."

28. Paul D. Wegner, *The Journey from Texts to Translations: The Origin and Development of the Bible* (Grand Rapids, MI: BridgePoint Books, an imprint of Baker Books, 1999), p. 221.

29. A number of helpful guides present the steps for evaluating the evidence such as J. Harold Greenlee's *Scribes, Scrolls & Scripture: A Student's Guide to New Testament Textual Criticism* or the more recent Paul D. Wegner's *A Student's Guide to Textual Criticism of the Bible.*

30. A helpful guide in this endeavor is Jack Finegan's *Encountering New Testament Manuscripts: A Working Introduction to Textual Criticism.*

31. I owe the substance of this discussion to the example in J. Harold Greenlee, *Scribes, Scrolls, and Scripture: A Student's Guide to New Testament Textual Criticism* (Grand Rapids, MI: Eerdmans, 1985), p. 81.

Chapter 14—What Should We Believe About the Original Bible?

Epigraph: Dennis Bratcher, "The Problem with Autographs," edited excerpt from *The Modern Inerrancy Debate*, CRI/Voice Institute (July 13, 2006, www.cresourcei. org/autograph.html).

1. Bart D. Ehrman, *Misquoting Jesus: The Story Behind Who Changed the Bible and Why* (San Francisco: Harper San Francisco, 2005), p. 5.

2. Ehrman, p. 11.

3. This "mistake" of Ehrman was first identified, as far as I know, by David H. Warren of Heritage Christian University in his paper "Was the Text of the New Testament in a State of Flux During the First and Early Second Centuries?: An Evangelical Response to the Oxford 2004/2005 Study" (Paper presented at the 58th Annual Meeting of the Evangelical Theological Society, Washington DC, November 17, 2006), p. 9.

4. This claim was made by Jack Rogers of Fuller Seminary and Donald McKim, a United Presbyterian minister, in their book *The Authority and Interpretation of the Bible: An Historical Approach* (New York: Harper and Row, 1979). For an evaluation of their proposal see John D. Woodbridge, "Biblical Authority: Toward an Evaluation of the Rogers and McKim Proposal," in *Biblical Authority and*

Conservative Perspectives: Viewpoints from Trinity Journal, ed. Douglas Moo (Grand Rapids, MI: Kregel Publications, 1997), pp. 9-64.

5. Ehrman, p. 10.

6. Ehrman would also contend that it is impossible to reconstruct the original, making the witness of our present text unreliable. If one cannot accept the text as a source of truth, even in the original, as does Ehrman, then any help the doctrine of inspiration in the original would have for the Christian is indeed pointless.

7. *The Gideon,* January 1994, pp. 12-13, as cited at "inerrancy survey" in "sermon illustrations" at www.bible.org.

8. However, in Acts 13:20 Paul approximates the chronology between the period of the Patriarchs and that of the Judges. For more on this see Eugene Merrill, "Paul's Use of 'About Four Hundred Fifty Years' in Acts 13:20," *Bibliotheca Sacra* 138 (1981), pp. 246-257.

9. This has also been defended in the past by some Protestants. See, for example, E.W. Grinfield, *An Apology for the Septuagint in Which Its Claims to Biblical and Canonical Authority Are Briefly Stated and Vindicated* (London: William Pickering, 1850).

10. Walter C. Kaiser Jr., *The Old Testament Documents: Are They Reliable & Relevant?* (Downers Grove, IL: InterVarsity Press, 2001), pp. 27-28.

11. Personal correspondence from Daniel B. Wallace, October 14, 2006.

12. The way a bilingual learns a language and maintains their native tongue also affects their translation ability. For example, one person may grow up with both languages and as a result be less proficient in both of them, while another person may learn a second language, and then not use their first language for some time, losing some proficiency.

13. James Patrick Holding, "Inerrancy and Human Ignorance: Why We Could Not and Cannot Have Inerrant Copies and Translations of the Bible" (www.tektonics.org/gk/inerrancy.html).

14. Martin Hengel, *Studies in Early Christology* (Edinburgh: T&T Clark, 1995), pp. 57-58.

15. John J. Brogan, "Can I Have Your Autograph?," *Evangelicals and Scripture: Tradition, Authority and Hermeneutics,* eds. Vincent Bacote, Laura C. Miguélez, and Dennis L. Okholm (Downers Grove, IL: InterVarsity Press, 2004), p. 111.

16. Brogan, pp. 109-110.

17. Frederic G. Kenyon, *The Story of the Bible,* 2nd ed. (Grand Rapids, MI: Eerdmans, 1967), p. 113.

Acknowledgments for Photographs

Permission to reproduce the following photographs is gratefully acknowledged.

Replica of stone tablet containing the Ten Commandments: photo by author, courtesy Bible Society, Jerusalem.

Author in genizah of the Jewish synagogue at Masada: photo by Paul Streber.

Page of Aleppo Codex: photo by author, courtesy British Library.

Page of Codex Leningradensis: courtesy National Library of Russia, St. Petersburg.

Nash Papyrus: courtesy University of Cambridge Library, Cambridge, UK.

Author in Dead Sea Scroll Cave 4 at Qumran: photo by Paul Streber.

Dead Sea Scroll Cave 1 at Qumran: photo by Rick Schuller.

Biblical Dead Sea scroll (Psalm Scroll) from Cave 11: courtesy Shrine of the Book, Jerusalem, Israel.

Septuagint, Codex Vaticanus: courtesy Vatican Library, Vatican City.

Septuagint, Codex Sinaiticus: photo by author, courtesy British Library, London, UK.

Page of Codex Alexandrinus: photo by author, courtesy British Library, London, UK.

Samaritan priests with Samaritan Pentateuch at Mt. Gerizim, Shechem: courtesy Alexander Schick, Bibelausstellung Sylt, Germany.

Syriac Peshitta: courtesy British Library, London, UK.

Reproduction of earliest portion of Gospel of John (from Rylands Papyri): courtesy Alexander Schick, Bibelausstellung Sylt, Germany (original in John Rylands Library, University of Manchester, UK).

Portion of Gospel of John (from Bodmer Papyri): courtesy Alexander Schick, Bibelausstellung Sylt, Germany.

Earliest copy of Jude and 1 and 2 Peter (from Bodmer Papyri): photo by author, courtesy Bible Society, Jerusalem, Israel.

Codex Vaticanus: close-up of John 1:1-14: courtesy Vatican Library, Vatican City.

Codex Sinaiticus: courtesy British Library, London, UK.

Konstantin von Tischendorf: courtesy Alexander Schick, Bibelausstellung Sylt, Germany.

Greek Orthodox monks with codex at St. Catherine's Monastery at Mt. Sinai: courtesy Alexander Schick, Bibelausstellung Sylt, Germany.

Silver amulet containing the oldest text of the Hebrew Bible: photo by author, courtesy Israel Museum, Jerusalem, Israel.

Tools of the scribe: photo by author, courtesy Cairo Museum, Egypt.

Name of God (YHWH) in paleo-Hebrew script in Hebrew Dead Sea Scroll biblical manuscript: courtesy Alexander Schick, Bibelausstellung Sylt, Germany.

Constantine, first Christian Emperor of Rome: photo by author, courtesy Istanbul Museum, Turkey.

Papyrus codices containing Gnostic documents from Nag Hammadi: courtesy Coptic Museum, Egypt.

Gospel of Thomas from Nag Hammadi: courtesy Coptic Museum, Cairo, Egypt.

Four Gospels (Codex Washingtonensis): courtesy Freer Gallery of Art, Smithsonian Institution, Washington, DC.

Temple Mount (Jerusalem, Israel), possible site of hidden manuscripts: courtesy, Israel Government Press Office, Jerusalem, Israel.

Remains of a Byzantine church, Pella (now in Jordan), possible site of hidden manuscripts: photo by author.

Recommended Reading

Please note: The works in this list reflect differing views on the subjects they cover. However, most do represent a conservative interpretation. These works are included because of the information they present as well as the perspective they bring to the discussion of the text.

Reference Works

Brown, Michelle P., ed. *In the Beginning: Bibles Before the Year 1000.* Washington DC: Freer Gallery of Art and the Arthur M. Sackler Gallery, 2007.

Gilmore, Alec. *A Concise Dictionary of Bible Origins and Interpretation.* New York: T&T Clark, 2006.

Price, J. Randall. *Secrets of the Dead Sea Scrolls.* Eugene, OR: Harvest House Publishers, 1995. Explains significance of the Dead Sea Scrolls to the Old and the New Testament.

Soulen, Richard N., and R. Kendall Soulen. *Handbook of Biblical Criticism,* 3rd ed., rev. and exp. Louisville, KY: Westminster/John Knox Press, 2001.

The Origin of the Bible

Barrera, Julio Trebolle. *The Jewish and the Christian Bible: An Introduction to the History of the Bible,* tr. Wilfred G.E. Watson. Grand Rapids, MI: Eerdmans, 1998.

Wegner, Paul D. *The Journey from Texts to Translations: The Origin and Development of the Bible.* Grand Rapids, MI: BridgePoint Books, 1999.

Old Testament Text

Kaiser, Walter C. Jr. *The Old Testament Documents: Are They Reliable & Relevant?* Downers Grove, IL: InterVarsity Press, 2001.

Toorn, Karel van der. *Scribal Culture and the Making of the Hebrew Bible*. Cambridge, MA: Harvard University Press, 2007

New Testament Text

Bauckham, Richard. *Jesus and the Eyewitnesses: The Gospels as Eyewitness Testimony*. Grand Rapids, MI: Eerdmans, 2006.

Bock, Darrell L., and Buist M. Fanning, eds. *Interpreting the New Testament Text: Introduction to the Art and Science of Exegesis*. Wheaton, IL: Crossway Books, 2006.

Bruce, F.F. *The New Testament Documents: Are They Reliable?* 5th rev. ed. Downers Grove, IL: InterVarsity Press, 1974. Dated, but still helpful.

Metzger, Bruce. *The Text of the New Testament: Its Transmission, Corruption and Reception*, 3rd ed. New York: Oxford University Press, 1992.

Canonicity

Beckwith, Roger T. *The Old Testament Canon of the New Testament Church*. Grand Rapids, MI: Eerdmans, 1985.

Bruce, F.F. *The Canon of Scripture*. Downers Grove, IL: InterVarsity Press, 1988.

Dungan, David L. *Constantine's Bible: Politics and the Making of the New Testament*. Minneapolis: MN: Fortress Press, 2007.

McDonald, Lee Martin. *The Biblical Canon: Its Origin, Transmission, and Authority*. Peabody, MA: Hendrickson Publishers, Inc., 2007.

McDonald, Lee Martin, and James A. Sanders, eds. *The Canon Debate*. Peabody, MA: Hendrickson Publishers, 2002.

Historical Jesus

Bock, Darrell, L. *Jesus According to Scripture: Restoring the Portrait from the Gospels*. Grand Rapids, MI: Baker Academic, 2005.

———. *Studying the Historical Jesus: A Guide to Sources and Methods*. Grand Rapids, MI: Baker Books, 2004.

Evans, Craig A. *Fabricating Jesus: How Modern Scholars Distort the Gospels*. Downers Grove, IL: IVP Books, 2006.

Komoszewski, J. Ed, M. James Sawyer, and Daniel B. Wallace. *Reinventing Jesus: What the Da Vinci Code and Other Novel Speculations Don't Tell You*. Grand Rapids, MI: Kregel Publications, 2006.

Neufeld, Thomas R. Yoder. *Recovering Jesus: The Witness of the New Testament*. Grand Rapids, MI: Brazos Press, 2007.

Pate, C. Marvin, and Sheryl L. Pate. *Crucified in the Media: Finding the Real Jesus Amidst Today's Headlines.* Grand Rapids, MI: Baker Books, 2005.

Witherington, Ben III. *What Have They Done with Jesus?: Beyond Strange Theories and Bad History—Why We Can Trust the Bible.* San Francisco: Harper San Francisco, 2006.

Alternative Christianities

Bock, Darrell L. *The Missing Gospels: Unearthing the Truth Behind Alternative Christianities.* Nashville, TN: Nelson Books, 2006.

Wright, N.T. *Judas and the Gospel of Jesus: Have We Missed the Truth About Christianity?* Grand Rapids, MI: Baker Books, 2006.

Textual Criticism

Brotzman, Ellis R. *Old Testament Textual Criticism: A Practical Introduction.* Grand Rapids, MI: Baker Books, 2002.

Greenlee, Harold. *Introduction to New Testament Textual Criticism.* Grand Rapids, MI: Eerdmans, 1964. Dated but still helpful.

Harrison, R.K., Bruce K. Waltke, D. Guthrie, and G.D. Fee. *Biblical Criticism: Historical, Literary and Textual.* Grand Rapids, MI: Zondervan, 1978.

Wegner, Paul D. *A Student's Guide to Textual Criticism of the Bible: Its History, Methods & Results.* Downers Grove, IL: Varsity Press Academic, 2006.

Bible Translations

The Dead Sea Scrolls Bible: The Oldest Known Bible, Translated for the First Time, eds. Martin Abegg Jr., Peter Flint, and Eugene Ulrich. San Francisco: Harper San Francisco, 1999. English translation of the biblical manuscripts of the Dead Sea Scrolls arranged in the canonical order of the Hebrew Bible.

New English Translation (NET) Bible 1st ed. (Biblical Studies Press, 2005). The first translation that includes the translator notes providing the explanation for the textual decision rendered for each disputed reading (60,932 notes total). It is also the first digitally produced version for the Internet and is available for free download at www.netbible.com. It is available also in standard bindings. Valuable because it follows the method of textual criticism that seeks to restore the original text and continually updates its text based on new evidence and scholarly input.

Person Index

Subject Index

Abiathar (High Priest)
> problem in Mark 2:26 240
>
> view of Bart Ehrman 242

Agrapha 162

Aleppo Codex
> burning of 59
>
> date of 59
>
> significance of 64-65
>
> site of 58

Alexandrian canon/manuscripts 150, 228, 234, 236, 275 n23

Alternative ("Lost") Christianities
> and Gnostic Gospels 188
>
> and Gnosticism 161, 175, 188-191
>
> and orthodoxy 164-165, 193
>
> *Da Vinci Code* views on 14
>
> hypothetical creations 191, 193
>
> New School 20, 190
>
> publication of Bart Ehrman on 28, 159, 166

Apocrypha
> canonicity of 138-39, 148, 152-54
>
> definition of 133
>
> description of 136
>
> divisions of 137
>
> in Dead Sea Scrolls 145-46
>
> list of 134-35
>
> significance of 133

Apographs 33, 257

Apologists (heresiologists) 121, 123, 160, 164-65, 171, 187, 189, 193

Aramaic (language and texts) 62, 71, 73, 215, 248, 257

Archaeology
> and discovery of manuscripts 47, 84, 160, 188, 213-16
>
> evidence of continuity of scribal tradition 273
>
> use in biblical studies 103, 104, 105

Archetype
> and genealogical solidarity 229
>
> definition of 97
>
> in relation to autograph 224-25, 275

Ark of the Covenant 38, 39, 46, 47, 90, 92, 143, 213, 256

Autograph
> alleged discoveries of 211-13, 215, 219
>
> and archetype 97, 224
>
> as inspired edition 35, 100
>
> definition of 31, 33-34
>
> destination of (New Testament) 214, 216
>
> in Chicago Statement 34-35
>
> inerrancy of 239-50
>
> loss of 44-53, 216
>
> materials used for 44
>
> Mosaic 39
>
> of Jeremiah 101
>
> reasons no need exists for 251-59
>
> recovery of 211-36

Biblical text
> development of (Old Testament) 88-96
>
> Islamic view of 29, 118, 184, 196, 208
>
> original (Hebrew) order of 206
>
> variants in

Byzantine (text type) 207, 211, 227-28, 234, 236, 275 n20

Canon
> and early Church Fathers 148-50

About the Author

Randall Price holds a master of theology degree from Dallas Theological Seminary in Old Testament and Semitic Languages, a PhD from the University of Texas at Austin in Middle Eastern Studies, and has done graduate study at the Hebrew University of Jerusalem in the fields of Semitic Languages and Biblical Archaeology.

He is Distinguished Professor of Jewish Studies at Liberty University and Professor of Archaeology and Biblical History at Trinity Southwest University. He has conducted numerous archaeological excavations in Israel, including serving as Director of Excavations at Qumran, site of the community that produced the Dead Sea Scrolls.

As President of World of the Bible Ministries, Inc., a nonprofit organization dedicated to reaching the world with a biblical analysis of the past, present, and future of the Middle East, Dr. Price speaks to international audiences through conferences and lectureships each year.

Dr. Price has authored or coauthored some 20 books on biblical subjects as well as contributing various articles to the *New Eerdmans Dictionary of the Bible*, edited by Noel David Freedman. He has also been the executive producer and on-screen host of five films for television based on his books, as well as appearing on numerous television documentary series, including *Ancient Secrets of the Bible, Mysteries of the Unexplained*, and on television specials such as *Uncovering the Truth about Jesus* and on programs for the History Channel. Dr. Price and his wife, Beverlee, have five children and reside in Texas.

World of the Bible Ministries, Inc.

World of the Bible Ministries, Inc., is a nonprofit Christian organization dedicated to exploring and explaining the past, present, and prophetic world of the Bible through an analysis of archaeology, the Middle East conflict, and biblical prophecy. Three ministries comprise this organization to accomplish this practical purpose:

World of the Bible Productions—produces new books, online studies, and documentary films on biblical backgrounds and biblical prophecy for international outreach through distribution and media, and publishes the *World of the Bible News & Views* newsletter.

World of the Bible Seminars—the speaking ministry of Dr. Randall Price through conferences in churches and organizations, and college, university, and seminary lectureships.

World of the Bible Tours—offers customized annual pilgrimages and study tours that allow participants to experience the reality of the world of the Bible, as well as archaeological excavation opportunities in Israel (optional university credit available).

To find out more about our products, request a free subscription to our newsletter, or receive a brochure of current tours to the Bible lands, or to contact Dr. Price for speaking engagements, you can reach us at:

Web site:	**www.worldofthebible.com**
E-mail:	**wbmadmin@itouch.net**
Address:	**World of the Bible Ministries, Inc.**
	P.O. Box 827
	San Marcos, TX 78667-0827
Toll free (in US):	**(866) 604-7322**
Phone:	**(512) 396-3799**

Other Books by Randall Price

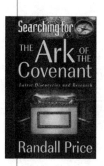

Searching for the Ark of the Covenant

Enshrouded in centuries of history, legend, and mystery, the Ark of the Covenant has captured the imaginations of people around the world. But for all its fame, most people still wonder what happened to it, whether anyone has actually seen it, and where it might be today.

Join Dr. Price in a fast-paced journey to several continents, many diverse cultures, and four millennia of history as you trace the fascinating path the Ark has taken to its present hiding place.

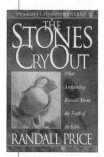

The Stones Cry Out

Recently uncovered ancient artifacts shed light upon the lives of the patriarchs, the Ark of the Covenant, the fall of Jericho, the existence of King David, and more. A fascinating survey of recent finds in Bible lands, with more than 80 photographs affirming the incontrovertible facts that support biblical truth. (Video and DVD also available.)

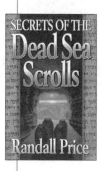

Secrets of the Dead Sea Scrolls

Find out about the technology that helps translators with previously unreadable Scroll fragments, supposedly "secret" Scrolls in hiding, the furious debate about who rightfully owns the Scrolls, and efforts to find more Dead Sea Scrolls. Includes never-before-published photographs. (Video and DVD also available.)

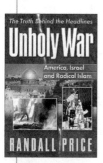

Unholy War

Why does strife continue in the Middle East? How is it connected to terrorist attacks on Western nations? In this popular book, Dr. Price provides a concise, fascinating look at the problems and the players in the Middle East.

Fast Facts® on the Middle East Conflict

In a helpful Q-and-A format with maps, charts, and sidebars, admired author and expert in Middle Eastern studies Randall Price counters misconceptions with the truth behind the headlines and a fascinating timeline of the conflict.

The Battle For the Last Days' Temple

Many Jews long to rebuild the Temple destroyed in the Roman conquest of AD 70. But the site is now dominated by the Muslim Dome of the Rock and Palestinians claim the Jews have no previous history at the site. Randall Price provides fascinating answers based on archaeological evidence, historical records, and exclusive interviews with those at the forefront of the Temple movement.

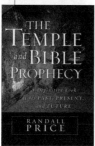

The Temple and Bible Prophecy

Are the biblical prophecies about a future temple merely symbolic, or do they point to a new physical Temple and even a restored scrificial system? And are Israel's current preparations to rebuild the Temple truly a significant sign of the end times? This comprehensive study of the Jewish Temple helps readers answer these questions and more.